POP ICONS *and* BUSINESS LEGENDS

"Hank Moore is a thought leader. Cognizant of the past, he weaves the accomplishments of others into dynamic strategies. I've worked with him and admire his writings."

—**George P. Mitchell**, Chairman of Mitchell Energy & Development. Developer of The Woodlands and downtown renovation in Galveston.

"Hank Moore truly embodies the concept of the Renaissance Man, from his worldly connections and involvement to his almost eerie sense of business acumen, in forecasting trends and patterns of commerce. To those of us who deal in the often delicate balance of customer and company, it is blessing to have, in Hank Moore, a resource we can depend on for fair, statesmanlike and balanced observation. I count him as a valued business friend."

—**Dan Parsons**, President, Better Business Bureau

"Every book that Hank Moore writes is a keeper. That's because of his thought leadership and ability to target what is paramount. Houston Legends is not only required reading, it is blessed reading for those of us who are Houstonians and those around the world who wish they were. Hank Moore brings out the grits and guts of these pioneers like nobody else could. You will be recommending this book to your friends."

—**Anthony Pizzitola** MBA, CFM, CBCP, MBCI, Quality Assurance Manager—Jones Lang LaSalle.

"Hank Moore knows more people than a person who just got elected as President of the United States, and more importantly he knows how to bring out their traits. I don't know how he does it."

—**George W. Strake Jr.**, Chairman-President of Strake Energy, Inc.

"Hank Moore works miracles in changing stuck mindsets. He empowers knowledge from without by enthusing executives to reach within."

—**Dino Nicandros**, Chairman of the Board, Conoco.

"Mr. Moore is one of the true authority figures for business and organization life. He is the only one with an Ethics Statement, which CEOs understand and appreciate."

—**Ben Love**, Vice Chairman, Chase Bank.

"Hank Moore's Business Tree™ is the most original business model of the last 50 years."

—**Peter Drucker**, business visionary.

"Always ahead of the trends, Hank Moore's insights are deep, applicable beyond the obvious."

—**Lady Bird Johnson**, former First Lady of the United States.

"Hank Moore provides fresh approaches to heavily complex issues. His step-by-step study of the business layers makes sense. It shows how much success one could miss by trying to take shortcuts. There cannot be a price put on that kind of expertise."

—**Roy Disney.**

"How can one person with so much insight into cultural history and nostalgia be such a visionary of business and organizations? Hank Moore is one of the few who understands the connection."

—**Dick Clark**, TV icon.

"Hank Moore is a million dollar idea person. He is one of the few business experts whose work directly impacts a company's book value."

—**Peter Bijur**, Chairman of the Board, Texaco.

"30 minutes with Hank Moore is like 30 months with almost any other brilliant business guru. He's exceptional, unlike any other, and with a testimonial list to prove it. As a speaker, he's utterly content rich, no fluff, no 'feely-touchy' nonsense, right to the point and unashamed to tell the truth. There is nobody better. Every CEO needs him."

—**Michael Hick**, Director, Global Business Initiatives.

"I could not have wished for a better boss and mentor in my first professional job than Hank Moore. He leads by example, and taught me valuable lessons not only about business, but also professionalism and ethics that have stood me well throughout my career. Indeed, when I was in a position to mentor others, I've often repeated "Hank Moore stories" to my staff, and they've all heard of my first boss. Over time, I grew to understand more and more that Hank Moore treats others with respect, and thereby commands respect. I was privileged to be trained by this creative and brilliant thinker who gets more accomplished in a day than most do in a week."

—**Heather Covault**, Media Relations Manager, Writer, Web Editor at Kolo, Koloist.com.

"Hank Moore brings alive the tales of these important individuals in a rich and detailed way that affords us all the opportunity to appreciate their contributions to our world and way of life. Well researched and experienced, Legends reflects Hank's personal relationships with those legends shaping the past, present, and future. Legends is a must read."

—**Nathan Ives**, Strategy Driven.com.

"Hank Moore has a wealth of knowledge. Not only is he fascinating to talk with, he's a fabulous writer as well. I'm so glad that he put all of his extensive knowledge of pop culture and business history down in a book for generations to come. Now we can all have access to the amazing stories behind many of the histories, corporations and who's who. Thanks Hank for sharing these wonderful stories. You Rock."

—**Kathryn C. Wheat**, author of the book *Networking: Naked and Unafraid*.

POP ICONS
and BUSINESS
LEGENDS

History of Commerce
and Heritage of Culture

*Back-stories of the innovators, inventors,
inspirers and influencers.*

HANK MOORE

New York

POP ICONS *and* BUSINESS LEGENDS
History of Commerce and Heritage of Culture
Back-stories of the innovators, inventors, inspirers and influencers.

Published in New York, New York, by Morgan James Publishing. Morgan James and The Entrepreneurial Publisher are trademarks of Morgan James, LLC.
www.MorganJamesPublishing.com

The Morgan James Speakers Group can bring authors to your live event. For more information or to book an event visit The Morgan James Speakers Group at
www.TheMorganJamesSpeakersGroup.com.

Shelfie

A **free** eBook edition is available
with the purchase of this print book.

CLEARLY PRINT YOUR NAME ABOVE IN UPPER CASE

Instructions to claim your free eBook edition:
1. Download the Shelfie app for Android or iOS
2. Write your name in **UPPER CASE** above
3. Use the Shelfie app to submit a photo
4. Download your eBook to any device

ISBN 978-1-63047-843-8 paperback
ISBN 978-1-63047-844-5 eBook
ISBN 978-1-63047-845-2 hardcover
Library of Congress Control Number:
2015916779

Cover Design by:
Rachel Lopez
www.r2cdesign.com

Interior Design by:
Bonnie Bushman
The Whole Caboodle Graphic Design

In an effort to support local communities and raise awareness and funds, Morgan James Publishing donates a percentage of all book sales for the life of each book to Habitat for Humanity Peninsula and Greater Williamsburg.

Get involved today, visit
www.MorganJamesBuilds.com

Habitat
for Humanity®
Peninsula and
Greater Williamsburg
Building Partner

Dedicated to Joan Wilhelm.

TABLE OF CONTENTS

ACKNOWLEDGEMENTS

Special dedication to the Bill & Melinda Gates Foundation, on behalf of humanity.

Special dedication to the Ford Foundation, for education, learning and wisdom.

Special dedication to the Carnegie Foundation, for community and cultural enrichment.

Remembrances to some of the icons and legends whom I knew and worked with: Steve Allen, Herb Alpert, Mary Kay Ash, Frankie Avalon, Burt Bacharach, James Baker, Malcolm C. Baldridge, Lucille Ball, Peter Bijur, Dr. Michael Debakey, Tony Bennett, Chuck Berry, Peter Bijur, Sonny & Cher Bono, Walter Brennan, George R. Brown, Harold Burson, George & Barbara Bush, Glen Campbell, Al Capp, Diahann Carroll, Johnny Cash, John Chancellor, Winston Churchill, Dick Clark, John & Nellie Connally, Mike Connors, Dr. Denton Cooley, Howard Cosell, Stephen Covey, Walter Cronkite, Philip B. Crosby, Walt Cunningham, Jimmy Dean, Michael Dell, W. Edwards Deming, Roy Disney, Fats Domino, Hugh Downs, Peter Drucker, Michael Eisner, Duke Ellington, Farrah Fawcett, Ella Fitzgerald, Eva Gabor, John Glenn, Bob Gooding, Max Gotchman, Billy Graham, Merv Griffin, Andy Griffith, Dr. Norman Hackerman, Florence Henderson,

Audrey Hepburn, Don Herbert (Mr. Wizard), Gerald Hines, Ima Hogg, Bob Hope, Ron Howard, Lee Iacocca, Lady Bird Johnson, Lyndon B. Johnson, Chuck Jones, Barbara Jordan, Larry Kane, Robert Keeshan (Captain Kangaroo), Don Knotts, Keith Landers (Johnny Dee), Brenda Lee, Jack Lord, Ben Love, Clare Boothe Luce, J. Willard Marriott, Dean Martin, Bill Mauldin, Glenn McCarthy, Rod McKuen, Marshall McLuhan, Ed McMahon, Harris & Carroll Masterson, George & Cynthia Mitchell, Mary Tyler Moore, Bill Moyers, Joe Namath, Rick Nelson, Dino Nicandros, Earl Nightingale, Roy Orbison, Patti Page, Fess Parker, Bert Parks, Little Richard Penniman, Tom Peters, Elvis Presley, Andre Previn, Vincent Price, Cactus Pryor, Dan Rather, Maureen Reagan, Robert Reed, Burt Reynolds, Nelson Riddle, Anthony Robbins, Kenny Rogers, Eleanor Roosevelt, Diana Ross, Darrell Royal, Colonel Harland Sanders, Vidal Sassoon, Peter Senge, Frank Sinatra, Robert Smith (Buffalo Bob), Steven Spielberg, Roger Staubach, Gale Storm, Ed Sullivan, Danny Thomas, Mel Torme, Jack Valenti, Gore Vidal, Barbara Walters, Dottie Walters, Dionne Warwick, Jack Welch, Lawrence Welk, Gus & Lyndall Wortham, Robert Young.

Also, acknowledgements to Imad Abdullah, Tom Arbuckle, Jim Bardwell, Robert Battle, Ann Dunphy Becker, Betty Bezemer, Judy Blake, Tom Britton, Sarah Buffington, Tony Castiglie, Glenn Chisman, George Connelly, Mike Contello, Rob Cook, John Cruise, Jenna & Michael Devers, Louise Dewey, Deborah Duncan, Dr. Ron Evans, Mike Flory, Felix Fraga, Yomi Garnett, Martin Gaston, Douglas Gehrman, Sonia Guimbellot, John Harris, Phillip Hatfield, Royce Heslep, Michael Hick, Mary Higginbotham, Richard Huebner, Susan & Robert Hutsko, Hiett Ives, Chris Kelso, Soulat Khan, Jon King, Dan Krohn, Kirby Lammers, Nancy Lauterbach, Torre Lee, Steve & Barbara Levine, Mike Linares, Lissa Lundberg, Jackie Lyles, Ben Madry, Hon. Tammy Collins Markee RCC, Aymeric Martinola, Wayne Mausbach, Kathleen McKeague, Eugene Mikle, Julie Moore, Phil Morabito, Howard Partridge, Dan Parsons, Monte Pendleton, Tom Perrone, Anthony Pizzitola, Travis Posey, Tamra Battle Rogers, Donna & Dennis Rooney, Mike Rosen, Rob Rowland, Rita Santamaria, Rick Schissler, Jack Shabot, John Solis, Al Spinks, Bill Spitz, Maggie Steber, Rod Steinbrook, Gail Stolzenburg, George Strake, Jane Moore Taylor, Rich Tiller, Linda Toyota, Kathryn van der Pol, Cameron Waldner, Louie Werderich, Kathryn C. Wheat, Robert Willeby, Melissa Williams, Ronald Earl Wilsher, Tom Ziglar.

Chapter 1
POP CULTURE WISDOM

I nfluences affecting our society, cultural upbringing, business concepts and working style.

Most people are more products of pop culture than they are of training. Business dilemmas, solutions and analyses are framed first in the field of reference (pop culture teachings of their youth) and then reframed in modern business context.

Working with companies, I have realized that presenting organizational strategies as an extension of previously-held pop-culture values gets more understanding, comprehension, attention and support. Most leaders of today's corporations grew up in the 1950s-1980s. I have conducted countless strategy meetings where leaders cannot articulate business philosophies, but they can accurately recite lyrics from "golden oldie" song hits, TV trivia and advertising jingles.

Being one of the rare business advisors who is equally versed in pop culture, I found that bridging known avenues with current realities resulted in fully articulated corporate visions. Many a Strategic Plan was written by piecing together song fragments, nostalgic remembrances and movie scenarios, then were aptly converted into contemporary corporate nomenclature.

When we recall the messages of the songs, movies and books of the 1930s, 1940s, 1950s, 1960s, 1970s, 1980s and 1990s, we realize that today's adults were formerly taught in their youths to:

- Think Big Picture.
- Conceptualize your own personal goals.
- Understand conflicting societal goals.
- Fit your dreams into the necessities and realities of the real world.
- Find your own niche, do your thing.
- Do something well and commit to long-term excellence.
- Seek truths in unusual and unexpected sources.
- Share your knowledge, and learn further by virtue of mentoring others.

How individuals and organizations start out and what they become are different concepts. Mistakes, niche orientation and lack of planning lead businesses to failure. Processes, trends, fads, perceived stresses and "the system" force adults to make compromises in order to proceed. Often, a fresh look at their previous knowledge gives renewed insight to today's problems, opportunities and solutions. I developed the concept of integrating Pop Culture Wisdom with management training and business planning over the last 40 years.

From 1958-1982, I produced many entertainment documentaries for radio, comprising anthologies of pop music. I emceed concerts with stars like Elvis Presley, Duke Ellington, Ella Fitzgerald, Little Richard, Kenny Rogers, The Beach Boys, Roy Orbison, Simon & Garfunkel, Nelson Riddle, Dionne Warwick and Andre Previn. I produced videos with stars from Audrey Hepburn to Vincent Price, plus television public service announcements. That was another lifetime ago.

For the longest time, I didn't let my business clients know about my years as a radio DJ, status as a musicologist and experiences in pioneering radio's "golden oldie show" formats. I didn't think that it lent credibility to wise business insights. However, years of experiences with corporate leaders made me come full circle and start integrating pop culture lingo into the conversations, consultations and planning processes.

All business leaders agreed that no road map was laid out for them. Executives amassed knowledge "in the streets," through non-traditional sources. Few lessons made sense at the time and, thus, did not sink in. When repackaged years later, executives vigorously enjoyed the rediscovery process. The previously overlooked became sage wisdom. Knowledge they were not ready to receive as youngsters before became crystal clear in later times.

Looking for Role Models

All of us are products of the mass culture in which we grew up. This permeates our careers and every other aspect of our lives. We are a confluence of many factors:

- Societal expectations, dreams, failures and also-rans.
- Events beyond our control.
- Mass media variations on home and family.
- Fads and foibles.
- Legitimate goals versus fancies.
- Music.
- Perceptions.
- Realities.
- Movies.
- The educational system, not to be confused with lifelong education.
- What we perceive other families have that we do not.
- Social changes and advances in global cultures.
- Television.
- Technology.
- Changing roles that people play in interfacing with each other.
- What constitutes self-improvement.

The same holds true for business and careers. If pop culture was a confusing mish-mash of mixed messages, then so was our business education, or lack of it. Rarely were we taught about such things as:

- Codes of personal conduct.
- Tiers of professionalism.
- The dues paying process.
- Contributing directly and indirectly to the bottom line.
- Expectations of executives.
- Sophisticated nuances of being a successful executive.
- Empowering teams.
- Benchmarking performance, yours and that of others.
- Observing trends and changes in society, the economy and the marketplace.
- Becoming an active participant, rather than just an observer.
- Championing-mastering change, rather than falling victim to it.
- Standing for something…and being counted-acknowledged.
- Mentoring others.
- Having original ideas.
- Learning how to think for yourself.
- Thinking for yourself gives you the advantage to make clear decisions.
- Carrying decisions into actions.
- Recognizing the positive by-products of effective decisions.
- Becoming a leader and sustaining leadership potential.
- Effecting a career Body of Work.
- Leaving something meaningful behind.
- Continuing to produce, rather than becoming a relic reflection of yourself.

The Ideal Parents

Most of us have fantasized the possibility of our parents being other people. Sometimes, idolized parents were those who already were attached to our friends. Most often, role models were symbols of people we didn't know but wanted to be like.

Businesses operate the same way as individuals. What looks good on the outside is what we must have and become. Tactics are commonly devised to get what we perceive that someone else has and look like what we assume they appear to be. Perception becomes reality. The process of chasing the perception becomes an obsession for businesses of all sizes until reality sets in.

With the advent of television in the 1950s, it was natural that TV families would be held up as ideals. We jokingly wonder how June Cleaver could do the housework in her fancy dress, high heels and pearls. We just knew that Harriet Nelson would make more delicious meals than our own mothers did. The families on TV situation comedies were all white, middle-class, carried traditional family structures and were mostly based in mythical small towns.

The realities behind the facades now make for fascinating insights:

- Harriet Nelson could not really cook. She had grown up in hotels and was accustomed to ordering room service.

- Ozzie Nelson had no job on TV, and his wife didn't work outside the home. No explanation was ever made about their means of support. Though his character appeared light on screen, Ozzie Nelson was the true guru of that show. In my mind, he stands with Desi Arnaz as one of the behind-the-scenes geniuses of TV.

- There was dysfunctional behavior, even though we didn't recognize it as such. When Danny Thomas yelled at his kids and spit coffee on the living room floor, it was couched in wisecracks.

- Women were severely stereotyped. Many TV wives appeared to be subservient…yet pursued their own pro-active courses. Laura Petrie always got her way. Lucy Ricardo pursued adventures with her friend Ethel Mertz. And mother did really "know best," though society would not quite position it that way in the 1950s. Nonetheless, women learned subtle ways to master the system, within the confines of good humor.

- While Western sheriffs won at the shootouts, the issues of good versus bad were overly simplistic. Life is mostly shades of gray, which tough strength does not work well against.

- Behind the guns and action, the Westerns taught lessons of empowerment and team building. On "Wagon Train" and "Rawhide," people had no choice but to get along and work together. As a team, they fought the elements and usually won.

- Gangsters always got their just deserves in movies and on cop TV shows. We were taught that crime does not pay and were shown the price for violating property and safety. Jack Webb, Broderick Crawford and other tough cops put the baddies in their place, in no uncertain terms.

Recalling Heroes, Molding Our Values

People's formative years influence their business careers. Heroes and role models of movies, TV shows, literature and music are forever held in our hearts. Whether consciously or not, we mirror our role models in everyday life. When the chips are down, pop culture mentorship really comes to our rescue. Deep inside, Roy Rogers and Dale Evans, Sky King, The Lone Ranger, Captain Midnight, Robin Hood, Zorro, Wonder Woman and others live within us.

Leadership skills were developed through playing games, from house to football. Concepts of the team contributing toward an organizational goal were the highlight of sports, youth clubs and group outings.

We now realize that many of our childhood idols had demons of their own. Keeping up appearances and being interchangeably confused with their on-screen characters led many a performer toward personal abuse, career burnout and eventual ruin. Not many taught us about going the distance. Too many actors and singers had short-term careers. That was the design of the system. In business, we must not follow pop culture and train ourselves to last, prosper and get better with age.

As we get older and more cynical, society tends to shoot down its media heroes and watches them stumble and fall, sometimes with interest and joy. We don't expect any of them to measure up to past pedestal status. When one falls from grace, we may either repudiate our past allegiance or justify unrealistic ways to keep them perched up on high. Having met many major performers and media heroes, I know that raw talent does not directly translate to business savvy and people skills. The Paul McCartneys of the world, who successfully embody it all, are few and far between.

One of my first career idols was Dick Clark, another man who is smart and accomplished in many facets. He had just debuted on "American Bandstand." I was in the fifth grade and started working at a radio station, determined to be Texas' answer to Dick Clark. A mentor reminded me that none of us should go through life as a carbon copy of someone else. We can admire and embody their qualities but must carve out a uniqueness all our own. Good advice from a 24-year-old Bill Moyers, who stands for me as an ever-contemporary role model.

Values and Ethics with a Pop Culture Spin

Great scriptwriters and songwriters have stuck with us. Our views of humanity were shaped by folk and pop songs. The sense of purpose, dedication to an end result and relishing of victory bring to mind many adventure films, westerns and epic dramas of our youth. We were taught and believe that good things come to those who wait, that good people get rewarded and that evil defeats itself. Whether we articulate them to others, we carry inward values, ethics, quests and senses of dramatic conclusion.

Corporate executives do not get a rulebook when the job title is awarded. They are usually promoted on the basis technical expertise, team player status, loyalty and perceived long-term value to the company. They are told to assume a role and then draw upon their memory bank of role models. Top executives have few role models in equivalent positions. Thus, they get bad advice from the wrong consultants.

In the quest to be a top business leader, one quickly reviews how poorly corporate executives were portrayed to the mass culture:

- J.R. Ewing ("Dallas") sold every member of his family and work force down the river. He is hardly a CEO role model, though many "good old boys" think how he operated was perfectly acceptable.
- Alan Brady ("Dick Van Dyke Show") practiced nepotism with his brother-in-law, Mel Cooley. Brady yelled at everyone and was especially abusive to Mel, in front of others. Creativity was determined by his will. All were expected to parrot his "vision."
- Lou Grant ("Mary Tyler Moore Show") drank on the job, was brash, threatened termination, asked pervasive questions and sometimes dated co-workers.
- Charlie Townsend ("Charlie's Angels") was never around. He left his staff to their own devices and to supervise themselves. The reasons most employees do not perform as expected is they are given insufficient direction and time with a mentor, not knowing what is expected of them.
- It was never revealed where John Beresford Tipton ("The Millionaire") earned all that money that he gave away to total strangers, in order to study their behaviors.

- Economic accountability was not a consideration in TV families. They lived well, but we rarely saw the relationship between workplace output to quality of life. How did Mike Brady ("The Brady Bunch") afford to feed a family of eight, especially with his wife staying at home and not working? He seemed to stay at home much more than the average successful architect.

- In reality, most TV lead characters were the employees of someone else. The boss was the brunt of the jokes. Fear of being disciplined was openly communicated to viewers as part of the territory in earning one's way in life. For example:

- Ralph Kramden ("The Honeymooners") was not considered to become a supervisor, nor a leader. He exhibited a defeatist attitude that probably kept him from being successful.

- Certain characters did their jobs in such a way as that the bosses fell in love with them and eventually married them. Witness Katy Holstrum ("The Farmer's Daughter"), Agent 99 ("Get Smart") and Jeannie ("I Dream of Jeannie"). At one time, some women went into business with such an unrealistic view.

Then, there were those who fostered the notion of "do as I say, not as I do." For example:

- We never saw psychologist Bob Hartley ("Bob Newhart Show") conferring with colleagues, attending professional symposia, authoring academic papers or seeking professional help. When he wasn't in session, he was joking with the receptionist and the dentist.

- Editor Perry White ("Superman") threatened young Jimmy Olsen, "Don't call me chief," when mentoring the eager reporter would have amplified Olsen's service to The Daily Planet. Alas, Olsen was always a tagalong and did not develop as a seasoned reporter, stalling his career.

- Marshal Simon Cord (played by Henry Fonda) was always out of town. His "Deputy" (played by Allen Case) was a shop keeper, who became the town's part-time law and order by default. Part-time jobs and careers are not the same thing.

Money was rarely an issue. We rarely saw families just scraping by, as were most Americans. "The Real McCoys" were farmers, with wealth in spirit and positive will.

There were unexplained quirks, showing insufficient resources necessary to do business:

- All the detectives on "77 Sunset Strip" drove the same car (a Ford convertible). How did the others get around and earn their livelihood, if a car was essential equipment?
- Steve McGarrett ("Hawaii Five-0") drove the same car (a 1967 Mercury Monterey) year after year. With his arrest record, why didn't the department upgrade his equipment?
- Jim Anderson was an insurance agent on "Father Knows Best." Yet, he never made evening calls…only working days. Thus, he couldn't sell that many policies and missed his marketplace…not being available at peak times that his customers were.
- Ricky Ricardo worked in a nightclub and always went to work during the day, usually being home most evenings. Try to figure that one!

Speaking Their Own Language

I've been in meetings recently where the following expressions were used to express some business context: "emergency bat turn" (for a market correction), "groovin' on a Sunday afternoon" (for a profit-sharing plan), "gypsies, tramps and thieves" (for marketplace competition), "a failure to communicate" (for personnel problems) and "head 'em up, move 'em out" (for creating a company rollout). Certainly, younger people had no clue of this jargon. Baby boomers did.

Every age demographic has its own pop culture lingo. We even borrow old ones and dust them off periodically for modern nomenclature, including these fad expressions that were hot at the time:

Would you believe (from "Get Smart")
A silly millimeter longer (from a cigarette commercial)
Let me make this perfectly clear (from Richard Nixon)

Get while the getting's good

Putting on the dog

Heavens to Mergatroid

See you later, alligator

All dolled up

That's the most

Stepping out

What a drag

Hot rod

Gun moll

What a bummer

Tell it like it is

Groovy

Rat fink

Peace, Brother

Right on

Black is Beautiful

Far out

Have a nice day

Time to rock and roll

Keep on keeping on

Sooky (have mercy, baby)

Tubular

Make my day

Shop till you drop

Doofus (acting silly)

Geek

Biker babe

Groupie

Talk to the hand

Don't go there

Changing with the Years

There are seven stages in people's willingness to adopt new perspectives:

1. Cluelessness or Apathy. Henry Ford said, "90% of the American people are satisfied." Will Rogers said, "Mr. Ford is wrong. 90% of the people don't give a damn." Content with the status quo. Taking a vacation from thinking. Not interested in learning more about life or seeing beyond one's realm of familiarization.

2. Basic Awareness. Latent readiness. Not moved to think differently, take risks or make decisions until circumstances force it. 90% don't care about specific issues until events that affect their lives force them to care about something. 5% affect decisions. 5% provide momentum.

3. Might Consider. The more one gathers information, they apply the outcomes of selected issues to their own circumstances. Begin learning through message repetitions.

4. Taking in Information. Something becomes familiar after hearing it seven times. Gains importance to the individual through accelerated familiarity. The more one learns, the more one realizes what they don't know. At this plateau, they either slide back into the denial level of cluelessness or launch a quest to become mature via learning more about life.

5. Beginning to Form Opinions. Triggering events or life changes cause one to consider new ideas, ways of thinking. Survival and the need-desire for self-fulfillment causes one to form strong desires to learn. Cluelessness and inertia are no longer options and are now seen as backward and self-defeating.

6. Thinking and Analyzing. Changing paradigms. Behavioral modification ensues. There are ways we used to think and behave. We do these things differently now because we have learned preferable ways that cause better outcomes. Thus, we don't revert to the old paradigms.

7. Behavioral Change and Commitment. Advocating positions. Creating own original ideas. Holding and further developing insights. Commitment to change and personal growth. Willing-able to teach and share intellect and wisdom with others.

Becoming Your Own Role Model

Amidst these entertaining analogies is a confluence of ideas in each of our heads. Few of us had modeling for life and career. We learned early glimpses of life from

TV. Along the way, we absorbed others, always influenced by the misperceptions of pop culture.

It is difficult to inventory all the images, sort perceptions versus realities and look new ways at old business tenets. This progression of statements, validations and commitments is the premise of this book, which is just the same approach utilized when I work with corporate clients on strategizing and visualizing their future:

- Examine where you came from.
- Retread old knowledge.
- Apply teachings to today.
- Honestly evaluate your path to progress thus far.
- Affix responsibilities, goals and benchmarks to all intended progress.
- Find creative new ways to approach and conduct business.
- Proceed with zeal, commitment, creative instinct and boundless energy.
- Achieve and reflect upon successes.
- Learn three times more from failure than success.
- Plan to achieve and succeed in the future.
- Never stop researching, planning, executing and evaluating.
- Benchmarks of one phase, project or series of events drive the research and planning for the next phase.
- Futurism is not an esoteric concept. After all, It's Almost Tomorrow. Actually, that phrase first appeared as the title of a song in 1955. But then, the present always is the dawn of a new golden oldie future.

Quotable Quotes

Poems, Prayers and Promises
"Big girls don't cry. That's just an alibi. Walk like a man, fast as you can. Walk like a man, my son." Frankie Valli and The Four Seasons (1962)

Letters, We Get Letters
"A line a day when you're far away. Little things mean a lot. Give me your heart to rely on." Kitty Kallen (1954)

We'll Remember Always

"Freedom's just another word for nothing left to lose." Kris Kristofferson (1967)

"When you move real slow, it seems like mo', cause it's alright." Curtis Mayfield (1963)

"The Ballroom prize we almost won. We will have these moments to remember." The Four Lads (1955)

"Diamonds, diamonds, pearls galore. She buys them at the five and ten cent store. She wants to be just like Zsa Zsa Gabor. Even though she's the girl next door." Dion (1963)

Planning & Anticipation

"And in the end, the love you take is equal to the love you make." The Beatles (1969)

Chapter 2

POP ICONS

Tribute to Dick Clark

Dick Clark inspired widespread nostalgia and cultural interaction in our culture. Those of us who have known and worked with him will never forget his humor, his sense of fairness, his encouraging ways, the optimistic disposition, the gut instinct and the lasting impacts that he made on our later successes.

I started out my career by aspiring to be like Dick Clark. Thanks to great mentors, I learned to be my own best self, a visionary thinker and a repository of great case studies. I appeared on radio and TV with him, as well as on conference stages. It was he who encouraged your own leadership qualities, because your success ultimately honored him.

Dick Clark grew up working in a radio station in Utica, NY, perfecting the talk and the interest in music. He realized that music styles changed rapidly and that their cultural impact affected. When opportunity came calling, he was ready, willing and able. He replaced other DJ's as host of a local bandstand show at WFIL-TV in Philadelphia, PA, switching his musical emphasis from big bands and easy listening music to the emerging rock n' roll. His bandstand show was a runaway hit and quickly was picked up by the ABC-TV network as a daily after-school show aimed at teens.

The success of "American Bandstand" spawned a weekly TV music variety series from New York, "The Dick Clark Beechnut Show," which in turn inspired concert tours, "The Dick Clark Caravan of Stars." He appeared in movies, as a teacher in "Because They're Young" and a doctor in "The Young Doctors." He was clean cut, respectful and mannerly, thus bringing legitimacy to rock n' roll. With the celebrity, he was hired to guest-star as an actor in TV shows such as "Stoney Burke," "Adam-12," "Honey West," "Branded," "Ben Casey," "Coronet Blue" and "Burke's Law." He played the last villain on the last episode of the "Perry Mason" weekly TV series.

The 1963 move from Philadelphia to Hollywood, CA, launched Dick Clark Productions. Though "American Bandstand" was owned by the network, he mounted what became a 50-year span of programs that he owned, produced and nurtured, including "The People's Choice Awards," "Where the Action Is," "Live Wednesday," "American Dreams," "The Happening," "New Year's Rocking Eve," "Academy of Country Music Awards," "Super Bloopers and Practical Jokes," "American Music Awards," specials, TV movies, game shows and more.

To go to his office and have meetings was like being in a museum. You sat at his desk in antique barber chairs, wrote on roll-top desks and enjoyed furnishings from nostalgic shops. Big band music played from a Wurlitzer juke box, and classic cars adorned the parking lot.

These are some of the principles that I developed myself but credit being inspired by Dick Clark. I've taught them to others and shared with him as well:

- As times change, the nature of "nostalgia" changes. Each entertainment niche may not be your "cup of tea," but relating to others will create common bonds and exhibits leadership.
- People are more products of the pop culture than they are of formal business training. They make strategic decisions based upon cultural

memories. I would ask corporate executives to articulate core values, and they could only recite meaningful song lyrics, movie lines and quotes. That's why I developed the Pop Culture Wisdom concept, to interpolate from the cultural icons into business jargon and workable policies.

- Companies and industries need to embrace change sooner, rather than becoming a victim of it later. The entertainment industry is the best at being flexible, spotting new trends, changing with the times, packaging creative concepts and leading cultural charges. Other industries could well learn from the entertainment business practices.

- Applying humility and humanity helps in bringing people together. Music is something that everyone relates to. Finding common ground about the zeal and joys inherent in running a company results in better buy-in and support of the goals.

- A lot of people in show business asked Dick Clark for advice. He had a lot of wise business sense, and the best came from gut instincts. My gut is usually right. If something feels wrong, then it is. If it is a good move to make, then I cite precedents as to what led to that recommendation. Trusting your gut comes from long experience, for which there are no shortcuts.

- Dick Clark was good about treating the teenagers as friends and with respect. He never came across as a scolding parent but rather as a friendly uncle. Long-term business success is a function of developing stakeholders and empowering them to do positive things with your company.

- Dick Clark Productions had a select list of projects. The take-back for business is to grow in consistent fashion, sustaining the down times with realistic activities.

- I recommend that organizations periodically revisit their earlier successes. Learn from case studies elsewhere in the marketplace. Review what you once did correctly and how your competitors failed. It is important to link nostalgia to the future. We can like and learn from the past without living in it.

Dick Clark liked to celebrate the successes of others. I've found that reciting precedents of successful strategy tends to inspire others to re-examine their own. Here are some other lessons that he taught us:

- Be a mentor and inspire others.
- Learn as you grow.
- Periodically celebrate the heritage.
- Be inclusive.
- Be ethical.
- Give the public more than you need to.

I'll close this tribute to Dick Clark with some of the songs from American Bandstand that have applicability to business strategy:

- "Did you ever have to make up your mind? It's not often easy and not often kind. Did you ever have to finally decide? Say yes to one and let the other one ride? There's so many changes and tears you must hide." John Sebastian and the Lovin' Spoonful (1965)
- "Do you know the way to San Jose? In a week or two, they'll make you a star. And all the stars that ever were are parking cars and pumping gas." Sung by Dionne Warwick. Written by Burt Bacharach & Hal David (1968)
- "Don't you want me baby? You know I can't believe it when I hear that you won't see me. It's much too late to find you think you've changed your mind. You'd better change it back or we will both be sorry." The Human League (1982)
- "How will I know if he really loves me? Tell me, is it real love? How will I know if he's thinking of me? If he loves me, if he loves me not." Whitney Houston (1986)
- "See the girl with the diamond ring. She knows how to shake that thing. See the girl with the red dress on. She can dance all night long." Ray Charles (1959)
- "What is love? Five feet of heaven in a pony tail…the cutest pony tail that sways with a wiggle when she walks." The Playmates (1958)

- "What's your name? Is it Mary or Sue? Do I stand a chance with you? It's so hard to find a personality with charms like yours for me. Ooh wee." Don and Juan (1962)

- "Each night I ask the stars up above, why must I be a teenager in love?" Dion and the Belmonts (1959)

- "Wouldn't it be nice if we were older? Wouldn't it be nice to live in the kind of world where we belong? Happy times together, we'd be spending. Maybe if we think and wish and hope and pray, it might come true." The Beach Boys (1966)

- "I've looked at life from both sides now. Those bright illusions I recall. I really don't know life at all." Judy Collins (1968)

- "There ain't no good guys. There ain't no bad guys. There's only you and me, and we just disagree." Dave Mason

- "Life goes on, after the thrill of living is gone." John Mellencamp (1982)

- "I've found the paradise that's trouble-free. On the roof's the only place I know, where you just have to wish to make it so." Sung by The Drifters. Written by Carole King and Gerry Goffin (1962)

Nourishing a Definitive Body of Work Through the Burt Bacharach Songbook.

Just as companies have books of business and corporate cultures, so do individuals, who in turn populate and influence organizations. This section looks through the prism of music and salutes the famed composer Burt Bacharach as the analogy for a fine, rich and definitive Body of Work.

At the beginning of my career, I was a radio DJ. I started in 1958, a golden period for music. Because Payola was looming as an issue in our industry, we were required to keep logs of the songs that were played, containing the labels on which they appeared, the names of the composers and other information. In today's industry, that would all be on spreadsheets. However, the manual writing of spreadsheets gave us the chance to digest and learn from the information, developing the skills to better program for our audience. To this day, I can look at the label of a record and, judging by the serial number, can tell you its date of release.

A bunch of records were in the Top 40 at that time: "Magic Moments" by Perry Como, "Story of My Life" by Marty Robbins, "The Blob" by the Five Blobs,

"Another Time Another Place" by Patti Page and "Hot Spell" by Margaret Whiting. I zeroed into the fact that the music composer of all these diverse hits was Burt Bacharach, though the lyricists were different names.

It occurred to me that this was a talent to watch, as I was already familiar with established composers such as George Gershwin, Cole Porter, Irving Berlin and others. I sensed early-on that Bacharach would belong in that upper echelon on Tin Pan Alley icons. Concurrently, I became familiar with the work of other young emerging music composers, such as Carole King, Buddy Holly, Paul Anka, Barry Mann, Neil Sedaka, John Lennon and Paul McCartney.

Throughout the 1960s, the music of Burt Bacharach and lyricist Hal David was everywhere. In the rock era, there were still hits and radio airplay for easy listening music, ballads, movie title songs and the like. The playlists were balanced and gave the public a full array of musical styles.

One could spot a Bacharach tune because it had a definable style. Bacharach himself played piano on and conducted many of the important hits. His arrangements fit the performers and needs of each piece. Yet, the hits had identifiable traits of a Bacharach production. Many talented artists wanted to record his songs, with his arrangements. The public sought out recordings with his hits. All of that represents Body of Work for a composer. Through the 1960s and 1970s, Bacharach broadened and experimented in creative directions. There was a Broadway show, a TV musical revue, movie soundtracks and movie tie-in tunes. He hosted TV specials and performed concerts of his music.

In the decades of the 1980s, 1990s and 2000s, newer fans and younger generations kept discovering Burt Bacharach. His old songs spoke to them, were updated and re-recorded. He collaborated with other musical talents (Elvis Costello, Carole Bayer Sager and James Ingram). Every decade, he kept getting rediscovered and re-recorded. There were tribute concerts and retrospectives. The Body of Work stood the test of time and appealed to wider audiences.

With the renewed interest in Burt Bacharach came the reissues of recordings. With the popularity of CDs came the retrospectives of his early work. Being a Bacharach fan, I acquired the compilations and fell in love with a whole new earlier Body of Work.

There were songs that I had played on the radio but had not realized that they were by Burt Bacharach. These included "You're Following Me" by Perry Como, "Be True to Yourself" by Bobby Vee, "Keep Me in Mind" by Patti Page, "Heavenly" by Johnny Mathis, "Take Me to Your Ladder" by Buddy Clinton, "Along Came Joe" by Merv Griffin, "Mexican Divorce" by The Drifters, "The Night That Heaven Fell" by Tony Bennett, "Blue on Blue" by Bobby Vinton and "Don't You Believe It" by Andy Williams.

I started discovering all those songs from Bacharach's early Body of Work that I had never heard before. As a Bacharach fan since 1958, I found myself in the same company as the younger music fans who have discovered his work and found relevance to their contemporary lives. My own personal favorites from these compilations (highly recommended that you hear, buy and download) include:

- "I Looked For You" by Charlie Gracie.
- "Too Late To Worry" by Babs Tino and Richard Anthony.
- "Long Day, Short Night" by The Shirelles, Dionne Warwick and Dawn Penn.
- "With Open Arms" by Jane Morgan
- "Sittin' in a Tree House" by Marty Robbins
- "The Answer to Everything" by Sam Fletcher
- "Thirty Miles of Railroad Track" by the Hammond Brothers

What I found in these musical gems was magical. Many of those songs stood on their own merits, serving the needs of the performers at the time. They served as building blocks for what became the definitive Bacharach sound.

That is the way that I am with business wisdom. I continually dust off old chestnuts and reapply them for clients, in my books, through my speeches and in sharing with mentees. The case studies become the substance of what we provide future clients. We benefit from going back and learning from our own early Body of Work, assuming that we strategized our career to be a long-term thing, as Burt Bacharach did. Everything we are in business stems from what we've been taught or not taught to date. A career is all about devoting resources to amplifying talents and abilities, with relevancy toward a viable end result. Failure to prepare for the future spells certain death for businesses and industries in which they function.

I'll close by adding business analogies to some Burt Bacharach song hits:

- "A House Is Not a Home" Organizations do not come with corporate cultures. They have to be nurtured. That's the subject of Chapter 6 in my book, "The Business Tree."
- "Walk On By" Just because it is available business does not mean it is the best available. Go beyond the low-hanging fruit.
- "There's Always Something There to Remind Me" Go back through your old files. Uncover what inspired you in the first place. It becomes the beacon toward your future.
- "Errand of Mercy" People can speak on your behalf and should be encouraged to do so. That does not absolve you from authoritatively stating your own case.
- "They Long To Be Close To You" Success breeds more success. That signals the need to weed out those who will take unfair advantage. Some networkers are users.
- "Odds and Ends" Go back and examine your company's strengths, weakness, opportunities and threats.
- "What the World Needs Now" Ethics and social responsibility must be parts of the business strategy.
- "Knowing When to Leave" The way that we end business relationships is just as important as the manner in which they begin.
- "Don't Make Me Over" Branding is NOT strategy. Every way in which a company markets must be commensurate and fit under definable business strategies.
- "That's Not the Answer" When consultants peddle "solutions," that's a vendor term for what they have to sell. Companies need to determine what they, and real business advisers will get them to that awareness.
- "There Goes the Forgotten Man" If someone is identified by one job, then that's not a Body of Work
- "Any Day Now" Perseverance pays off. That's how businesses survive and go to the next plateau.

- "My Little Red Book" Having a network of friends and resources is important.
- "The Windows of the World" We are a global economy and must learn the business protocols of others. Going global is essential, and there are nuances to its effectiveness.
- "Arthur's Theme, Best That You Can Do" Employees should be encouraged to be their best. Empowered work teams are more valuable to the organization. Effective leaders encourage people to be their best, and it will benefit the company. That's the subject of Chapter 7 in my book, "The Business Tree."
- "Living Together, Growing Together" Collaborations, partnering and joint-venturing are the most important new trend in business. That's the subject of Chapter 8 in my book, "The Business Tree."
- "That's What Friends Are For" Category 6 in my Business Tree book looks at forces outside your company that can profoundly affect the climate in which you do business. Learn how to identify and nurture your stakeholders.
- "Loneliness Remembers What Happiness Forgets" We learn three times more from failure than success. Learning from failures is how successful strategies are built. That's the subject of Chapter 9 in my book, "The Business Tree."
- "Overnight Success" Learn to go the distance. Most overnight successes reflect many years of dues-paying.
- "Turn On Your Heartlight" When the company functions at its best, then it continues setting higher sites. Organizations in the right business for the right reasons tend to practice continuous quality improvement. That's the subject of Chapter 10 in my book, "The Business Tree."

A rich and sustaining Body of Work results from a greater business commitment and heightened self-awareness. None of us can escape those pervasive influences that have affected our lives, including music and the messages contained in songs. Like sponges, we absorbed the information, giving us views of life that have helped mold our business and personal relationships.

Lessons from The Monkees Apply to Success

It was the night of February 9, 1964. Davy Jones stood backstage at the Ed Sullivan Theatre in New York City. As a teenage actor and singer, he was in the cast of the Broadway hit "Oliver," starring British singer Georgia Brown. That was the night that The Beatles invaded America, starring on CBS-TV's "Ed Sullivan Show." There were other acts on the bill that night, including comedian Frank Gorshin, singer Tessie O'Shea, the comedy team of Charlie Brill & Mitzi McCall and the "Oliver" cast to perform scenes from the show for the TV audience.

Jones watched the Beatles perform in their American television debut and mused that he would like to get a gig like that one day. He in fact did two and a half years later, as a cast member in a TV sitcom that was inspired by The Beatles' movie "Hard Day's Night."

Hollywood responded to Beatlemania by putting together a group of actors to play a Beatles type teenage pop group. "The Monkees" was primarily a TV sitcom, and it was produced by Columbia-Screen Gems, whose other hits included "Bewitched," "I Dream of Jeannie," "Gidget" and "The Flying Nun." Stars Michael Nesmith and Davy Jones had music in their repertoire. Mickey Dolenz and Peter Tork were actors who portrayed pop musicians.

The songs were written by Tommy Boyce, Bobby Hart, Neil Diamond, Carole King, John Stewart and other top talents. The recordings featured studio musicians. The Monkees tended to the sitcom and lip-synced two songs per episode, one of them done in a new, original format: as a music video.

Once The Monkees debuted on NBC-TV, they were an instant hit. They primed the pre-teen market for such later luminaries as Herman's Hermits, Paul Revere & the Raiders, The Cowsills and The Partridge Family. The TV show spawned concert tours, and The Monkees had to learn to play instruments. There were guest shots, product tie-in's, merchandising and Monkees fan clubs. All this activity jelled with The Monkees, and it became the prototype for other pop acts packaged as big business.

Arguably, music videos were invented as theatrical shorts. Staging pop hits was popularized in the 1950s by NBC-TV's "Your Hit Parade." Variety shows such as Sullivan's brought the top recording acts to TV audiences. But it was The Monkees who set the prototype for music videos, which MTV later patterned its format.

Monkee Michael Nesmith not only was the creative juice behind music videos, but his mother was another trailblazer in the business world. As a secretary in Dallas, Texas, she invented the office product Liquid Paper.

Critics said that The Monkees were cute mop-tops (with Davy Jones being the cutest). They were lambasted for not playing their own music. As the group took control of their instruments on stage, they began receiving respect as legitimate musicians. Their success helped to fund charitable causes.

The Monkees lasted only two seasons on NBC-TV. There was "Head," the Monkees movie. There were recordings and concert tours that outlasted the series. Monkee members Nesmith and Jones had solo careers. Periodically, The Monkees would reunite for nostalgia tours.

There are four basic kinds of companies:

1. Those who created the original concept. The people who created the widget then proceed to run the widget manufacturing and distribution enterprise. The Monkees were a spoof of The Beatles, who created the widget. Yet, The Monkees created the music video component and the laughter-friendly audience acceptance of what was formerly mis-understood.

2. Companies who take someone else's concepts, perfect them and deliver them to new and different marketplaces than had the original widget firm. The Monkees went into living rooms. Parents saw them as "sons," when they were more leary of The Rolling Stones, The Animals, The Doors and other rock groups. The Monkees reached wider audiences, thus priming the pump for other comparable sitcoms.

3. Companies with a short life in the marketplace. They are nurtured as assets to be expanded in other directions, flipped to other sellers or taken to other levels. Though they only ran two seasons, "The Monkees" has been rerun ever since. They turned up on cable TV, VHS tapes and DVD box sets. Remarketed music sets continued to sell on records, tapes, CDs and Internet downloads. The Monkees' two-year stint in the original market has extended to 45 years in the after-market.

4. Companies that team with others, creating a synergy and diversified holding that individual players could not achieve on their own. This embodies the most important dynamic of modern business:

Collaborations, Partnering and Joint Venturing (discussed in Chapter 8 of my book, The Business Tree™). The Monkees led to "Michael Nesmith's Elephant Parts," which led to MTV music videos. Many TV shows (comedies and dramas) have since incorporated music video inserts. Monkees money helped bankroll Woodstock and music videos by other artists.

The Monkees were that rare business enterprise that applied to all four categories of business. Then there is the dynamic of casting the right actors to play the right parts. Most musical groups came together by happenstance, many playing good music but not possessing charm and charisma. Alas, The Monkees as a study on better ways to conduct business.

I end with words of wisdom from the masters:

- "Cheer up sleepy Jean. Oh what does it mean to a Daydream Believer," recorded by The Monkees.
- "Another Pleasant Valley Sunday here in status symbol land," recorded by The Monkees.
- "Words that never were true, spoken to nobody but you. Words with lies inside, but small enough to hide till your playing was through," recorded by The Monkees.

And some other golden oldies lyrics, for good measure:

- "Hey life, look at me. I can see through reality. Now I see life for what it is. It's not a dream. It's not a bliss. It happened to me, and it can happen to you." "The Happening" (1967) sung by Diana Ross & the Supremes
- "Don't make me over. Now that I'd do anything for you. Don't pick on the things I say, the things I do. I'll always be by your side, whenever you're wrong or right. Accept me for what I am. Accept me for the things that I do." Burt Bacharach & Hal David (1962)
- "When it's time to change, you've got to rearrange." The Brady Bunch (1972)
- "I was so much older then. I'm younger than that now." Bob Dylan (1966)

- "Kicks just keep getting harder to find. And all your kicks aren't bringing you peace of mind. Before you find out it's too late, you better get straight." Paul Revere & the Raiders (1966)

Remembering Great Mentors

One never forgets their first mentor. I have had several great ones, who in turn taught me the value of passing it on to others. That's why I advise businesses, write books, speak at conferences and more.

That first great mentor sticks with you always. Mine was legendary humorist and media figure Cactus Pryor. I started working for him in 1958, at KTBC Radio in Austin, TX. Cactus was the program director and morning radio personality. His show, filled with humor, humanity and music, was the natural lead-in to "Arthur Godfrey Time," which we carried from the CBS Radio Network.

Cactus was 34 at the time that he began mentoring me. He had grown up around show business. His father, Skinny Pryor, owned a movie theatre and entertained audiences with comedy routines during intermissions. Cactus was inspired by all that he saw. He joined KTBC as a disc jockey in 1945, becoming program director. When the station signed on its TV station on Thanksgiving Day, 1952, Cactus was the first personality on the screen. He welcomed viewers and introduced the first two programs, the University of Texas vs. Texas A&M football game, followed by the "Howdy Doody Show" from the NBC-TV Network.

Cactus had been doing his morning show from his home, with his kids as regulars, with the repartee being similar to Art Linkletter interviewing children. Early in 1958, he was doing his morning show back in the studio. I started as his regular on Saturday mornings, and he gave me segments to do. From him, I learned valuable lessons. You cannot be a carbon copy of everyone else. He wanted me to like and respect Dick Clark but not become a clone of him. Being one of a kind is a long quest. He wanted me to set my own tone and not be labeled by others.

From Cactus Pryor and a 24-year old newscaster named Bill Moyers, I learned that if you take the dirtiest job and do it better than everyone else, you will become a solid expert. In the good old days of regulated broadcasting, stations had to keep logs of the music, to avoid the hint of Payola (a growing controversy at the time). I kept the logs and learned about the music, the record companies, the composers and much more.

Stations also had to perform Community Ascertainment by going into the community, inquiring about issues, and assuring that broadcasting addressed those issues. That's where I learned to file license renewals. That's where I learned the value of public service announcements and public affairs program, which deregulation precluded broadcasting from doing. From that mentoring, I fell in love with the non-profit culture, the organizations and the client bases affected by them. Community Ascertainment inspired me to the lifelong championing of not-for-profit groups and their fine works. From that experience, I still advise corporations to set up non-profit foundations and do good deeds.

The early days of television were creative. Cactus hosted a local variety show on Channel 7. He interviewed interesting locals, showcased local talent and did comedy material. One of his advertisers was an appliance store and, while showing the latest TV sets, Cactus kicked their screens to demonstrate their rugged qualities. When the station left its first temporary home at the transmitter atop Mount Larson, Cactus was carried out in the chair in which he was sitting, a symbol that the variety show would move to the new studio at the corner of 6th and Brazos.

Cactus began developing special characters, with unique personas. That first year in which I worked with him, he created a puppet, Theopolous P. Duck. It was inspired by Edgar Bergen's characters. Mr. Duck delivered jokes with a cultured accent. He appeared in comedy spoof segments on local KTBC-TV shows, such as "Now Dig This" (hosted by Ricci Ware), "Woman's World" (hosted by Jean Covert Boone) and the "Uncle Jay Show" (hosted by Jay Hodgson).

During that time, he developed a famous sign-off phrase. Network stars had their own, such Garry Moore's "Be very kind to each other." Cactus used the phrase: "Thanks a lot. Lots of luck. And thermostrockamortimer." He joked that his made-up term meant "go to hell." But really, he wanted to tantalize people into thinking bigger thoughts and being their best.

Cactus loved to play on words, giving twists to keep the listeners alert. He used turns of phrases such as "capital entertainment for the capitol city" and "that solid sound in Austin town." In talking breaks for our sister station (KRGV), he said "that solid sound in the valley round."

He taught me how to deliver live commercials and to ad-lib. In those days, we would do live remotes for advertisers, inviting people to come out, get prizes and meet us at the external location. Doing such remotes got us appearance fees, and they really drew for the advertisers.

Through the remotes, I learned how to feed lines and develop the talent to speak in sound bites, as I do for business media interviews to this day. I was with Cactus at a remote for Armstrong-Johnson Ford. The out-cue was to describe the 1959 Ford model. Cactus said, "It's sleek and dazzling, from its car-front to its car-rear." That was a cue for the studio DJ to play a commercial for the Career Shop, a clothing retailer. Today, when I use nouns as verbs and place business terms out of context to make people think creatively, I'm thinking back to Cactus Pryor.

One remote on which I joined Cactus was for the fourth KFC franchise in the United States. We got to interview Colonel Harland Sanders on his new business venture. Little did I know that, 20 years later, KFC would be a corporate client of mine, and I would be advising them how to vision forward, following the Colonel's death.

Music programming was important to Cactus Pryor and, thus, to me. Mentees of his understood and advocated broad musical playlists, with the variety to appeal broadly. Under a "service radio" format, different day-parts showcased different musical genres. He believed that virtually any record could be played, within context. One of the programming tricks that I taught him was to commemorate Bing Crosby's birthday each May by playing "White Christmas" and other holiday hits out of season, which got the listeners fascinated.

In those days, you could play rock n' roll hits from the KTBC Pop Poll, a list that was circulated to local record stars as a cross-promotion. There were also positions in the "clock" devoted to easy listening artists, instrumentals, country cross-overs and what Cactus called "another KTBC golden disc, time tested for your pleasure."

Cactus liked rock n' roll but wanted to see that easy listening records got proper attention. He would indicate his interest in notes on the green shucks that encased the records. As a write this section, I'm holding "Many a Time," a 1958 release by Steve Lawrence, an easy-listening star who was beginning to also be considered a teen idol. Here's the dialog from this record jacket: "Plug hard as hell. Experiment to see if we can get it on the Pop Poll. Cactus." One of the DJ's wrote, "How hard is hell?" Cactus wrote a reply, "Hard, ain't it hard." Steve Lawrence would subsequently have many teen hits ("Pretty Blue Eyes," "Portrait of My Love," "Go Away Little Girl," "Walking Proud." etc.).

Humor was the beacon over everything that he did. Cactus began recording comedy records, such as "Point of Order" on the Four Star Label and still others for Austin-based Trinity Records. He began writing a humorous newspaper column, "Cacti's Comments."

Besides his radio work, Cactus Pryor got bookings as an after-dinner speaker. In the early years, he gave comedy monologues and historical narratives. Always lively and entertaining, he inspired audiences to think the bigger ideas and look beyond the obvious. I follow his tenets in delivering business keynotes and facilitating think tanks and corporate retreats.

His gigs got more humorous. Cactus created different personas, replete with costume and makeup. His first was a European diplomat who had the same voice and inflection as Theopolous P. Duck. He would deliver funny zingers, often touching upon political sacred cows. Then, he would peel off the mustache and ask, "Ain't it tacky?" He would then divulge that he actually was humorist Cactus Pryor from Austin, Texas. The act was well accepted and perfected during the era when our boss, Lyndon B. Johnson, was President of the United States.

Cactus did national TV variety shows. He was the "other Richard Pryor." He continued developing characters and entertaining audiences up through the 1990's, when his son Paul had begun doing the circuit as well. Paul is a funny satirist as well, something that I had known back when he was a school buddy of my sister Julie.

John Wayne called Cactus "one of the funniest guys around" and invited him to appear in two classic Wayne movies, "The Green Berets" and "The Hellfighters." I recall visiting Cactus on the set of "The Green Berets" in Benning, Georgia, and seeing him keep stars John Wayne, David Janssen, Jim Hutton and Bruce Cabot in stitches in between shots and poker games.

Though national fame beckoned, he kept his roots in Austin, claiming, "There is no way to follow laughs onstage but with pancakes at City Park." He stayed in his beloved Centex community. He did write books on Texana and history. There were contributions to the news-talk stations.

These are some lasting things that I learned from my first mentor (Cactus Pryor), and I've shared them with corporations and audiences all over this world:

- A great mentor, teacher and role model need not be from the same strata as those whom he or she inspires.
- Top executives must set high standards to which others aspire, including themselves. We must train people to be trustworthy.
- A Body of Work takes time, energy, resources and lots of heart to produce. This holds true for any company-organization and for any person.
- Defining what is good taste is a matter of judgment, perspective and experience.
- The process of amassing life and professional skills is ongoing.
- As an integrated process of life skills, career has its place.
- Whatever measure you give will be the measure that you get back.
- Getting and having are not necessarily the same thing.
- One cannot live entirely through work.
- One doesn't just work to live.

And these are some of the insights that I have developed, inspired by his early mentoring:

- Never assume that people place high priorities on anything other than meeting their immediate needs. After they've used you, they'll forget you.
- Set boundaries soon and often. Otherwise, it haunts you for the rest of your life and clouds your productivity. Do not place too much focus on what you wish you had said, done and accomplished.
- See through show-boaters. Those who brag about contacts rarely have a clue. Dreamers and schemers are allowed to get by because of other people's gullible, undiscerning and unsophisticated natures.
- Learn to say no without apologizing. Say it neutrally and strongly. Mean it.
- Put things in a crisis mode to illustrate your points. That's what lawyers do. Couch planning as the only way to avert a crisis. Expect the best, but prepare for the worst. 85% of the time, proper planning averts crisis.
- Etiquette is a direct reflection of what people were/were not taught. Their trustworthiness is reflected in the way they handle themselves, via walking etiquette, elevator etiquette, telephone handling, meeting skills

and networking etiquette. People who we think should know better often do not.

- Don't make the margin of profit too low. Once you set low perimeters, people see them as the top ends. They will cut and skim. They will see you as the low-cost provider.
- Senior corporate executives, especially those who rose to the rank of CEO, have had to adapt more in their careers than young people who never rise past mid-management. When young people want it all now and think they know enough, older people are wise enough to see the longer perspective.
- Things are never simple for one who must make decisions and policies. Many factors must be weighed.
- One cannot always go the path that seems the clearest. One who thinks differently and creatively will face opposition. With success of the concept, it gets embraced by others, who claim to have been visionary all along.
- Shepherding good ideas and concepts does not get many external plaudits. The feeling of accomplishment must be internal. That is a true mark of wisdom.

I met Steven Spielberg in 1970 at the beginning of his film directing career. I was at Universal Studios, interviewing Robert Young on his TV series "Marcus Welby, M.D." Young felt that his young TV episode director (Spielberg) would be one of the superstars of Hollywood, and he was right. Spielberg had this distinguished five-year career, directing three made-for-TV movies and episodes of shows like "Columbo," "The Bold Ones," Rod Serling's Night Gallery" and "Name of the Game." This prepared him for a dynamic movie career. What we do in our salad days sets the tone for magnificent career achievements.

Pop Icons Collage.

Author Hank Moore is pictured with Dick Clark. Photo taken in 1976.

Author Hank Moore is pictured with Sonny and Cher. Photo taken in 1967.

Chapter 3

ICONS AND LEGENDS
FOR CHILDREN

K ids are an important part of the population. They symbolize our love, protection, hopes, dreams and accomplishments.

Industries catering to children are a vital, thriving part of the economy. From food to sports programs, from day care to tutoring, from clothing to entertainment and from toys to other merchandise, kids represent at least 35% of business activity.

The number of children under the age of 18 in the U.S. is expected to grow by 7 million over the next 10 years, from 75 million to 82 million. Business opportunities will grow accordingly. The same is true for population growth on the other end of the age spectrum, seniors. There are 57 million children in the U.S., who spend $100 billion on their own, buying food, drinks, candy, movies, clothing, sports, electronics and video games. What their parents and other family members spend on them is four-fold, covering housing, furniture, transportation, activity programs, tutoring, appliances, computers and vacations. The international market for children's products and services is expected to grow steadily.

The business trends expected to dominate the kids' market in the future include multi-function toys and accessories, retro toys with a modern appeal, organic foods and drinks with reusable packaging, adult electronics stylized for children, multi-lingual programs, party entertainment, products addressing special needs, pop-culture themed products, problem-solving products and children's business cards and websites.

There are stages in the development of children as customers and consumers. From age 1, they accompany parents and observe. From age 2, they begin asking for things and make connections to what they've seen advertised. From age 3, they accompany parents and begin selecting items (more than half asking for specific brands). From age 4, they learn to pay as the customer. From age 5, they make independent buying decisions and purchases.

Healthcare institutions serving children deliver care that identifies, assesses, treats and supports children and their families. They focus on early help and prevention, reducing the escalation of disease and promote recovery and stimulating long-term opportunities and outcomes.

Education centered tutoring programs, from localized providers to national networks such as Sylvan Learning. Recreation for children is served through a host of day camps, art institutes, sports programs and leadership development.

Icons and legends related to children are a much beloved part of pop culture. Every era has them, and adults carry those feelings and memories from their childhoods forever. These are some of the areas where business icons and legends serve the important children's market.

Toy Legends

Toys are used for play, for education and for creative expression by children. It is said that children will play with whatever they find available. The oldest mechanical puzzle came from Greece in the 3rd Century B.C. As children were seen as themselves rather than as extensions of their parents, the manufactured toy industry started in the 18th Century. The first board games were produced in the 1750's. 19th Century toys had educational purposes, including puzzles, books, cards and board games. In 1817, the kaleidoscope was introduced.

In the 1860s, girls played with dolls, and boys played with marbles and toy trains.

In 1900, production began on Meccano, predecessor to the erector set and tinker toys. In the 1920s, Dinky Toys manufactured die-cast toy cars, ships, trains and toy soldiers. Synthetic rubber from World War II turned into silly putty. In 1943, Richard James experimented with springs for his military research, the result becoming the Slinky. Play-Doh was first created as a wallpaper cleaner. The 1950s brought Lego's Rubik's Cube, Mr. Potato Head and The Action Man.

Mattel Toys was founded in 1945 in Segundo, California, by Harold Matson and Elliot Handler. Mattel's Barbie Doll was named after Handler's daughter. Mattel produces Fischer-Price, Monster High, Hot Wheels, Matchbox, Masters of the Universe, American Girl dolls, board games and WWE Toys. It introduced such products as Chatty Cathy in 1960, See N' Say in 1965, Hot Wheels in 1968 and home game video consoles in the 1980s.

The original inductees into the National Toy Hall of Fame in 1999 were Barbie, Crayola Crayons, erector sets, Etch A Sketch, the Frisbee, the hula hoop, Lego's, Lincoln Logs, marbles, Monopoly, Play-Doh, the Radio Flyer wagon, roller skates, teddy bears, Tinker Toys, the View-Master and the yo-yo.

Inducted in 2000 were bicycles, jacks, jump ropes Mr. Potato Head and Slinky. Inducted in 2001 were Silly Putty and Tonka Trucks. Inducted in 2002 were the jigsaw puzzle and Raggedy Ann. Inducted in 2003 were alphabet blocks and checkers. Inducted in 2004 were G.I. Joe, the rocking horse and Scrabble. Inducted in 2005 were Candy Land, the cardboard box and the jack-in-the-box. Inducted in 2006 were Easy Bake Oven and Lionel trains. Inducted in 2007 were the Atari 2600, Kite and Raggedy Andy. Inducted in 2008 were the stick, the baby doll and the skateboard. Inducted in 2009 were the ball, Game Boy and Big Wheel. Inducted in 2010 were The Game of Life and playing cards. Inducted in 2011 were Hot Wheels, the doll house and the blanket. Inducted in 2012 were Star Wars action figures and dominoes. Inducted in 2013 were Chess and the rubber duck. Inducted in 2014 were little green army men, bubbles and Rubik's Cube.

And then there is the retro market for kids who grew up. Old toys and memorabilia have long been a staple of antique stores and flea markets. The internet era brought as Ebay and other websites that sell the memories of childhoods, all eras.

Literature for Children

Comic strips began appearing in newspapers in the late 19th Century. The first to appear was "The Yellow Kid." Early 20th Century comic strips appearing in newspapers included "The Katzenjammer Kids," "Gasoline Alley," "Pogo," "Winnie Winkle," "Little Annie Rooney" and "Barney Google and Snuffy Smith."

One of the most popular comic strips centered on a girl named Little Orphan Annie. It was created in 1924 by Harold Gray, taking the name from an 1885 poem. It followed the adventures of 11-year-old Annie, her dog Sandy and her benefactor Oliver "Daddy" Warbucks. "Little Orphan Annie" ran as a radio show from 1930-1942. Two movies were based upon the comic strip. In 1977, it became a Broadway musical Actresses who played Annie onstage included Andrea McArdle, Sarah Jessica Parker, and Alyssa Milano. In the 1982 movie version, Annie was played by Aileen Quinn.

Other comic strips with special appeal to kids included "Beetle Bailey," "Buck Rogers," "Tarzan," "Dennis the Menace," "Dick Tracy," "Henry," "Terry and the Pirates," "Mother Goose and Grimm," "Prince Valiant," "Flash Gordon," "Mandrake the Magician," "The Lone Ranger," "The Green Hornet," "Batman," "Donald Duck," "Fritz the Cat," "Moon Mullins," "Peanuts," "Amazing Spider-Man," "Garfield," "B.C." and "Mutts."

Comic books were popular with kids from the 1930's through the 1960's. It began with the introduction of Superman in 1938. DC Comics specialized in super heroes. Dell published monthly editions based on cartoons, TV shows and movies. Classics Comics covered great books, with pictures and condensed texts. Marvel Comics symbolized the renaissance of superhero and science-fiction stories, from the 1970's forward to the present day.

Magazines for children included the Weekly Reader, Jack and Jill, National Geographic for Kids, Boys' Life, Kids World, Quiz Kids, Cricket and Recess Kids.

Books for children trace roots back to the mid-18th Century. "A Little Pretty Pocket Book" by John Newberry was published in 1744. It contained rhymes, picture stories, games for the pleasure and a diary for the kids to record their daily activities. "Practical Education: The History of Harry and Lucy" in 1780 urged children to teach themselves.

In the early 19th Century, Danish author and poet Hans Christian Andersen traveled Europe and collected fairy tales. The Brothers Grimm followed suit, recalling interesting stories from German heritage. These were followed by "Norwegian Folktales" and "Swiss Family Robinson" in 1812.

Books for children shifted to realism, fantasy and adventures. "Tom Brown's School Days" appeared in 1857. Lewis Carroll's "Alice in Wonderland" was published in 1865. Louisa May Alcott's "Little Women" was published in 1868. Mark Twain released ""Tom Sawyer" in 1878. Joel Chandler Harris released "Uncle Remus" in 1880. "The Adventures of Pinnochio" was published in 1883. Robert Louis Stevenson wrote "Treasure Island" and "Kidnapped" in the 1880's. Rudyard Kipling's "The Jungle Book" came in 1894.

The 20th Century brought some beloved classics: Frank Baum's "The Wonderful Wizard of Oz" (1900), J.M. Barrie's "Peter Pan" (1911), A.A. Milne's "Winnie the Pooh" (1926), Laura Ingalls Wilder's "Little House in the Big Woods" (1932), J.R.R. Tolkien's "The Hobbit" (1937), Dr. Seuss's "And To Think That I Saw It on Mulberry Street" (1937), C.S. Lewis's "The Chronicles of Narnia" (1950), E.B. White's "Charlotte's Web" (1952), Dodie Smith's "101 Dalmations" (1956), Roald Dahl's "Charlie and the Chocolate Factory" (1964) and J.K. Rowling's "Harry Potter" (1997).

Little Golden Books was founded in 1942 by Georges Duplaix as a children's book subsidiary of Simon and Schuster. Bank Street College of Education's Writers Laboratory became source material for the books. One of its first releases, "The Poky Little Puppy," is still sold today and looks essentially the same. The company produced Little Golden records, tapes, toys, CD-roms and games. Some books were adapted from other children's icons, including Disney, Sesame Street, The Muppets, Mister Rogers, Barbie, Power Rangers and youthful personalities.

The Disney Influence

Walt Disney started his career as an artist at a newspaper in Kansas City. He met cartoonist Ubbe Iwerks, and they formed a company. They made advertisements, and Disney was inspired into a career in animation. Disney produced the "Newman Laugh-O-Grams," followed by "Alice Comedies" and then "Oswald the Lucky Rabbit." Losing the rights to Oswald, Disney and Iwerks developed a new character, Mickey Mouse, who soon topped "Felix the Cat" as the most important cartoon character.

With the success of Mickey Mouse came the "Silly Symphonies" series, which later inspired the feature-length film "Fantasia." The Symphonies spawned The Three Little Pigs, Donald Duck, Goofy and Pluto. "Snow White and the Seven Dwarfs" in 1937 was Disney's first feature film. Later came "Three Caballeros," "Alice in Wonderland," "Peter Pan," "Lady and the Tramp," "Sleeping Beauty," "Sword in the Stone," "Bambi," "101 Dalmations," "The Aristocats" and many others. Disney produced spirit films during World War II and later true-life adventure features. Some features included animated and live-action scenes, including "Song of the South" and "So Dear To My Heart."

This quote summarizes the Disney philosophy: "When you wish upon a star. Makes no difference who you are. Your dreams will come true." Voiced by Jiminy Cricket, in the Disney movie classic "Pinnochio" (1941).

The 1950s brought Disney Studios into live-action scripted movies, including "Treasure Island," "20,000 Leagues Under the Sea" (starring Kirk Douglas), "Old Yeller" (starring Tommy Kirk), "The Great Locomotive Chase" (starring Fess Parker) and "Light in the Forest" (starring James MacArthur and Carol Lynley). The 1960's brought audiences "Polyanna," "The Parent Trap" (Hayley Mills starring in the original, Lindsay Lohan starring in the remake), "Mary Poppins" (starring Julie Andrews), "Babes in Toyland" and "The Monkey's Uncle" (starring Annette Funicello).

Disney conceived a theme park in California, Disneyland, which would embrace his studios characters, stories and fans. While raising money to build it, he agreed to produce a television series, "Disneyland," later retitled "Walt Disney Presents" and "Walt Disney's Wonderful World of Color." The park opened in 1955 and was a hit, inspiring in 1971 Disney World in Orlando, Florida.

The Disney TV series remained a popular attraction for decades, running on the ABC and NBC networks. The show was a mix of recycled material from his shorts and movies, original dramas, promotions for new Disney films and compilations of subject material. It spawned Davy Crockett, a major craze that in turn spawned feature films, coon skin caps, toy merchandising, recordings and personal appearances for stars Fess Parker and Buddy Ebsen. Disney produced two other TV series, "The Mickey Mouse Club" and "Zorro."

Business extensions have included Buena Vista Distributing, Disneyland Records, vacation resorts, water parks, Imagineering services and cable networks.

Inspired by Disney, other entertainment companies specializing in children and the family trade have operated successfully. They brought us movies, TV shows, merchandising, theme parks and a lot of great memories.

TV Shows for Children

Television became the window on the world for Baby Boomer children. The TV set was the babysitter in an era where both parents worked outside the home. It was also the source of education and inspiration for kids.

The first kid shows were live participation series. "Howdy Doody" set the tone for the TV industry, with its Peanut Gallery of kids, the likeable Buffalo Bob Smith as the host, puppet Howdy Doody as the kid hero, Clarabell the Clown and a cast of characters in the mythical village of Doodyville.

The success of Howdy Doody spawned many other series for kids and with kids as participants. These included "The Paul Winchell & Jerry Mahoney Show," "Kukla, Fran & Ollie" (Burr Tillstrom, Fran Allison), "The Quiz Kids," "Super Circus," "Rootie Kazootie," "The Pinky Lee Show" (starring a former burlesque comic who later inspired Pee Wee Herman), "The Soupy Sales Show," "Andy's Gang" (Andy Devine), "The Gumby Show," "Shari Lewis Show," "The Magic Land of Allakazam" (Mark Wilson) and "Beany and Cecil."

Some TV hosts had multiple series. Jack Barry hosted "Juvenile Jury" and "Winky Dink and You." He went on to host the quiz show "Twenty One," which was investigated and found to have been rigged. Some shows were educational. "Watch Mr. Wizard" featured Don Herbert teaching science experiments to kids in the studio. "Ding Dong School" was hosted by Dr. Frances Horwich.

There were shows filled with entertainment but also teaching messages. The biggest was "Captain Kangaroo," hosted by Robert Keeshan, who had previously played Clarabell the Clown on "The Howdy Doody Show." Fred Rogers hosted "Mister Rogers' Neighborhood," first on Pittsburgh TV, then on Canadian TV and mostly on PBS. "Sesame Street" has been running on PBS since 1969, produced by the Children's Television Workshop, featuring music, comedy, education and a host of guest stars. Sesame spawned other PBS shows, including "The Electric Company," "Zoom," "Newton's Apple," "Barney and Friends," "Dragon Tales," "Teletubbies," "Cailou," "Clifford the Big Red Dog,"

"Arthur," "Dinosaur Train," "Peg+Cat" and "Curious George." Jim Henson's characters were on "Sesame Street" and then spun off into movies and their own series, "The Muppet Show."

In the 1950s, there were several live-action dramatic shows with appeal to kids and families. These included:

- "Captain Video," starring Richard Coogan, Don Hastings and Hal Conklin.
- "Space Patrol," starring Ed Kemmer and Lyn Osborne.
- "Tom Corbett, Space Cadet," starring Frankie Thomas and Jan Merlin.
- "The Roy Rogers Show," starring Roy Rogers Dale Evans and Pat Brady.
- "The Hopalong Cassidy Show," starring William Boyd and Edgar Buchanan.
- "The Gene Autry Show," starring Gene Autry and Pat Buttram.
- "Annie Oakley," starring Gail Davis, Brad Johnson and Jimmie Hawkins.
- "Buffalo Bill Jr.," starring Dick Jones, Nancy Gilbert and Harry Cheshire.
- "Sky King," starring Kirby Grant, Gloria Winters and Ron Hagerthy.
- "Rocky Jones, Space Ranger," starring Richard Crane.
- "Lassie," starring Jan Clayton, Tommy Rettig and George Cleveland, later re-cast with June Lockhart, Jon Provost and Hugh Reilly, still later re-cast with Robert Bray as the ranger.
- "Captain Gallant of the Foreign Legion," starring Buster Crabbe, Fuzzy Knight and Cullen Crabbe.
- "Captain Midnight," starring Richard Webb, Sid Melton and Olan Soule.
- "Fury" (starring Peter Graves, Bobby Diamond and William Fawcett).
- "Tales of the Texas Rangers," starring Willard Parker and Harry Lauter.
- "Adventures of Rin Tin Tin," starring Lee Aaker and James Brown.
- "The Adventures of Robin Hood," starring Richard Greene.
- "My Friend Flicka," starring Johnny Washbrook, Gene Evans and Anita Louise.
- "Circus Boy," starring Mickey Dolenz (later becoming one of The Monkees).
- "Shirley Temple's Storybook."

Cartoon shows in the 1950s often included features that had been shown in movie theatres, including "Popeye," "Mighty Mouse Playhouse," "Woody Woodpecker Show," "Mr. Magoo," "Heckle and Jeckle Show," "Bugs Bunny Show." "Porky Pig Show" Road Runner Show" and "The Pink Panther Show."

William Hanna and Joseph Barbera had produced cartoons at MGM studios, notably Tom and Jerry. In 1957, they formed an independent company to produce cartoon series for television. Their shows set the tone for what other cartoon producers would do on television for the next three decades. Their hit shows included "Ruff and Reddy," Huckleberry Hound," "Quick Draw McGraw," "Yogi Bear," "The Flintstones," "Top Cat," "The Jetsons," "Magilla Gorilla," "Secret Squirrel," "The Banana Splits" and "Josie and the Pussycats."

Popular animated series of the 1960s and 1970s included "Matty's Funday Funnies," "Rocky & Bullwinkle," "King Leonardo and His Subjects," "The Alvin Show," "Calvin and the Colonel," "Fireball XL-5," "Tennessee Tuxedo," "Jonny Quest," "Linus the Lionhearted," "Underdog," "Atom Ant," "The Fantastic Four," "George of the Jungle," "Dudley Do-Right," "Hot Wheels," "H.R. Pufnstuf," "Scooby-Doo," "The Bugaloos," "Lancelot Link, Secret Chimp," "The Reluctant Dragon and Mr. Toad," "Sabrina and the Groovy Goolies," "Deputy Dawg," "Lidsville," "Sabrina, the Teenage Witch," "Kid Power" and "Sealab 2020."

There were cartoon shows based on such entertainment icons as "The Beatles," "The Lone Ranger," "King Kong," "The Monkees," "Superman," "Off to See the Wizard," "Spider Man," "The Archie Show," "The Jackson Five," "The Osmonds" and "The Brady Bunch."

The cable era brought audiences Nickelodeon. It started in 1977 as Pinwheel and changed in 1979 to Nickelodeon. Since 1985, it has shared its channel space with Nick at Nite, showing classic TV reruns. Nick's popular shows included "SpongeBob Square Pants," "Mr. Wizard's World," "Clarissa Explains It All," "Teenage Mutant Ninja Turtles," "The Ren and Stimpy Show," "Are You Afraid of the Dark," "The Fairly Odd Parents," "Dora the Explorer," "Power Rangers," "I-Carly," "Jimmy Neutron," "Degrassi," "Johnny Bravo" and "Blues Clues." Since 1985, it has shared its channel space with Nick at Nite, showing classic TV reruns, in turn spawning TV Land, Nick Jr. and Teen Nick.

Icons and Legends Who Were Children: Young Inventors

This section covers kids and teens who were icons and legends themselves. This reviews the actors, singers and youthful inventors who created iconic bodies of work. Most of them continued to accomplish throughout their lives. It was the child in them that led them toward iconic activities. Let's review some of the great child icons who have been an important part of our lives and society.

Horatio Adams knew that his father Thomas had purchased a lot of Mexican chicle with the intent of producing a rubber substitute. Horatio, then 13, found an alternate use, designing chewing gum. He developed gumballs and convinced the local druggist to dispense them.

Alexander Graham Bell was 18 when he began developing a way to transmit speech. His "harmonic telegraph" evolved into the telephone.

Benny Benson was 13 in 1926, living in an orphanage in Chignik, Alaska. The state held a contest to design the flag, and his artwork was chosen from 700 submissions across the territory. It became the official flag when Alaska became a state in 1959. For designing it, Benson won a $1,000 scholarship, a watch and a trip to Washington, D.C. In 2013, the 100th anniversary of his birth, the Alaska Legislature renamed the Kodiak Airport in his honor.

Henry Bessemer was 17 in 1830, producing as his first invention embossed stamps for use on title deeds. This made the illegal use of title stamps impossible, thus producing more revenue for the British government.

Joseph Armand Bombardier was 15 in 1922, living in Quebec, Canada. Spending winters in the snow, he added a sleigh frame and hand-whittled propeller to his father's old model T car. Thus evolved the snowmobile.

Louis Braille was accidentally blinded as a child. While attending a school for the visually impaired in Paris, Braille was 15 when he created a system using raised dots instead of letters.

Sarah Buckel was 14 in 2006 and loved to decorate her school locker but didn't want to scrape it clean at the end of the year. She chose patterns and devised Magnetic Locker Wallpaper.

Peter Chilvers was 12 in 1958 when he created the first sailboard, used in windsurfing.

Sam Colt was attending a boarding school at age 15. Wishing to get popular with the other kids, he made a firework and discharged it outside. Years later, he adapted the concept, and it became the revolver gun.

Jacob Dunnack was 8 in 2000 when he invented the Bat Ball, a system to store baseballs inside the bat.

Thomas Alva Edison was 17 in 1862, producing as his first invention a telegraphic repeating instrument, while working as a telegraph operator.

Frank Epperson was 11 in 1905 when he left his drink, a mixture of water and powdered soda on the porch overnight, during which time it froze in the cold weather. He called this delicacy the "Epsicle." 18 years later, Frank made it for his kids, and they called it "Pop's Sicle." In 1923, he commercialized the product, developing various flavors (30 now on the market, with orange being the most popular).

Philo Farnsworth was a 14-year old boy in Idaho when he drafted the first sketch of what would later become electronic television.

Fabian Fernandez-Han was 12, living in Conroe, Texas, when he invented the Oink-A-Saurus app to help kids to save and draw money from their piggy banks.

Abigail Fleck was 8 years old in 1993 when she and her father were cooking in their home in St. Paul, Minnesota. Abbey devised an innovative way to cook bacon, and they founded a company to sell their product, the "Makin' Bacon."

Benjamin Franklin loved to swim and was 11 years old when he invented flippers for the hands. The device was later adapted as flippers for the feet.

Cassidy Goldstein was 11 in 2001 when she developed Crayon Holders, maximizing their use via plastic tubes. The Intellectual Property Owners Education Foundation named her the 2006 Youth Inventor of the Year.

Suzanna Goodin, at 6 years of age, was tired of cleaning the cat food spoon. She invented an edible spoon shaped cracker.

Chester Greenwood was 15 in 1874 when creating his first invention, earmuffs, which were made by his factory for the next 60 years. Greenwood created more than 100 other inventions.

Kathryn Gregory was 10 in 1994, playing in the snow when the cold began to affect her wrists. To keep her hands and forearms warm, she invented fuzzy sleeves called Wristies. After testing them out on members of her Girl Scout troop, KK and her mother launched a business to produce them. She was the youngest person ever to appear on the QVC Channel, selling Wristies. In 2010, after finishing college, she became CEO of Wristies, Inc.

Robert Heft was a 17-year-old high school student in 1958. As a class project, he proposed adapting the American flag to increase to a 50-star design. His teacher gave him a B-minus but promised to increase the grade if he could get the U.S. Congress to endorse the idea, which they did. The U.S. flag contained 48 stars since 1912. In 1959, with the annexation of Alaska, the flag briefly carried 49 stars. In 1960, with the annexation of Hawaii, the flag went to 50 stars.

Taylor Hernandez was 10 in 2005, inventing "Magic Sponge Blocks," which would safely stack without hurting children when they fall.

Param Jaggi was 15 in 2008 when taking a driver's education course in Plano, Texas. Watching the car exhaust, he got the idea for a small device that plugs into the muffler. He created a device to utilize algae to convert carbon dioxide from automobile exhaust into clean oxygen. In 2011, his sustainable design won the International Science Fair, beating out 1,500 other applicants.

Margaret Knight was 12 in 1849, working at a cotton mill. She developed a safety mechanism that made it impossible for a shuttle to leave the loom. She later made 90 inventions and carried 26 patents, including the rotary engine, flat-bed paper bag machine and a5waterproof protector for women's skirts.

Chelsea Lannon was 8 in 1994 when she received a patent for the Pocket Diaper, which holds a baby wipe and powder puff. She got the idea while helping her mother change a sibling's diapers.

Jeanie Low was 11 when she invented the Kiddie Stool, which fits under the sink so that children can unfold it and stand on it in order to reach the sink on their own.

Hart Main was 13 in 2010 when he created Man Can candles in recycled soup cans, using as seed money the $100 earned from his newspaper route in Ohio. The early cans were emptied at local soup kitchens.

Cyrus Hall McCormick was 15 in 1824 when he developed a lightweight cradle for carting harvested grain. In 1831, he invented a horse-drawn device to cut small grain crops, known as the reaper.

George Nissen was 16 when he designed the first trampoline in his parents' garage.

Blaise Pascal was educated by his father, who was a French tax collector. In 1642, at the age of 19, Blaise created an adding machine for his father. It was able to add two decimals together and subtract. He made 50 of them, but nobody was interested in them at the time. Pascal's invention evolved 300 years later into the modern calculator. In 1968, the programming language PASCAL was named after him.

Robert Patch was 6 when in 1957 he invented a toy truck that can be disassembled and can be rebuilt into different kinds of trucks.

Ryan Patterson was 17 in 2002 when he invented a glove with special sensors that translate the hand motions of sign language into written words on a digital display.

Kelly Reinhart was 6 years old in 1998 when her parents challenged her to draw a new invention. Inspired by cowboy gun holsters, Kelly drew a thigh pack in which kids could carry their video games. At the age of 10, she started her own non-profit organization to teach other kids how to be inventors.

Ralph Samuelson was 18, living in Minnesota and wanted to create something like snow skiing on the water. He took two wooden boards and bent the ends by boiling them in a kettle. He is recognized as inventing water skis.

Becky Schroeder was 10 in 1972 when she tried to do homework in her mother's car, living in Toledo, Ohio. As it got dark, she created a way to see the paper better. She used phosphorescent paint to cover an acrylic board. At age 12, she received a patent for her Glo-Sheet invention, the youngest female to receive a U.S. patent.

Joe Shuster and Jerry Siegal conceived on Superman when they were still in high school.

Pamela Sica was 14 when inventing a push-button device that raises the floor of a car, enabling easier removal of cargo.

Richie Stachowski was 11 when he went with his family on vacation to Hawaii in 1996. He devised the Water Talkie, a device that facilitates swimmers talking with each other, pointing out the wondrous sights viewed underwater. He pitched his idea to Toys R Us and got an order for 50,000 units. With his family, he founded a company to produce them, Short Stack LLC. At 13, his company was sold to Wild Planet Toys.

Theresa Thompson (age 8) and her sister Mary (age 9) in 1960 invented a solar tepee for a science fair project, calling it the Wigwarm. They are the youngest sisters ever to receive a U.S. Patent.

Anton van Leeuwenhoek was 16 in 1648 when he developed improvements to the microscope.

George Westinghouse was 19 when he got his first patent in 1865, for the rotary steam engine.

Spencer Whale was 6 years old in 1998 when he visited a children's hospital. He then created a toy car with an attached IV pole, facilitating kids playing while receiving medicines. Several hospitals now have Kid Care Cars and Trucks.

Icons and Legends Who Were Children: The Performers

Christina Aguilera began singing at age 8, becoming one of the pop superstars as a singer and songwriter. She has been ambassador for the United Nations' World Food Program and holds a star on the Hollywood Walk of Fame. She is a staple of the NBC-TV series "The Voice."

Julie Andrews became a singing star at age 12 in England. In her 20's, she headlined Broadway in "My Fair Lady" and "Camelot." She reigned in the movies for three decades, including "Mary Poppins" and "Victor/Victoria."

Freddie Bartholomew started performing at age 3 in England. He moved to the U.S. when he was 10, under contract to MGM for such films as "David Copperfield," "Anna Karenina," "Little Lord Fauntleroy," "The Devil is a Sissy" and "Captain's Courageous." Then came teenage film roles. In his 20's, he went into television as a director, producer and executive.

Jimmy Boyd burst on the music scene at age 9, signing "I Saw Mommy Kissing Santa Claus." He sang other kid record hits. As a teenager, he appeared on the TV sitcom "Bachelor Father."

Michael Burns worked steadily as a child and teenage actor, beginning at age 12 and appearing on "It's a Man's World," "Dobie Gillis," "Wagon Train," "Twilight Zone," "The Bionic Woman," "Gunsmoke," "The Big Valley," "Streets of San Francisco," "Police Woman," "Dragnet" (as Blue Boy) and many other shows. He earned his doctorate in European history and became a professor at Mount Holyoke College.

Kirk Cameron began acting at the age of 9. At 15, he starred on TV's "Growing Pains." Now, he is an evangelist minister. He was honored by Indiana Wesleyan University, inducted into their Society of World Changers.

Jackie Coogan made millions of dollars working as an actor in the silent screen era. His best known film was 1914's "The Kid" with Charlie Chaplin. Following the revelation that his parents squandered most of the money that he earned, the California Legislature enacted the Coogan Law, requiring a portion of child earnings be applied to a "blocked trust" savings account. In later years, another former child actor, Gary Coleman, sued his adoptive parents and former business manager over poor management of his trust.

Jackie Cooper was a child actor at MGM in the 1930s, then played teen parts in the 1940s. He starred in TV sitcoms "The People's Choice" and "Hennessy" in the 1950s and 1960s, becoming a respected Hollywood studio executive and director in later years.

Celine Dion began her singing career at age 5, composing her first song at age 12. She became the first Canadian to receive a gold record in France, when she was 15. She began the ascent to pop superstar status at age 18. After three decades, she is a major headliner at concerts.

Patty Duke started appearing at age 10 on the CBS-TV soap opera "The Brighter Day." She then played Helen Keller in the Broadway play "The Miracle Worker," reprising the role for the film version. At age 16, she was given her own TV series, "The Patty Duke Show." She played two parts in the popular sitcom that is ranked as one of the top 50 TV shows of all time. Then came the films "Valley of the Dolls" and "Me Natalie." She returned to TV in 1970 for "My Sweet Charlie," the first of countless TV movies in which she starred over the next 40 years. From 1985-1988, she served as President of the Screen Actors Guild. Her 1990 autobiography was entitled "Call Me Anna."

Jodie Foster began her career at age 3 as the Coppertone girl in TV ads. She began appearing on TV series, starring at age 12 in ABC's "Paper Moon." Then came kid roles in films such as "Alice Doesn't Live Here Anymore" and "Taxi Driver." Then came Disney films and a distinguished adult acting career, including "Contact" and "Silence of the Lambs." At one point, she put the acting career on hold in order to pursue schooling at Harvard University. She remained an actor on Hollywood's A-list and became a film director, capping a 50-year career.

Annette Funicello began her career at age 12 as one of the Mouseketeers on ABC-TV's popular Disney series "Mickey Mouse Club." She was discovered by Walt Disney at a dance recital in Burbank, California. She appeared in the "Spin and Marty" serials and Disney's "Zorro" series. She recorded many records for the Disneyland label, with 1959's "Tall Paul" putting her on "American Bandstand." Then came Disney movies "The Shaggy Dog," "Babes in Toyland," "The Misadventures of Merlin Jones" and "The Monkey's Uncle." In her 20's, Annette starred in the "Beach Party" movies with Frankie Avalon. She was the TV spokesperson for Skippy Peanut Butter. She evolved into the role model for other teenage idols. At age 50, Annette was diagnosed with multiple sclerosis and was still a positive role model for the way that she valiantly lived with the disease over the next 20 years.

Judy Garland began singing at age 2. As a teenager, she became one of MGM's top stars, notably in "The Wizard of Oz." As an adult, she became a major concert attraction, one of the greatest singers of the 20th Century.

Debbie Gibson became a major recording artist at age 15, with pop classics including "Only in My Dreams," "Out of the Blue," "Foolish Beat," "Shake Your Love" and "Staying Together."

Melissa Gilbert was the darling of 1970's TV, beginning at age 10 as Laura Ingalls Wilder on NBC's "Little House on the Prairie." She went on to star in countless TV movies. From 2001-2005, she served as President of the Screen Actors Guild.

Barry Gordon was a child singer and actor in the 1950s, appearing with such greats as Jack Benny. He had a successful teen acting career in the 1960s and evolved into film production and management. From 1988-1995, he served as President of the Screen Actors Guild.

Lesley Gore was 16 when she burst on the music scene with the #1 hit "It's My Party." She continued a long string of hits, dubbed the essential Girl Group Singer. For five decades, she kept the tradition of teen pop ballads alive, including "You Don't Own Me," "Maybe I Know," "Judy's Turn to Cry," "That's the Way Boys Are," "She's a Fool" and "Sunshine, Lollipops and Roses."

Jennifer Love Hewitt started singing at age 3 at rodeos in her native Waco, Texas. She began performing professionally at age 10 in TV commercials and in the Disney Channel series "Kids Incorporated." She appeared in films and starred in the TV series "Ghost Whisperer" and "Criminal Minds."

Ron Howard started acting at age 3. He appeared on "The Andy Griffith Show" as Opie Taylor, from age 6-14. Then came movies such as "The Music Man" and "The Courtship of Eddie's Father," plus guest starring roles on top TV series such as "Dr. Kildare." This author met Ron Howard in 1971, when he was a 17-year-old actor on Henry Fonda's TV series, "The Smith Family," talking then about his intention to become a movie director. Then he appeared in the box-office smash "American Graffiti," followed by the gigantic TV series "Happy Days." Then Howard became one of the film industry's steadiest and most respected directors of the last three decades.

Michael Jackson grew up in a musical family. His father Joe Jackson had sung with two popular 1950s groups, The Falcons and The Flamingos. Joe put together a group of his sons, The Jackson Five. They were discovered by Diana Ross when Michael was 11 and signed to the prestigious Motown label. The hits rolled at Motown and later at Epic Records. Michael became a solo performer, quickly being dubbed the King of Pop. His stylized records and music videos of the 1980's became the benchmarks around which the industry grew. His sister Janet started singing at age 7 and also evolved into one of the music industry's top stars.

Beyoncé Giselle Knowles is one of the world's current superstars. She was born in Houston, Texas, and performed in singing and dancing competitions as a 9-year-old child. She rose to fame in the 1990s as lead singer of R&B girl-group Destiny's Child. Beyoncé released her debut solo album in 2003, earning five Grammy Awards and featuring two number-one singles, "Crazy in Love" and "Baby Boy." After disbanding Destiny's Child in 2005, she released a second solo album, including the hits "Irreplaceable" and "Beautiful Liar." She ventured into acting, with a Golden Globe-nominated performance in "Dreamgirls" (2006), and starring roles in "The Pink Panther" (2006) and "Obsessed" (2009). Her portrayal of Etta James in "Cadillac Records" (2008) influenced her third album. Other records are critically acclaimed, and she remains an all-time crowd pleaser in concert.

Brenda Lee started singing professionally at age 11. She was known as Little Miss Dynamite and belted out so many teen anthems: "I'm Sorry," "Rocking Around the Christmas Tree," "As Usual," "All Alone Am I," "Johnny One Time,"

"Sweet Nothings," "Break It To Me Gently," "Fool #1," "My Whole World Is Falling Down," "Thanks A Lot," "I Want To Be Wanted," "Too Many Rivers" and others.

Frankie Lymon was 13 when he sang the chart-topping hit record, "Why Do Fools Fall in Love." He and his group, The Teenagers, had other soulful hits. Lymon was a role model for Michael Jackson.

Jerry Mathers headlined the TV sitcom "Leave It To Beaver." One of his great lines as the precocious Beaver Cleaver: "Things are never quite the same when you try to go back to the past. That's like when you leave gum on the window sill overnight and try to chew it the next morning."

Hayley Mills was a daughter of English theatre royalty. Walt Disney gave her a contract to star in major studio films, including "Pollyanna," "The Parent Trap" and "Summer Magic."

Alyssa Milano began her career at age 12, later co-starring on the TV sitcom "Who's the Boss." As an adult, she starred on TV's "Charmed." She is now a goodwill ambassador for UNICEF.

Dickie Moore started performing at age 4 in the "Our Gang" comedies. As a child actor, his films included "Oliver Twist," "Madame X," "My Bill," "Little Men" and "The Blue Bird." At age 16, he gave Shirley Temple an on-screen kiss. He has owned a public relations firm and married actress Jane Powell.

Margaret O'Brien started appearing in movies at age 4 and was under contract to MGM. She appeared in "Meet Me in St. Louis," "Babes on Broadway," "Journey for Margaret," "The Canterville Ghost," "Little Women," "Glory," "Our Vines Have Tender Grapes," "Jane Eyre" and "The Secret Garden."

Mary Kate Olsen and Ashley Olsen were sensations in the ABC-TV sitcom "Full House." When the show started, the twins were six months old, alternating in the role of Michelle Turner. They continued through the eight-year run of "Full House" and hosted their own TV special. The Olsen twins were personified in a series of books and videos appealing to pre-teen girls, including "Double, Double, Toil and Trouble," "How the West Was Fun," "It Takes Two" and "When in Rome." They starred in a later TV series, "Two of a Kind."

Donny Osmond started singing at age 4. With his talented brothers, they were performing at Disneyland when they were discovered by singer Andy Williams. They appeared on the Williams TV show and then became top recording artists in the 1970s.

Marie Osmond debuted as part of her brothers' act on the Andy Williams Show when she was 4. Her first hit record, "Paper Roses," came when she was 14. She began hosting the Donny & Marie Show on ABC-TV at age 17. She appeared in the Broadway musicals "The King and I" and "The Sound of Music." She has hosted TV shows, appeared in concerts and is currently the TV spokesperson for Nutri-System.

LeAnn Rimes began performing at age 5, performing in musical theatre in Dallas. By age 9, she was an experienced singer and had a major record deal at age 14. She has since become a country music superstar with pop cross-over appeal and international stature.

Mickey Rooney started performing in vaudeville at age 4. As a child actor, he headlined MGM movies in the 1930s, 40s and 50s. He was America's top box office draw in 1938, when he was 17. As an elder statesmen of Hollywood, Rooney lived well into his 90's.

Kurt Russell was a child actor in the 1960s, beginning by appearing with Elvis Presley in "It Happened at the World's Fair." As a teen, he headlined Disney movies, a film domination that has continued for four decades.

Britney Spears began performing at age 12.

Taylor Swift began performing at age 11, becoming one of the world's current superstars.

Shirley Temple started performing at age 6 and was America's hottest box office draw in 1935 and 1936. Her cute films saved her studio from bankruptcy. She became a Hollywood ambassador to a world that was weary from the Great Depression. She evolved into teen roles in films and later hosted a TV series, "Shirley Temple's Storybook." She ran for Congress and later served the U.S. in the diplomatic corps. Upon being honored at the Oscars in her 80's, Shirley said, "My best advice for performers is to start young."

Justin Timberlake began performing at age 12.

Stevie Wonder started performing at age 11 as a child singer. He was one of the Motown hit makers. Because of his writing talents, Wonder became one of the respected musical performers of the last five decades.

Natalie Wood was a talented star in 1940s films such as "Miracle on 34th Street." In the 1950s, she was a teen actress on TV and in films. She grew into a respected adult movie star, with hits including "Rebel Without a Cause," "Splendor in the Grass," "West Side Story," "Gypsy," "Sex and the Single Girl," "Love With the Proper Stranger," "The Great Race," "This Property is Condemned," "Penelope" and "Inside Daisy Clover."

The Great Kid Oriented TV Shows

Child performers have been prominently featured in top TV series, consisting of family situation comedies and heart-warming dramas.

"The Brady Bunch" (1969-1974) is a pop culture phenomenon, symbolizing blended families that are so prevalent in modern society. The parents were played by Robert Reed and Florence Henderson, and Ann B. Davis played the housekeeper. The kids were played by Barry Williams, Maureen McCormick, Christopher Knight, Eve Plumb, Mike Lookinland and Susan Olsen. It came back as a variety show, then again as a sitcom. There were records, books and more memorabilia. Brady mania has remained with us. Here is wisdom from the Brady Bunch:

- "Nobody has smooth sailing all the time."
- "Some of us are good at one thing. Others are good at another."
- "If you keep your eyes open, opportunities will present themselves."
- "Sometimes, when we lose, we win."
- "When it's time to change, you've got to rearrange."

"The Donna Reed Show" (1958-1966) starred Donna Reed and Carl Betz as the parents. The kids were played by Shelley Fabares and Paul Petersen.

"Eight is Enough" (1977-1981) starred Dick Van Patten and Betty Buckley as the parents. The kids were played by Grant Gooeve, Lani O'Grady, Laurie Walters, Susan Richardson, Connie Needham, Willie Aames, Dianne Kay and Adam Rich.

"The Facts of Life" (1979-1988) starred Charlotte Rae as the housemother. The kids were played by Nancy McKeon, Lisa Whelchel, Kim Fields and Mindy Kohn.

"Family Affair" (1966-1971) starred Brian Keith as the father and Sebastian Cabot as the butler. The kids were played by Kathy Garver, Johnny Whitaker and Anissa Jones.

"Father Knows Best" (1954-1960) starred Robert Young and Jane Wyatt as the parents. The kids were played by Elinor Donahue, Billy Gray and Lauren Chapin.

"Flipper" (1964-1967) starred Brian Kelly. The kids were played by Luke Halpin and Tommy Norden.

"Full House" (1987-1995) starred Bob Saget, Dave Coulier, John Stamos and Lori Loughlin. The kids were played by Candace Cameron Bure, Jodie Sweetin, Mary Kate Olsen and Ashley Olsen.

"Gentle Ben" (1967-1969) starred Dennis Weaver and Beth Brickell as the parents. The kid was played by Clint Howard.

"Gidget" (1965-66) starred Don Porter as the father and Sally Field as the teenaged daughter.

"Leave It To Beaver" (1957-1963) featured Hugh Beaumont and Barbara Billingsley as the parents. The lead character was Beaver Cleaver, played by Jerry Mathers, with Tony Dow appearing as his brother Wally.

"Little House on the Prairie" (1974-1983) starred Michael Landon and Karen Grassle as the parents. The kids were played by Melissa Gilbert, Melissa Sue Anderson, Lindsay Greenbush and Sidney Greenbush.

"Make Room For Daddy/The Danny Thomas Show" (1953-1964) featured Danny Thomas and Marjorie Lord as the parents. The kids were played by Sherry Jackson, Rusty Hamer and Angela Cartwright.

"The Monroes" (1966-1967) was a Western, where a family of kids headed for a new life following their parents' deaths. Barbara Hershey played the oldest daughter and led the Monroe clan. The kids were played by Michael Anderson Jr., Tammy Locke, Keith Schultz and Kevin Schultz.

"The Partridge Family" (1970-1974) was about a family that recorded and appeared in concert. It was based on a real pop act family, The Cowsills. The Partridges featured two mega-important musical forces, Shirley Jones as the mother and David Cassidy as the teenaged rock star son. The other kids in the family made up the band, including Susan Dey, Danny Bonaduce, Jeremy Gelbwaks and Suzanne Crough.

"Saved By the Bell" (1989-1993) starred Mark-Paul Gosselaar, Mario Lopez, Tiffani Thiessen, Dustin Diamond, Lark Voorhies and Elizabeth Berkley as high school students.

"Seventh Heaven" (1996-2007) starred Stephen Collins and Catherine Hicks as the parents. The kids were played by Jessica Biel, Mackenzie Rosman, Beverley Mitchell, David Gallagher, Barry Watson, Lorenzo Brino and Nikolas Brino.

"Skippy the Bush Kangaroo" (1966-1970) starred Ed Devereaux as the park ranger. The kids were played by Tony Bonner, Ken James, Garry Pankhurst and Liza Goddard.

"The Waltons" (1971-1981) starred Ralph Waite and Michael Learned as the parents and Will Geer and Ellen Corby as the grandparents. The kids were played by Richard Thomas, Judy Norton, Eric Scott, Mary Beth McDonough, Jon Walmsley and Kami Cotler.

"Who's the Boss" (1984-1992) starred Judith Light and Tony Danza as the parents. The kids were played by Alyssa Milano and Danny Pintauro.

Many former child stars enjoyed long careers as nostalgia movie ambassadors and classic TV icons. They are role models from gentler times. These include Danny Bonaduce (from "The Partridge Family"), Angela Cartwright (from "The Danny Thomas Show," "The Sound of Music" and "Lost in Space"), Johnny Crawford (from "The Rifleman"), Karolyn Grimes (from "It's a Wonderful Life"), Billy Mumy (from "Twilight Zone" and "Lost in Space"), Donny Osmond, Marie Osmond, Butch Patrick (from "The Munsters"), Paul Petersen (from "The Donna Reed Show"), Lisa Loring (from "The Addams Family"), Mickey Rooney, Shirley Temple and Beverly Washburn.

Walt Disney hosted the Disneyland TV series. Categories of programs included Fantasyland, Frontierland, Adventureland and Tomorrowland.

Chapter 4

CHARACTER ICONS

I cons and legends are a part of pop culture. Every era has them. These characters are animated and live action. They appear is every media and evoke fond memories and life experiences.

The AFLAC duck has appeared in TV commercials for AFLAC Insurance since 2000.

The Ajax Pixies appeared in TV commercials for Ajax cleanser from 1948-1959. They were voiced by Hans Conreid, Joe Silver and June Foray.

Alfa-Bits Cereal has had several characters in its commercials: Truly Lovable (voiced by Jim Nabors), the Alpha-Bits Wizard, Alfie the Wonder Dog, Alpha Computer, Alpha Kids and Alphabet Letters.

Archie Andrews was created by Vic Bloom and Bob Montana in 1941. Archie was the main character in a long-running comic strip. His friends were Veronica Lodge, Betty Cooper, Jughead Jones, Cheryl Blossom, Reggie Mantle and Valerie Smith. The Archie youth adventures also appeared on radio, in comic books, in an

Archie TV series and in records by a group called The Archies (whose biggest hit was the #1 "Sugar Sugar").

Arnold the Pig was a character on the 1964-70 TV sitcom "Green Acres," starring Eddie Albert and Eva Gabor. Frank Inn trained Arnold and other animals appearing on the show.

Asta was the dog character who followed Nick and Nora Charles in the 1934-1947 "Thin Man" movie series (with William Powell and Myrna Loy), later on the 1957-1959 "Thin Man" TV series (with Peter Lawford and Phyllis Kirk).

AT&T's Lily Adams, the store manager who converses with customers, is portrayed by Milana Vayntrub.

Backyardigans is a cartoon series, covering the adventures and learning experiences of five animal children. It was created in 2004 by Janice Burgess.

Barney & Friends was created by Sheryl Leach in 1987, while she was considering shows that would be appropriate for her young child. She created a series of home videos, starring Sandy Duncan. The series was adapted as a cartoon series for PBS and spawned a Barney Fan Club and merchandising line.

Bartles & James Wine Coolers spokespersons (1985-1991) were portrayed by David Joseph Rufkahr and Dick Maugg.

Batman was created by Bob Kane and Bill Finger in 1939. He appeared in comic books, then on a radio series and in movie serials. In 1966, Batman was adapted to a TV series starring Adam West, a show with camp humor and lots of famous guest stars. The later movies returned Batman to his darker roots, starring Michael Keaton, Val Kilmer and Christian Bale.

Beetle Bailey was created by Mort Walker in 1950. The comic strip concerns the humorous hijinks of Beetle and his friends serving in the Army at Camp Swampy.

Betty Boop first appeared in 1930, headlining a series of cartoons produced by Max Fleischer. She emulated characteristics of singer Helen Kane and film star Clara Bow. She is regarded as a sex symbol of animation and an icon of the Jazz Age flappers.

Betty Crocker has been an animated character for General Mills since 1921.

Bevo is a longhorn steer and is the mascot of the University of Texas.

Big Bird is a pivotal character on "Sesame Street." It was created in 1969 by Jim Henson and Kermit Love and was portrayed by Caroll Spinney.

Big Boy in the 1970s commercials for Big Boy Restaurants was portrayed by Jonathan Winters.

The Bonny Maid appeared in TV commercials in 1949-1950 for Bonny Maid floor covering products, dressed in Scottish plaid. She was portrayed by Anne Francis.

Bonzo was a chimpanzee who appeared in the 1951 film comedy "Bedtime For Bonzo," starring Ronald Reagan.

Bucky Beaver advertised for Ipana Toothpaste in TV commercials from 1957-1959. He was voiced by Jimmie Dodd, who at the time also presided over "The Mickey Mouse Club."

The Budweiser Clydesdales are a group of horses who appear in promotions and TV commercials for the Anheuser-Busch Brewing Company. The three teams that tour the world are based in St. Louis, MO, Fort Collins, CO, and Merrimack, NH. The Budweiser Frogs appeared in TV commercials during the 1990s.

Bugs Bunny is the lead in a repertoire company of cartoon characters produced by Warner Bros. Pictures. Others include Daffy Duck, Porky Pig, Sylvester the Cat, Tweety Bird, Wile E. Coyote, The Roadrunner, Elmer Fudd, Foghorn Leghorn and Speedy Gonzales. They appeared in the Looney Tunes and Merrie Melodies series.

Buster Brown and his dog Tige began appearing in advertisements for Buster Brown Shoes in 1904.

BuzzBee represented Honey Nut Cheerios Cereal. He was voiced in commercials by Arnold Stang.

The Cabbage Patch Kids were created in 1978 by Xavier Roberts, a 21-year-old art student. Companies manufacturing the dolls at various times included Coleco, Hasbro, Mattel, Toys R Us, Play Along, Jakks Pacific and Wicked Cool Toys.

The California Raisins were cartoon characters in a series of TV commercials began in 1986 on behalf of the California Raisin Advisory Board. Their lead vocal was supplied by Buddy Miles. The Raisins were so popular that they released record albums, had a toy line and headlined their own primetime TV special (which was nominated for an Emmy award).

The Campbell Soup Kids have appeared in advertisements as far back as 1904.

Cap'n Crunch was a character appearing on cereal boxes and in TV commercials, created in 1963 by Jay Ward. His voice was supplied by Daws Butler.

Captain Kangaroo was a monumental children's TV show, debuting on CBS in 1955 and running for 30 years. The Captain was portrayed by Robert Keeshan. Other characters around the Treasure House were Mr. Green Jeans (portrayed by Hugh Brannum), Mr. Moose (portrayed by Cosmo Allergretti) and Mr. Baxter (portrayed by James E. Wall). The Captain's success inspired "Sesame Street" (the other great children's TV show).

Care Bears were created in 1981 by a licensee of American Greeting Cards. They expanded from cards to stuffed animals to movies to other merchandising.

Charlie Chan was the Oriental detective in a long series of movies in the 1930s and 1940s, starring Warner Oland and Sidney Toler.

Charlie McCarthy and Mortimer Snerd were the dummies operated by ventriloquist and entertainer Edgar Bergen. They graced radio shows, TV shows and movie short subjects in the 1930s, 1940s and 1950s.

Charlie the Tuna has represented StarKist Tuna since 1961, voiced originally by Herschel Bernardi.

The Chicken of the Sea Mermaid appeared in commercials for Chicken of the Sea Tuna. She was voiced by Darla Hood, formerly of "Our Gang/The Little Rascals."

The Chipmunks were created by Ross Bagdasarian in 1958, billing himself as David Seville. The Chipmunks were his voice on three parts, with the tape speed doubled. Their first hit record was "The Chipmunk Song," a Christmas classic. It was followed by other Chipmunks records, a Chipmunks TV series, more recordings and a movie. David Seville Jr. has carried on the Chipmunks tradition.

Chuck E. Cheese is the character that symbolizes the Chuck E. Cheese pizza restaurants.

Clarence the Cross Eyed Lion lived in a game preserve and enjoyed adventures with the kids in a movie and later a TV series called "Daktari."

Clifford the Big Red Dog is a children's book series by Norman Bridwell dating back to 1963. It established Scholastic Books, and Clifford became the imprint's mascot. The Clifford TV series on PBS has remained popular.

Columbo was a detective played in a long running TV series by Peter Falk.

The Coppertone Girl has appeared in advertisements for Coppertone sunscreen since 1944. In 1965, Jodie Foster appeared as the kid in Coppertone TV commercials.

Cornelius the Rooster appeared in commercials for Kellogg's Corn Flakes. He was voiced by Dallas McKennon in the 1950s and by Andy Devine in the 1960s.

Curious George was created in 1939 by Hans Augusto Rey and Margret Rey. The first book appeared in 1941, and many followed. Stuffed animals, films and the PBS cartoon series followed.

Dick Tracy was created as a comic strip by Chester Gould in 1931. Tracy fought crime, and characters were patterned to look like actual celebrities. Breathless Mahoney was patterned after Lauren Bacall. Dick Tracy ran as a radio series in the 1930s and 1940s. In the movies, he appeared in a serial and in several features. There was a Dick Tracy TV series and a cartoon series in the 1950s. In 1990, Warren Beatty played Dick Tracy in a movie, with Madonna as Breathless.

Dig 'Em Frog has represented Kellogg's Honey Smacks cereal since 1972. He has been voiced by Howard Morris.

Dora the Explorer was created in 2000 by Chris Gifford, Valerie Walsh Valdes and Eric Weiner as a children's TV series, followed by video games.

Dragon Tales was created in 1978 by Ron Rodecker. In 1997, Jim Coane found the sketches and developed it for television, going on PBS in 1999.

Duke the Dog has appeared on TV commercials since 1993, promoting Bush's Baked Beans. Duke's voice is supplied by Robert Cait.

The Easter Bunny is a folkloric symbol for Easter and was first mentioned in literature in 1682.

Elsie the Cow has been a symbol for the Borden Company since 1938.

The Exxon Tiger debuted in commercials in 1964 as the Enco/Esso Tiger.

Farfel the Dog represented Nestle's Quik from 1953-1965. He was portrayed by ventriloquist Jimmy Nelson.

The Flintstones was a 1960s cartoon series set in the stone age. It was created by William Hanna and Joseph Barbera.

Flipper was a bottlenose dolphin that appeared in two heartwarming movies and a TV series in the 1960s.

Flo has appeared in TV commercials for Progressive Insurance since 2008. She is portrayed by Stephanie Courtney.

The Florida Orange Bird was created in the 1970s by Walt Disney Productions to represent the Florida Citrus Commission.

Floyd D. Duck appeared in TV commercials for Bubble Yum Bubblegum.

Francis the Talking Mule was featured in seven movies in the 1950s, starring Donald O'Connor. The mule's voice was supplied by actor Chill Wills.

Freshup Freddie was created in 1957 by Walt Disney Productions for Seven Up.

The Frito Bandito was a cartoon character representing Frito's Corn Chips in the 1960s. He was voiced by Mel Blanc.

Frosty the Snow Man was portrayed in a 1950 song written by Walter Rollins and Steve Nelson and sung by Gene Autry. Frosty was later adapted to a TV special, which still runs as a Christmas classic.

Fury was a horse who took his master Joey (played by Bobby Diamond) on heroic adventures in the 1955-1961 TV series. Fury lived on a ranch owned by Jim Newton (Peter Graves) and Pete (William Fawcett).

Gentle Ben the bear was created in 1965 by Walt Morey, introduced in a book and adapted as a TV series, later as an animated series, plus feature films.

Geoffrey the Giraffe has represented Toys R Us since the 1960s.

The Gerber Baby was first drawn in 1927 by Dorothy Hope Smith.

The Grinch was created Dr. Dr. Seuss in 1957 for a book, also published in Redbook Magazine. Its cartoon adaptation "How the Grinch Stole Christmas" was produced in 1966 and still runs on TV every holiday season.

Hanna-Barbera Characters are important TV icons. William Hanna and Joseph Barbera were illustrators for MGM studios, drawing the Tom and Jerry cartoons. They launch an independent production company in 1957 with TV series starring Ruff & Reddy, Huckleberry Bound, Quick Draw McGraw, Yogi Bear, The Flintstones, The Jetsons, Wally Gator, Magilla Gorilla, Top Cat, Jonny Quest, Atom Ant/Secret Squirrel, Loopy De Loop, Space Ghost and others.

The Happy Cows have represented Real California Cheese since 1993.

The Happy Hotpoint Girl danced through TV commercials for Hotpoint Appliances in 1955. She was portrayed by Mary Tyler Moore.

Howdy Doody set the tone for children's TV shows, with its Peanut Gallery of kids, the likeable Buffalo Bob Smith as the host, puppet Howdy Doody as the kid hero, Clarabell the Clown and a cast of characters in the mythical village of Doodyville. It debuted on NBC in 1947 and ran until 1960.

The Incredible Hulk was created by Stan Lee and Jack Kirby in 1962. It appeared in comic books, later a TV series starring Bill Bixby and Lou Ferrigno and a feature film.

J. Fred Muggs was a monkey who appeared in the 1950s on NBC-TV's "Today Show," hosted by Dave Garroway. The monkey scampered around the studio and provided comic relief.

Jax Beer had a series of animated TV commercials in the late-1950s and early-1960s, voiced by the comedy team of Mike Nichols and Elaine May.

Jerry Mahoney was the dummy sidekick of ventriloquist and entertainer Paul Winchell.

The Jetsons was a 1962 cartoon series set in the space age. It was created by William Hanna and Joseph Barbera.

Joe Camel was an animated character who appeared for Camel Cigarettes from 1987-1997.

The Jolly Green Giant has represented Green Giant Vegetables since 1928. In the 1960's, he was voiced in TV commercials by Herschel Bernardi.

Jose Jiminez was a character created by Bill Dana, when he was appearing on "The Steve Allen Show" in 1959. Dana made a series of comedy records as the mythical character.

Josephine the Plumber appeared in commercials for Comet cleanser in the 1970s and 1980s. She was portrayed by Jane Withers.

The Keebler Elves have represented Keebler Snacks since 1968. They were voiced by Parley Baer.

Kermit the Frog was Jim Henson's first Muppet character, created in 1955. Henson performed Kermit from 1955-1990. Since 1990, Kermit has been performed by Steve Whitmire.

The Kool-Aid Kids have appeared in TV commercials for the powdered drink since the 1950s.

Lamb Chop was the puppet sidekick of Shari Lewis on her many TV shows (NBC and PBS) and concert appearances.

Lassie was the dog who helped people in trouble, bonded with families and inspired other animal oriented shows. Lassie was created by Eric Knight for his novel "Lassie Come Home." The book inspired a movie series, a radio series that ran from 1947-1950 and a TV series that ran from 1954-1973.

Leo the Lion was the mascot of MGM Studios. His magnificent roar opened the credits of all MGM pictures from the 1920s forward.

Li'l Abner was created by Al Capp in 1934. At its peak, it had 60 million readers in 900 U.S. newspapers, plus international distribution in 100 newspapers in 28 nations. It centered around life in Dogpatch with sweethearts Lil' Abner and Daisy Mae with their families. Its character Fearless Fosdick was a parody of Dick Tracy. The strip ran until 1977. It spawned movies and a Broadway musical.

Li'l Penny has represented Nike athletic shoes since 1996, voiced by Chris Rock.

Little Bear was created in 1957 by Else Holmlund Minarik for a series of children's books. Little Bear became a popular TV series in the 1990s.

The Little Old Winemaker represented Italian Swiss Colony Wine. In 1960s TV commercials, he was portrayed by Ludwig Stossel and voiced by Jim Backus.

Little Orphan Annie was created in 1924 by Harold Gray, taking the name from an 1885 poem. It followed the adventures of 11-year-old Annie, her dog Sandy and her benefactor Oliver "Daddy" Warbucks. "Little Orphan Annie" ran as a radio show from 1930-1942. Two movies were based upon the comic strip. In 1977, it became a Broadway musical Actresses who played Annie onstage included Andrea McArdle, Sarah Jessica Parker, and Alyssa Milano. In the 1982 movie version, Annie was played by Aileen Quinn.

Little Red Riding Hood was featured in stories told throughout Europe in the 10th Century. The earliest known printed version was in 1697 by Charles Perrault. Brothers Jacob and Wilhelm Grimm revised the story in their 1857 book. Other authored have adapted the tale, which has been told in movies, books, TV, a Broadway musical (1987's "Into the Woods") and even a 1966 hit record by Sam the Sham and the Pharaohs.

The Lone Ranger was created in 1933 by Fran Striker for a show on WXYZ Radio in Detroit, Michigan. Radio stars were George Seaton, Earle Graser and Brace Beemer. The Lone Ranger TV series from 1949-1957 starred Clayton Moore, with Jay Silverheels as his companion Tonto. The Green Hornet was also created by Fran Striker and was, in fact the Lone Ranger's cousin. The Green Hornet fought crime in comic books, movie serials and in a TV series starring Van Williams and Bruce Lee.

Lucky the Leprechaun was created in 1963 for the box of Lucky Charms cereal by General Mills.

M&M's characters were voiced in the 1960s and 1970s by Don Messick and Stan Freberg. They have also been voiced by Phil Hartman and Vanessa Williams. They are now voiced by J.K. Simmons and Billy West.

Mabel the Waitress appeared in commercials for Carling Black Label Beer from 1951-1958. She was portrayed by Jean Goodspeed.

Madge the Manicurist represented Palmolive dish detergent from 1966-1992. She was portrayed by Jan Miner.

The Maytag Repairman has represented Maytag Appliances since 1967. He was portrayed from 1967-1988 by Jesse White.

McGruff the Crime Dog was created for the Advertising Council and in public service announcements says "take a bit out of crime." He has appeared since 1978 for the National Crime Prevention Council.

Mickey Mouse is the lead in a repertoire company of cartoon characters produced by Walt Disney Studios. Others include Donald Duck, Pluto and the Three Little Pigs. Then there those in the features: Bambi, Lady and the Tramp, 101 Dalmations, Aladdin, The Lion King, The Aristocats, Mulan, The Sword in the Stone, The Little Mermaid, DuckTales, The Jungle Book, Dumbo, Fantasia, etc.

Mikey the freckle-faced kid represented Life Cereal from 1972-1981. He was portrayed by John Gilchrist.

Miss Piggy was created in 1974 for Jim Henson's "The Muppet Show," designed by Bonnie Erickson and performed by Frank Oz.

Mister Ed was a talking horse in the 1961-66 TV sitcom, starring Alan Young and Connie Hines. Ed's voice was supplied by actor Allan "Rocky" Lane. Ed was derived from a series of children's short stories that appeared in the 1930s in Liberty Magazine.

Morris the Cat has represented Nine Lives Cat Food since 1968, voiced by John Irwin.

Mother Nature appeared in commercials for Chiffon Margarine in the 1970s and 1980s. She was portrayed by Dena Dietrich, stating "it's not nice to mess with Mother Nature."

Mr. Clean debuted in TV commercials in 1958. He was created by Linwood Burton, a marine ship cleaning businessman, who sold the product to Procter & Gamble. Mr. Clean's voice was supplied by actor House Peters Jr.

Mr. Moto was the Japanese detective in a series of movies in the 1930s, starring Peter Lorre.

Mr. Owl has represented Tootsie Roll Pops since 1970, originally voiced by Paul Winchell.

Mr. Peanut has represented Planters Peanuts & Snacks since 1916.

Mr. Whipple appeared in commercials for Charmin bathroom tissue from 1965-1989. He was portrayed by Dick Wilson.

The Muppets (a blend of marionette and puppet) were created by Jim Henson in 1955, appearing on TV in Washington, D.C. from 1955-1961. They performed sketch comedy, appealing to audiences of all ages. The Muppets became regulars on "Sesame Street" and spun off to have their own TV series, movies, record albums and merchandising.

My Friend Flicka was a children's novel, written in 1941 by Mary O'Hara. It was a heartwarming story of a horse and the family that owned it. Flicka appeared in a 1943 movie starring Roddy McDowell and a 1956 TV series starring Johnny Washbrook.

Nipper the Curious Dog has represented RCA Victor since 1900. Chipper, a puppy version of Nipper, was introduced in 1991.

The Old Spice Sailor represented Old Spice Aftershave in the 1960s and 1970s. He was portrayed by John Bennett Perry.

Our Gang was a series of comedy short subjects featuring kids, produced by Hal Roach and MGM in the 1930s and 1940s. In the 1950s, the series was shown on television under the title The Little Rascals.

Peanuts characters by Charles M. Schulz in the comic strips and on television cartoons included Snoopy, Charlie Brown, Linus, Lucy Van Pelt, Schroeder, Patty, Violet Gray, Shermy, Pig-Pen, Sally Brown, Frieda, Woodstock, Peggy Jean, Marcy, Franklin, Rerun, Eudora and Peppermint Patty.

Peter Pan was created in 1902 by J.M. Barrie. It ran as a play in London from 1904-1913 and spawned a book in 1911. A film adaptation was produced in 1924. Walt Disney made an animated feature version of Peter Pan in 1953. Peter Pan became a smash Broadway hit in 1954, starring Mary Martin, for which she won a Tony Award. Ms. Martin reprised the role in a live TV version in 1954, which was so popular that it was restaged each year up through 1960. There have been other Peter Pan versions on stage and TV, starring Cathy Rigby, Allison Williams and others. In 1991, there was a live action film, "Hook," starring Robin Williams as Peter Pan, Dustin Hoffman as Captain Hook and Julia Roberts as Tinker Bell.

The Pink Panther was a cartoon character created for the opening credits of a 1963 film comedy. He was designed by David H. DePatie and Fritz Freleng. There were several spinoff Pink Panther movies, starring Peter Sellers and directed by Blake Edwards. The Pink Panther was so popular that a series of theatrical cartoons was produced. That led to a Pink Panther TV series. The character's famous theme song was written and recorded by Henry Mancini.

Pokemon was created in 1995 by Satoshi Tajiri. It began as a series of video games for Game Boy, then extended into a popular cartoon TCV series. It portrayed the exploits of kids who learn teamwork and mutual sharing. Merchandising included the trader cards, books and music.

Popeye was created by Elzie Crisler Segar and first appeared in a comic strip ion 1929. Four years later, Max and Dave Fleischer adapted Popeye and other characters for a series of theatrical cartoons. Popeye has appeared in comic books, TV, arcade games and movies.

Poppin' Fresh the Pillsbury Doughboy represented Pillsbury biscuits since 1965, voiced first by Paul Frees.

The Post Cereals Sugar Bear has appeared in commercials since 1949. He is voiced by Sterling Holloway (who also voiced Winnie the Pooh).

The Purple People Eater was a friendly alien from outer space who headlined a hit 1958 record, sung by Sheb Wooley.

Qantas Koala Bear has represented Qantas Airlines since 1967, voiced by Howard Morris.

The Quik Bunny has represented Nestle's Quik since 1973, voiced by Barry Gordon.

Rin Tin Tin was a dog who performed heroic deeds to save people in danger. He debuted in silent films in the 1920's and then appeared in children's books. From 1954-1960, he headlined a TV series, attached to a company of soldiers during Western days.

Rocky the Flying Squirrel and Bullwinkle the Moose were created by Jay Ward, Alex Anderson and Bill Scott. They headlined a cartoon series with great humor, which started in 1959. Other cartoon elements in the shows included Dudley Do-Right, Mr. Peabody's Improbable History and Fractured Fairy Tales. Segments later appeared on the "Hoppity Hooper Show." There was a movie version in 2000. TV Guide ranked Rocky and Bullwinkle as the sixth greatest TV cartoon of all time.

Ronald McDonald has represented McDonald's Restaurants since 1959. In early years, he was portrayed by Willard Scott. His name adorns the Ronald McDonald House, a program for patients at children's hospitals.

Rosie the Waitress appeared for Bounty Paper Towels in TV commercials from 1970-1990. She was portrayed by Nancy Walker.

Rudolph the Red Nosed Reindeer first appeared in a book by Robert L. May in 1939, a publication that he wrote on assignment from Montgo0mery Ward. May's brother-in-law, songwriter Johnny Marks, adapted Rudolph into a song, and it was a 1949 hit record for Gene Autry. The comic book series began in 1950 and the Little Golden Books series in 1958. The Rudolph TV special was produced in 1964 and still runs every holiday season.

Santa Claus was first dramatized illustrating in a poem in 1823. The image has been maintained through books, music, action figures and films.

Sarah Tucker told her friends about Cool Whip dessert topping in the 1960s and 1970s. She was portrayed by Marge Redmond.

The Simpsons was created by Matt Groening in 1986. The cartoon dysfunctional family appeared in shorts on "The Tracey Ullman Show" from 1987-1989, then got their own series on the Fox Network.

The Six Million Dollar Man was based upon the novel "Cyborg" by Martin Caidin. It spawned three TV movies and a series starring Lee Majors. The Bionic Woman was a spinoff series from 1976-1979 that starred Lindsay Wagner.

Skippy the Bush Kangaroo was an Australian version of heroic dogs headlining TV series. Skippy lived at a ranger station, and his series ran from 1966-1970.

Smokey the Bear has represented the United States Forest Service since 1944. He proclaims "only you can prevent forest fires."

The Snow Queen was created in 1844 by Hans Christian Andersen, published in the book "New Fairy Tales." The children's story illustrates good versus evil situations and has been adapted into several cartoons, movies and TV specials.

Snow White and the Seven Dwarfs headlined Walt Disney's first feature length animated movie, made in 1937.

The Snuggle Bear has represented Snuggles fabric softener since the 1990s. He was designed by Kermit Love and voiced by Corinne Orr.

Sonny the Cuckoo Bird appears in commercials for Cocoa Puffs. The original voice in the 1960's was Chuck McCann.

South Park was created by Trey Parker and Matt Stone in 1992, developed as two animated shorts and a cartoon TV series that debuted in 1997.

Speedy was a cartoon character that appeared in TV commercials for Alka-Seltzer from 1952-1964 and again since 2014.

Sponge Bob Square Pants was created by marine biologist and animator Stephen Hillenburg in the 1980s and developed it as a cartoon TV series in 1996. It debuted on Nickelodeon in 1999 and has won several awards.

Spuds MacKenzie was a dog who appeared in Bud Light TV commercials from 1987-89.

Steven Jackson was the character in the Dell Computers commercials, proclaiming "dude you're getting a Dell." He was portrayed by Benjamin Curtis.

Strawberry Shortcake is a character that appears on greeting cards, stuffed animals and other merchandising. The original design by Muriel Fahrion in 1977 led to a franchise that included movies and videotapes.

Superman was created by Jerry Siegel and Joe Shuster (high school students in Cleveland, Ohio) in 1933 and first appeared in comic books in 1938. The Superman radio series starred Bud Collyer. The TV series starred George Reeves. The movie series starred Christopher Reeve.

Taco Bell Dog was a chihuahua, representing Taco Bell from 1997-2000, voiced by Carlos Alazraqui.

Teletubbies was created by Anne Wood Andrew Davenport in 1996 as a TV series targeting pre-school children.

Tony the Tiger has represented Kellogg's Frosted Flakes cereal since the 1950s. He has been voiced by Dallas McKennon, Thurl Ravenscroft and Lee Marshall.

Toucan Sam has represented Kellogg's Froot Loops cereal since 1952. He has been voiced by Mel Blanc, Paul Frees and Maurice LaMarche.

The Trix Rabbit has represented Trix Cereal since 1959, originally voiced by Mort Marshall.

Uncle Ben has represented Uncle Ben's Rice since 1946.

The Vlasic Stork has represented Vlasic Pickles since the 1970s.

The White Knight has appeared in commercials for Ajax detergent since 1963.

Wizard of Oz characters included Dorothy, the Scarecrow, Tin Woodman, Cowardly Lion, Toto, Wicked Witch and the Wizard.

Willy Wonka was created by Roald Dahl in 1964 for his book "Charlie and the Chocolate Factory." In films, Willy was portrayed by Gene Wilder in 1971 and Johnny Depp in 2005.

Winnie the Pooh was created by British author A.A. Milne in 1924. There were other books, including "The House at Pooh Corner," which was the title of a 1971 Kenny Loggins song recorded by the Nitty Gritty Dirt Band. Walt Disney produced a "Winnie the Pooh" cartoon feature in 1965, with Winnie's voice supplied by Sterling Holloway. Many lines of Pooh character stuffed animals, games and toys have been produced over the years.

Wonder Woman was created in 1941 by William Moulton Marston for DC Comics. In 1975, a TV series based on Wonder Woman was developed, starring Lynda Carter. The character has since appeared in "Justice League" superhero cartoon series.

Woody Woodpecker was created in 1940 by Walter Lantz and Ben Hardaway, appearing in a theatrical cartoon series. Woody spawned a hit song in 1948 (recorded by Kay Kyser) and moved to TV in 1957.

Media Milestones.

Chapter 5
STORIES AND STRATEGIES
OF THE ICONS

No matter how much planning one does (which I strongly advocate and facilitate for clients), many things just happen. Accidents that work are called strokes of genius. Daily business is shaped by eccentricities, external influences and chance occurrences. By studying some of them, we gain insight into what modern business could be.

During a visit to the United States in the 1960s, Soviet Premier Nikita Khrushchev placed his hand on the tail fin of a Cadillac limousine. With seeming innocence, he asked, "What does this thing do?"

Elliott and Ruth Handler founded a toy company known as Mattel, Inc. They had a daughter named Barbie, who played with paper dolls, pretending that she was a mommy. Ruth watched her child play and got the idea for a doll with accessories, pretending to be an independent adult. Thus was born the largest selling doll in the history of the world, the Barbie Doll.

For those wondering the practical applications of outer space technology and research, look to items now normally found in the home, notably pocket calculators and microwave ovens.

So many odd-but-true happenings created the lifestyle that the populace embraced. Pop art, inventions, fashions, fads, and natural obsessions have contributed more to molding a society than textbook lessons. Historians continue to ponder the effects of pop culture.

As times change, the nature of nostalgia changes. While it is fun to remember the old days, we realize that pop art and culture set the rules by which we live as adults. Each generation relates to different phases of pop culture.

In 1965, a young woman in New York suggested to her boyfriend, a printer, that he make posters with Humphrey Bogart's picture. He acquired a negative for free, bought some cheap paper, and printed a batch of posters. Next, he ran a few ads to promote the pop-art posters.

Some kids came into a Greenwich Village bookstore, inquiring about the Bogart posters. The owner found the printer and bought his supply. The printer left town to take a long weekend. When he returned, the phone was ringing. The bookstore had sold more than 1,000 Bogart posters and needed more to be printed. Realizing they were sitting on a goldmine, the printer and the bookstore owner formed Personality Posters. Thus, the celebrity poster boom began.

The atomic bomb is responsible for many societal reactions and phenomena, the most surprising being the bikini bathing suit. Rumors spread during post-World War II research that the world would end soon. Fashion designers scheduled the "ultimate" show with the most daring styles. One model shocked the world by wearing a skimpy two-piece suit. The costume—now accepted swimwear—was named for Bikini Atoll, location of bomb testing.

President John F. Kennedy was asked by a Life Magazine reporter for a list of his favorite books. Kennedy was a known intellectual who reportedly read one book every day. When the list included the Ian Fleming novel, "From Russia With Love," the James Bond spy story craze hit America.

Hungarian design professor Erno Rubik devised a multi-colored puzzle in the mid-1970's. Each of six sides has nine squares, with each row able to rotate around its center. When solved, each side is one color. There are 43 quintillion possible positions. Least possible moves to solve is 20. Rubik's Cube sold billions of units in its heyday. Knowledge of group theory and algorithms is useful.

Witness these fabulous firsts:

- The first product to carry the union seal was the cigar (1874).
- Franz Schubert wrote 1,000 musical works but left only one symphony unfinished.
- The Beatles used to write all their hit songs within a two-hour window.
- Ohio is the birth state of the most U.S. Presidents (seven).
- The last teenager to rule England was Queen Victoria.

How Cities Got Their Names

Albany, NY

New York's first capital was Beverwyck when it was a Dutch fur-trading outpost. English settlers renamed it Albany in honor of the Duke of Albany, who later became King James II.

Albuquerque, NM

An early provincial governor named the town after Francisco Fernández de la Cueva, a Spanish officer who also served as Viceroy of New Spain and later Viceroy of Sicily. One of the Viceroy's aristocratic titles was the 8th Duke of Alburquerque, a town in the province of Badajoz, Spain.

Atlanta, GA

In the early 1840's, Atlanta called itself Marthasville, after former governor Wilson Lumpkin's daughter Martha. The name changed to Atlanta in 1847. Some claim that Martha Lumpkin's middle name was Atalanta. Others say it was inspired by Greek mythology's Atalanta.

Austin, TX

After Texas won independence from Mexico, the new republic needed a capital. The town of Waterloo was renamed in honor of Stephen F. Austin, hailed as the Father of Texas.

Azusa, CA

This was a made-up name for the town in California, symbolizing that has everything from A to Z, in the USA.

Baltimore, MD

Named after Cecilius Calvert, the second Lord Baltimore, the first Proprietary Governor of Maryland, 1632-1675.

Boston, MA

Colonists named Boston, MA, after Boston, Lincolnshire, England.

Buffalo, NY

The original settlement was located on Buffalo Creek.

Charlotte, NC

North Carolina's largest city gets its name from German Princess Charlotte-Mecklenburg-Sterlitz, who is best remembered as Queen consort of British King George III. Early settlers named the city in her honor, which is why Charlotte still has the nickname "the Queen City."

Chicago, IL

Chicago comes from the French pronunciation for "shikaakwa," which means "wild garlic" in the Miami-Illinois language.

Cincinnati, OH

Territorial governor Arthur St. Clair changed the name in 1790 from Losantiville to Cincinnati to honor the Society of the Cincinnati, an organization of former Continental Army officers.

Cleveland, OH

It is named for General Moses Cleaveland, surveyor and investor for the Connecticut Land Company, who led the first group to settle in the area in 1796. He oversaw planning of the early town, then headed back to Connecticut a few months later and never returned to the city bearing his name.

Denver, CO

Colorado's capital is named for James W. Denver, who served in Congress, fought in the United States Army and served as Governor of the Kansas Territory. He only visited the city twice, in 1875 and 1882.

Detroit, MI

The Motor City gets its name from the French word Detroit (strait), due to its position along the strait connecting Lake Erie to Lake Huron.

Fort Worth, TX

General Williams Jenkins Worth was a soldier in the American victory in the Mexican-American war. After Worth's 1849 death from cholera, the War Department named the new fort for the late war hero.

Fresno, CA

The Spanish word Fresno is used for the white ash trees that are plentiful in the area around the San Joaquin River.

Kingwood, TX

Kingwood was a suburb built in 1970 to accommodate Houston's new Intercontinental Airport. It was a joint venture by the King Ranch and Friendswood Development Company.

Las Vegas, NV

Las Vegas is Spanish for "the meadows." Spanish settlers found green pastures and natural wells that supported plant life in the area, and they also gave the city its name.

Los Angeles, CA

Spanish settlers originally called the settlement "The Town of Our Lady the Queen of Angels of the Little Portion." The official name was eventually shortened to El Pueblo de la Reina de Los Angeles and eventually became Los Angeles.

Macon, GA

Macon was named for Nathaniel Macon, who served in Congress from 1791-1815, serving as Speaker of the House. Many of the city's early settlers were transplants from North Carolina, they named their city after their old local hero. There are towns and counties bearing Macon's name in Missouri, Illinois, Alabama, Tennessee, Georgia and North Carolina.

Memphis, TN

Memphis was originally a shipping hub on the Mississippi and borrowed its name from another famous river port: Egypt's ancient capital of Memphis on the Nile.

Miami, FL

The southern Florida city is named after the Mayaimi, a Native American tribe that lived around Lake Okeechobee until the 18th century.

Minneapolis, MN

In 1852, a school teacher combined the Sioux word "mni" for "water" with the Greek word "polis" for "city," paying tribute to the town's lakes.

Missouri City, TX

Land developers in St. Louis created a development in Texas, to attract customers.

New Orleans, LA

French settlers originally dubbed it Nouvelle-Orleans in honor of Phillippe II, Duke of Orleans, who was Regent of France at the time of the city's founding.

Orlando, FL

Orlando Reeves owned a plantation and sugar mill a bit north of what became the city. Settlers found where Reeves had carved his name in a tree and believed that it was a grave marker to a soldier in the Seminole War and named their settlement for him.

Phoenix, AZ

Founder Darrell Duppa recognized that their site had been a Native American settlement and suggested Phoenix because their city would rise from the ruins of the former civilization.

Portland, OR

In 1845, settlers Asa Lovejoy and Francis Pettygrove wanted to name the settlement after their respective hometowns, Boston, MA, and Portland, ME. They settled their argument by flipping a penny. Portland won the contest, and the penny is still on display at the Oregon History Center.

Sacramento, CA

While exploring the northern part of California in the 19th century, Gabriel Moraga discovered what's now the Sacramento Valley and the Sacramento River. The area's beauty stunned Moraga so thoroughly that he declared, "Es como el sagrado sacramento" ("this is like the holy Sacrament"). Moraga named the river and the valley Sacramento, and the city's name followed.

San Antonio, TX

Spanish missionaries and explorers came to what is now San Antonio on June 13, 1691, feast day of Saint Anthony of Padua. They named their settlement in his honor.

Seattle, WA

Seattle gets its name from an English version of the name of Si'ahl, a Duwamish chief who was a valuable ally to the area's early white settlers.

Tomball, TX

Named for Thomas Ball, the attorney who helped bring the railroad there.

Topeka, KS

The word Topeka comes from the local Kansas and Iowa term for "to dig good potatoes." They were prairie potatoes, a staple of Native American diets tasting similar to turnips. Early settlers picked the name for the city because it was "novel, of Indian origin and euphonious of sound."

Truth or Consequences, NM

Named for a popular radio quiz show, hosted by Ralph Edwards.

Tucson, AZ

The name "Tucson" originates in the O'odham language of Arizona's Tohono O'odham tribe, meaning "at the base of the black hill," referring to the nearby mountains.

Waco, TX

Named after the Waco Indian tribe, as was radio station WACO.

PAMS, Music Provider

One of the great lines in pop culture is attributed to an imaginative business enterprise from Dallas, TX. It is "More Music," sung in happy, grandiose tones.

PAMS was the premier jingle producer for radio stations. During its three-decade run, PAMS created on-air identity music for radio stations worldwide. The dominance of jingles helped to define the radio formats, distinguish stations from each other and fed compatibly into the mix of recorded music of the era.

In the 1940s, radio stations featured live local variety shows. Stations employed house orchestras. Bill Meeks was a musician in the band at stations WRR and WFAA. In 1947, Gordon McLendon opened a new station in Dallas (KLIF), with Bill and his band hired to perform live. House bands backed singers on the variety shows, and they performed on live advertising jingles. The station ID jingles were happy, peppy and equivalent to the upbeat advertising spots. Meeks also sold advertising time.

In 1951, Meeks opened his own company, PAMS. It stood for Production Advertising Merchandising Service. They began recording advertising for a variety of clients, distributing beyond KLIF and to stations throughout Texas. The barter deal was that if stations aired clusters of PAMS client ads, then they would also get PAMS-produced ID jingles for each local station.

By the late 1950s, Top 40 radio formats were the trend, with disc jockeys playing the latest hits, and the jingles augmented local "house ads" (also known as "talking breaks"), giving the stations discernable image, which translated to higher ratings.

By the mid-1960s, the company's total focus was on generating new, annual, creative jingle packages. They were supplying stations all over the world. In the early days, PAMS served one station per market. Eventually, they serviced multiple stations in some markets due to differing jingle packages. Their jingle practice expanded to country, easy listening and soul music stations. They even produced jingle packages for TV stations.

PAMS experimented with sounds and concepts. There was the talking guitar. There were holiday-themed jingles. There were high school sports salutes in jingle form. There were even jingles for the weather, sports and public service announcements (integral in the good old days of regulated radio). The tone of the jingles was listener appreciation, community salute and a familial city culture.

In 1961, PAMS innovated its "My Home Town" concept (part of PAMS Series 16). Song length jingles were recorded about each city where PAMS supplied jingles. Their client radio stations partnered with local sponsors, pressed the jingles onto 45RPM records and promoted this hot release throughout their communities. The success of "My Home Town" spawned a second PAMS community appreciation package, 1962's "Having a Ball in (City-name)." There was even a hit record, "The Frito Twist," done by Bill Meeks, accompanied by the PAMS house band.

PAMS hit its peak in the late 1960s. The client list included WABC, WIL, KFWB, WLS, WXYZ and the BBC. Most major Texas radio stations bought and aired PAMS jingles, including KLIF, KBOX, KNUZ, KILT, KNOW, KCRS, WACO, KWKC, KOGY, KNIN, KBWD, KSPL, KGRI, WTAW, KEYS, KDLK and KDOK.

By the mid 1970s, the marketplace for PAMS jingles shrunk drastically. That was the time that groups began acquiring local radio stations and began automating the program, with generic jingles. As a result, the jingle industry shrank radically. PAMS suspended business in 1978. Other jingle companies picked up the remaining marketplace.

PAMS client stations were unique, and the trend toward homogenizing radio broadcasting did the listeners a disservice. The listeners of today do not remember the glory days of Top 40 radio, personality formats and unique jingle identities. Today's listeners do not know how much they lost from the powerhouse days, as punctuated by PAMS jingles.

The success of PAMS spawned a large colony of advertising, music production, film production and creative services companies in Dallas. Other jingle companies resulted from the PAMS influence. In turn, recording companies bore the fruit of the market for localized products and services. The prominence of PAMS had a powerful impact on broadcasting and music empires.

Learning From the Titanic

One of the greatest tragedies in history, the sinking of the Titanic, can be attributed to carelessness, insufficient planning and stubborn pride.

People went down with the ship while still quoting the ship's marketing hype, "Everybody knows this ship cannot sink." They really believed the spin and rationalized it as a false hope to avert disaster. They were so sure, thought tragedy could not happen to them, believed themselves to be invincible, had false senses of security and exhibited unnecessarily stoical behavior when confronted with the harsh realities of death.

In 1912, the Titanic, a Trans-Atlantic ship on its maiden voyage, hit an iceberg and sank. Though some people escaped by lifeboats, there were still 1,502 people killed.

If any of these had occurred, chances are that every life would have been saved. The Titanic would not have sunk if any of these precautions-actions had occurred:

- Management: had the ship's officers heeded one of the six iceberg warnings.
- Planning: had the ship's design required better lighting to see a potential collision.
- Timing: had the ship hit the iceberg 15 seconds sooner or 13 seconds later.
- Logistics: had the water-tight bulkheads been one deck higher.
- Supplies: if the ship had carried enough lifeboats.
- Regulations: had the distress signal to a nearby ship been heeded and acted upon.

Not only did the people die, but it was the end of an era in travel. Credibility toward steamships was shaken. Safety became more important in the luxury travel industry. Other forms of travel could serve customers better, faster and cheaper. Concern for corporate savings at the expense of quality was raised.

Learning from History

The basic cause of World War II was a failure to uphold the peace treaty following World War I. Countries let circumstances fester (notably the Hitler regime) that paying attention to and adhering to the peace treaty would have precluded.

"They can't hang you for saying nothing," quipped President Calvin Coolidge in the 1920's. He spent more time doing chores at his farm and taking long naps than taking care of the nation's business. Coolidge prided himself upon doing little and, thus, failed to see crises brewing during his presidency. This "keep your head in the sand" mentality is prevalent of people who move on and let others clean up the damage.

Throughout the 1920s, the U.S. spent $50 million per year in trying vainly to enforce the highly unpopular Prohibition Act. Bootleggers, racketeers and mobsters made billions of dollars and established footholds in territories that were impossible to retract. An unpopular law spearheaded by a zealous few was never really enforced, and its criminal perpetrators became "folk heroes" to many.

People at Work

The current success rate for organizational hires is 14%. If further research is put into looking at the total person and truly fitting the person to the job, then the success rate soars to 75%. That involves testing and more sophisticated hiring practices.

Retaining good employees, involving training, motivation and incentives, is yet another matter. According to research conducted by the Ethics Resource Center:

- Employees of organizations steal 10 times more than do shoplifters.
- Employee theft and shoplifting accounting for 15% of the retail cost of merchandise.
- 35% of employees steal from the company.

- 28% of those who steal think that they deserve what they take.
- 21% of those who steal think that the boss can afford the losses.
- 56% of employees lie to supervisors.
- 41% of employees falsify records and reports.
- 31% of the workforce abuses substances.

One out of every 20 employees has substance or alcohol abuse problems, with resulting behaviors which in turn adversely effect another 20 people in their lives. Employees with substance abuse problems cost their companies $7,000 per year in downtime or lost days, $9,500 in make-good and work redo and another $15,000 in opportunity and credibility costs to the organization. Companies with good Employee Assistance Programs reduce these high costs and retain the services of valuable workers.

The old adage says: "An ounce of prevention is worth a pound of cure." One pound equals 16 ounces. In that scenario, one pound of cure is 16 times more mostly than an ounce of prevention.

Human beings as we are, none of us do everything perfectly on the front end. There always must exist a learning curve. Research shows that we learn three times more from failures than from successes. The mark of a quality organization is how it corrects mistakes and prevents them from recurring.

Running a profitable and efficient organization means effectively remediating damage before it accrues. Processes and methodologies for researching, planning, executing and benchmarking activities will reduce that pile of costly coins from stacking up.

Analyzing the Music Industry and Changing Technologies

Forces in the recording industry have announced intentions to cease production of compact discs and convert their music marketing to digital downloads. That is a dangerous course of action and stands to further devastate a music industry that has systematically killed the golden goose over many years.

The CD issue (including those who advocate obliterating the medium) is symptomatic of the bigger watersheds that have crippled and ruined large chunks of the music industry:

- Not understanding the business basics.
- Taking decisions away from the creative people.
- Focusing only on the technology, not on the creative output.
- Not understanding the totality of the music industry, with recording as a prime stakeholder, not as the stake driver that it tries to be.
- Failure to learn from the past.
- The trends toward over-formatting of radio.
- Failure to understand and nurture the relationship with radio.
- Failure to understand and nurture the relationship with television.
- Deregulation of broadcasting.
- Failure to collaborate, bundle products or combine efforts to create and sustain advantage.
- Failure to understand and nurture relationships with the retailing industry.
- Failure to plan for the present.
- Trends toward homogenization of culture that resulted in drastic cuts in the quantity and quality of original music programming available.
- Trends away from utilizing and showcasing music.
- Trends away from spoken word and educational usage of recordings.
- The music industry responding to changes and uncertainty by scapegoating the wrong people.
- The international marketplace responding as entrepreneurs by taking up the slack and addressing the "missed opportunities" by the American music industry.
- Making knee-jerk decisions based upon partial information and wrong hunches.

In 1877, Thomas Edison introduced the cylinder, developed originally for business office use. It was the earliest Dictaphone, whereby messages were recorded by a needle on a rolling tube. In 1888, Emile Berliner invented the phonograph record, for the purpose of transporting music to consumers. Columbia Records (now Sony) was founded in 1898, followed by RCA Victor Records in 1901. Edison missed his chance to influence the recording industry by sticking with the cylinder medium, not converting to phonograph records until 1912 and finally getting out of the recording business in 1929.

The radio industry began as a multi-city network that piped recorded music into department stores. In 1920, the first radio sets sold by Westinghouse to promote its first station, 8XK in Pittsburgh, PA. In 1926, NBC Radio signed on the air, followed by CBS the next year. In addition to news and other entertainment shows, a large portion of radio programming was attributable to music, and a long growth relationship with the record industry was sustained. Stars came on variety shows to promote their releases, and the era of radio disc jockeys was firmly secured in the public culture.

The media of music distribution was the 78RPM record. It was bulky, breakable and limiting the amount of music on each side. Record companies put multiple discs into sleeves and began calling them "albums," the terminology still existing today. Those albums started as collections of "sides" but became thematic. Further packaging enabled various-artist albums and collections of "greatest hits" (those two categories currently accounting for half of all CD sales, a big chunk of business to be wiped out by going all-digital).

The two major labels went into research and development on non-breakable records that would play at slower speeds, with thinner grooves and more music on each side, producing a cleaner sound (without pops and scratches). The results were Columbia (owned by CBS) introducing the 33-1/3RPM long playing vinyl record in 1948 and RCA Victor (owned by NBC) introducing the 45RPM vinyl record in 1949. Why those speeds? They were combined derivatives of 78RPM, known by engineers as "the mother speed." Not surprisingly, today's CDs play at 78RPM, a technological updating of Emile Berliner's 1888 invention of the phonograph record.

The 1930s and 1940s were massive-growth periods for the recording and broadcast industries. Along came other record labels: Brunswick, Decca, Capitol, Coral and jazz imprints. Movie studios got into the record business. Entrepreneurs brought Atlantic, King and other labels to showcase black artists and country music (two major growth industries attributable to the interrelationship of radio and records). Then came the international recording industry, which is the major user of CD technology.

The 1950s saw exponential growth of the recording industry. There were more retail outlets for the music than ever before or ever since. One could buy music at every grocery store, department store and many unexpected locations. There was an industry of sound-alike records, sold at reduced prices. The result was that all families had phonographs, and music was going into cars via radio, thus stimulating record sales and thus encouraging other technologies to bring music into cars (emerging as homes in our mobile society).

The emergence of teens as the primary record buyers was fed by TV shows, increased disposable income and recording artists catering to younger audience. Due to broad radio playlists, there was ample airplay for every musical taste, and the record industry continued to grow. Independent record labels proliferated, as did recordings by local artists around the country.

With the British Invasion of the 1960s came the reality of the international nature of entertainment. To package and market emerging modern music, media were implemented to make the best possible sounds and reflect the plastic portability of youth traffic. Along came music available on cassette tapes, then 8-track tapes. The music industry experimented with Quadraphonic Sound, and that experiment fell flat after one year.

At every juncture, there were transition periods in the adoption and acceptance of new media. For the first 11 years of 45RPM records and LPs being manufactured, there were still 78RPM discs on the market. Throughout the tape formats, there were still records. With the advent of Compact Discs, there were still records and cassette tapes on the market. To now rush to conversion of all music to digital downloads is short-sighted and stands to kill markets and after-markets for CDs that still have another 20 years to run.

To kill the CD makes poor business sense. 78RPMs were phased out because better technology was developed. Quadraphonic was technology glitz but did not make good business sense. 8-track tapes were only meant to be an interim medium, until CDs were developed. CDs are the dominant medium and are economical to produce.

Killing CDs is contrary to the heart of the music business. CDs enable local bands to have records. Computer downloads are convenience items and impulse purchases. People's listening frequency and intensity is different (and significantly reduced) through computer downloads.

Nothing still says "record" like a CD in a plastic case, where the album is as much in the packaging as the content material on the disc. Lose the "record album," and the music industry will never be the same.

This is the juncture where the music industry must step back, analyze their decline over the last 30 years and understand the reasons why they must create new opportunities and move forward.

If I were advising the industry, I would steer them toward:

- Stimulating a culture where excellence in music would be encourages, thus improving the quantity and quality of music being recorded.
- Creating a music industry where the products would be more worth buying. There are still higher profits in album sales, rather than Internet song downloads (the modern equivalent to the 45RPM single).
- Thinking of music distribution in directions other than just the Internet.
- Stimulating the global record industry.
- Encouraging TV shows to once again have theme songs.
- Encouraging movies to get back to real musical soundtracks (not just the current drum crashing noise effects). This would re-boot the soundtrack album industry.
- Recognizing that nearly half of all record sales and downloads involves repackaging older music product for new audiences.
- Finding ways to promote local acts around the world.
- Working with radio programmers to get playlists expanded. Music has to have the interactive exposure via radio. Nurture programmers of internet radio shows as the best new opportunity for expanding music exposure.
- Understanding better the after-market of music resellers, and stimulate that series of opportunities for expanding the reach of musical products around the world.
- Recognizing downloads as "low hanging fruit." Do not put all your industry's distribution in one area, because that one area will always change.

The much-needed regeneration of the music industry to make a comeback and reclaim its past dominance takes time, energy, resources and lots of heart to produce. Couch planning as the only way to avert a crisis. Changing technologies does not equate to planning and strategy development.

One cannot always go the path that seems clearest. One who thinks differently and creatively will face opposition. With success of the concept, it gets embraced by others. Shepherding good ideas and concepts does not get many external plaudits. The feeling of accomplishment must be internal. That is a true mark of impactful changes and success.

Chapter 6

THE HISTORY AND
HERITAGE OF BUSINESS

C ommerce was created to advance society's basic needs, wants and aspirations. As time passed, business innovated, gave society more and created opportunities that previously never existed. People shifted attention and priorities as the nation colonized, explored, civilized grew, became a dominant world force and further innovated. The process of adaptation became the American Way.

The history of trade and commerce can be traced to ancient times, even before the Golden Age of Greece and the Roman Empire. Beginning in the 9th Century, the wilderness of Western Europe began populating. Distribution systems were developed, though often interrupted by periods of famine. People built forts at strategic locations for the transportation of goods. The agricultural systems grew to support increased populations. As demands for food products and luxury goods exhibited from town to town, trades, guilds and professional associations were formed to coalesce business opportunities.

Each time that disaster occurred, the rural areas were hurt, and the cities continued to grow. In the 15th Century, trade and business levels rose. Merchants began traveling from town to town to take orders, place goods and move goods. Craft guilds emerged, as cities became viable customers. Improved transportation stimulated the growth of port cities. The Spanish, Portugese, French and English began to search for additional trade in Africa, the Middle East and the New World. The merchants accrued sources of wealth, becoming economic and political influencers.

Christopher Columbus crossed the Atlantic and discovered the New World. Explorers were considered the first entrepreneurs, including Hernando de Soto and Francisco Pizzarro. French exploration affected the development of business history because of its heightened scales and affects on governments. Jean-Baptiste Colbert envisioned the roles of merchants and trade as essential to dominating society. Port cities on the Great Lakes and Gulf of Mexico became funnels to exploring the New World and merchant capitalism.

By the 16th Century, discovery and exploration flourished. The accumulation of capital became a virtue. Materialism became common in advancing societies. From English common law evolved the rights and sanctity of private property. Governments were not based on free enterprise, though they instituted regulations to address potential crises. Successful enterprises are the result of trendsetters, the refining processes, sales to marketplaces, attempts to refine the workforce and the output of goods and services.

British mercantilists established colonies at Jamestown, Massachusetts Bay, New York, Philadelphia, South Carolina and Virginia. Colonial merchants and enterprise systems developed regional characteristics, with trading centers stemming from the kinds of crops, products and goods produced. Early American manufacturing included weaving, candle making, soap production, leather crafts, iron and copper fabrication, shipbuilding and agricultural markets. Colonists sought protection of property, employment systems, fiscal responsibility, American re-export trade and investments in manufacturing processes.

Settling the continent served to create opportunities for business. During periods of the fights for independence, domestic industries grew, including textiles, farming, ironworks, cotton, food processing and agri-business.

John Rolfe planted and harvested tobacco crops in Virginia in 1612. Tobacco became the main source of revenue for Virginia, Maryland and North Carolina. British tobacco merchants sold the harvested crops for three times the cost to produce them. After the Revolutionary War, the growers established factories for the production of pipe and chewing tobacco. This then inspired the great tobacco empires that grew in the 19th Century.

In the early years of the United States, the building of passable roads and canals were essential to the development of business and commerce. Roads drew the settlements together, then expanded to accommodate the westward expansion. In 1824, Henry Clay's "American System" proposed a national economic development plan, coupled with protective tariffs to encourage American industry. In 1825, the Erie Canal was completed, resulting in more than 3,000 miles of inland waterways to open up new territories to settlement and commerce.

In the 19th Century, the American states became the largest free-trade zone in the world. Efforts were made to improve transportation, including canals, railroads, national highways, steamboats, the merchant marine and routes to the West. Expanded rail systems moved goods and served as primary consumer transportation.

In 1793, Eli Whitney invented the cotton gin. By 1815, cotton was the dominant Southern crop for export to textile mills being built in the North. In 1860, cotton accounted for two-thirds of the nation's exports.

Electricity was the major factor that transformed business, industrialization and quality of life in the 19th Century. It had been subject of speculation and fantasy until the 16th Century, when scientist William Gilbert studied electricity and magnetism, coining the term "electricus." In the 18th Century, Benjamin Franklin conducted studies into electricity. In 1791, Luigi Galvani published his study of bioelectricity, with electricity being the medium by which nerve cells pass signals to the muscles. In 1800, Alessandro Volta's battery provided a reliable source of electrical energy. In 1821, Michael Faraday invented the electric motor. In 1827, George Ohm analyzed the electrical circuit. In 1861, James Maxwell linked electricity and magnetism, and light.

In 1835, Samuel F.B. Morse's invention of the electromagnetic telegraph allowed long-distance communication. In 1843, Congress voted to construct telegraph lines. Morse later pioneered the submarine cable telegraph.

Electricity turned from scientific research into an essential tool of modern life, due to the inventions of Thomas Edison, Alexander Graham Bell, George Westinghouse and others. In 1879, Edison developed a successful incandescent lamp. Solid-state components were used in radios in the early 1900's, followed by invention of the transistor in 1947. Delivery of electricity stimulated power plants, municipal delivery stations and ancillary industries committed to powering up society (Edison Electric Light Company, General Electric, Westinghouse, Tennessee Valley Authority, etc.).

Early America witnessed the first industrial revolution. As farms could be operated by fewer workers, people took jobs in factories. Gradually, workers became acclimated to manufacturing schedules, time clocks and the effects of mass employment on family quality of life. By 1860, one-eighth of America's population was foreign born. Immigrants formed company towns in Pennsylvania, New Jersey, Connecticut and Rhode Island.

The gold rush in California in 1848-58 led to business opportunities and a boost to the economy. Shipping companies transported passengers, who stayed and settled the state. Agriculture, commerce, transportation and industry grew. The same was true for the Colorado gold rush a decade later. Gold, silver and copper mining industries became dominated by high-stakes capital investors.

Railroads transformed life and business opportunities. The first significant development was in 1865, when the first steel rails were manufactured. In 1893, the gasoline engine was invented. By 1900, there were six principal railroads, navigating 200,000 miles of track, travel industries and shipping services. America grew exponentially along the railroad routes. Cities of commerce sought rail service and depended upon it.

In 1867, Jesse Chisholm mapped out a route for herding cattle to market between Kansas and Canada. The cattle drives created towns and commerce hubs. In 1869, the first transcontinental railroad was completed. Horace Greeley was a newspaper editor who encouraged westward expansion. He set up a model town (Greeley, Colorado) but never visited it. These romanticized periods were factors in settling the Western states.

In 1878, forestry and farmland were big business. Hundreds of sawmills emerged, providing lumber for building communities. Land was given out at cheap prices to encourage building, and fortunes were made in the lumber industry.

Steel was the other building block of modern life, and fortunes were made in that industry too. By 1880, the Kelly-Bessemer process had become the dominant method of manufacturing steel.

The late 19th Century was rich in inventions. Christopher L. Sholes developed the typewriter. I.W. McGaffey invented the vacuum cleaner. John Oliver's chilled steel plow helped develop prairie agriculture. L.H. Wheeler developed windmills to serve areas which were previously uninhabitable. Andrew S. Hallidie invented an underground continuous cable and mechanical gripper. Joseph F. Glidden changed the face of the Great Plains with the invention of barbed wire, as water holes, roads and entire towns were fenced in.

In 1871, Henry Davidson in Great Britain invented the first amusement arcade game. In 1885, William T. Smith invented America's first arcade machine. In 1931, David Gottlieb introduced the first coin-operated pinball game machine. Bumpers were added in 1936 and flippers in 1947.In 1971, Nolan Bushnell wrote the program for the first computer video game. In the 1990s, virtual pinball played on a computer was introduced.

The founding fathers found there were costs associated with modern society, including wars and depressions. As consumption grew, so did the entrepreneurial spirit to create new goods and services. City dwelling gave rise to mass transit, suburbs, infra-structures and modifications to the marketplace. In the industrial age, monopolies led to anti-trust actions, which resulted in decentralization and regulations. Waves of deregulation led to crises, which later led to re-regulations.

The 20th Century was typified by the automobile and its support industries (energy, highways, retail and parts) as the most significant factors in commerce growth and development. In 1921, President Warren G. Harding proclaimed in that "the motor car has become an indispensible instrument in our political, social and industrial life."

Ransom Olds introduced the marketing of cars in 1901, produced to be affordable and convenient to operate. Henry Ford built his first car in 1896 and founded Ford Motor Company in 1901. Ford introduced assembly-line production and techniques in 1913. By 1914, the production of automobiles exceeded that of wagons and carriages for the first time. General Motors was founded in 1908 by William Durant, reflecting mergers of companies in order to offer cars in all price ranges. GM set the pattern of introducing new models each year. Walter Chrysler was president of American Locomotive Works and then joined GM in 1911, followed by founding his own corporation to make cars in all price ranges.

In 1929, the peak year of the auto boom, more than five million were sold. The industry produced trucks during World War I, and afterward the commercialization of truck production resulted. Bus production followed in the 1920's. Unionization came to the industry in the 1930's. During World War II, the industry retooled its production processes to include vehicles and machinery for military uses. Turmoil produced opportunities and change, which inspired systems of managing change. At each stage were burst of innovation.

Orville and Wilbur Wright did what others said could not be accomplished, developing the first heavy flying machine, thus launching the science of aviation. From the first successful flight at Kitty Hawk, North Carolina, in 1903, they spent years on experiments and refinements to airplanes. In 1909, France's Louis Bleriot flew across the English Channel.

Aircraft was first used by the military during World War I. The airline industry developed to carry mail on a contract basis. In 1927, Charles Lindbergh was the first to fly non-stop from New York to Paris in his plane "The Spirit of St. Louis." His flight increased the sense of adventure attached to airlines. Refinements in planes, safety considerations and dynamics of air travel led to the founding of commercial carriers, along with the building of facilities to accommodate air traffic. Juan Trippe was considered the father of American overseas commercial aviation.

Affordable energy was essential to the operation of automobiles and later aircraft. Over 40 percent of all energy consumption is by industry. In 1870, coal replaced wood as the primary energy for industrialization. In 1910, petroleum replaced coal as the primary energy source.

Leadership in the field of energy meant people of determination and vision, who saw in "black gold" the way of life that we now enjoy. In 1861, the first gusher came in Pennsylvania.

In 1862, John D. Rockefeller went to Ohio to investigate oil as an investment. He bought a refinery. In 1870, he formed Standard Oil of Ohio. By 1875, he owned large refineries in New York and Pennsylvania. In 1876, 90 percent of the oil business was under his control. At the end of his life, he donated generously to charity, at one time handing out dimes on the street to the less fortunate. In 1879, Chevron was founded as Pacific Coast Oil Company.

In 1901, Joseph Stephen Cullinan went into court in Beaumont, Texas, and got the right in advance to kill any marauder who might oppose his charge to clean up and quiet down in the skyrocketing boomtown. In 1901, oil was discovered at Spindletop, near Beaumont.

In 1903, William Stamps Farish and Robert E. Blaffer met at a boarding house in Beaumont. They joined forces to form a drilling partnership. The next year, they moved to Houston to concentrate on the nearby Humble field where oil was discovered in 1904. In the early years, they were so short of operating money that they lived in a shack in the fields. Blaffer put up his gold watch as security to guarantee payment of a drilling crew's wages. By 1908, they had become comfortably established. Harry Wiess knew the vast benefits of energy from the constant addition of knowledge through chemistry, physics and other sciences that are now applied to every product.

In 1911, Farish, Blaffer and Wiess joined forces with Ross Sterling and Walter Fondren in founding the Humble Oil & Refining Company. Humble became one of the giants in the industry through association with Standard Oil Company of New Jersey. Humble Oil became Enco-Esso, later Exxon and now ExxonMobil Corporation.

In 1902, Texaco was founded. In 1916, Gulf Oil was founded. In 1917, Phillips Petroleum was founded. In 1918, Sinclair Oil was founded.

Oil was difficult to transport on land. So, the pipeline was invented. Oil was difficult to transport by sea. Thus, the tank-ship was invented. Oil was difficult dangerous to refine. The most complex machinery was created to handle oil and gas safely, surely and cheaply.

Oil has grown even harder to find. Even airplane equipment is used to map huge underground areas for prospective oil bearing formations, while drilling in even the rough waters in the Gulf of Mexico and the Pacific Ocean.

Into the shoes of the pioneers of energy stepped such wildcatters as H.L. Hunt, Hugh Roy Cullen, George Strake, Glenn McCarthy and Sid Richardson. To them, the sky was not too high nor the earth too deep to hide oil from them. In 1921, they scoured South Texas reserves. In 1926, the West Texas oil industry was launched. In 1929 came the huge discoveries in Conroe's Cookfield Belt and the

Frio sands of the Gulf Coast. In 1926, natural gas was piped into Houston for the first time. It came from a field in Refugio. Up to that point, only manufactured gas had been available.

In 1930, engineer Roger Henquet opened a small office in a walk-up apartment house in Houston, as the only representative for a small radical type of service to the oil industry. The new company was Schlumberger Well Surveying Corporation. In 1930, the U.S. Schlumberger presence consisted of himself, one helper and one truck unit. The company that he introduced to oil operators is now spread all over the world and is one of the largest oil service organizations.

Since World War II, the chemical industry has boomed and grown until it is the largest manufacturing employer in Texas. The industry is a complex mixture of companies that produce chemical raw materials, basic chemicals, petrochemicals, agricultural chemicals, plastics, synthetic rubber, metals, drugs and household chemicals.

There were population shifts, typified by moves from farms to cities. Demographic changes led to the influx of women in the workforce. Cities experienced economic supremacy. With rapidly increasing affluence, wages were up, and consumer choices were up. All of these factors inspired business innovations and successes.

The fast food industry developed after World War II. Soldiers came home, and the Baby Boom resulted. Low-cost loans enabled many to buy homes in the suburbs. This stimulated the building of highway systems and freeways. On those roadways were shopping centers, the first retail outstretch since the strongholds of downtown business districts. This became a boon to the automobile and energy industries, with more cars on the roads, driving longer distances. To cater to all those cars and families, the roads became dotted with restaurants, featuring take-out items.

Local restaurants spread onto the roadways. Then followed the fast food chains. McDonald's began as a barbecue shop in 1940 in San Bernadino, California. In 1948, it was reorganized by brothers Richard and Maurice McDonald as a hamburger restaurant, featuring the "Speedee Service System." In 1955, Ray Kroc opened the ninth McDonald's franchise in Des Plaines, Illinois, and purchased the McDonald brothers' equity. Kroc grew the chain worldwide.

Whataburger was founded in Corpus Christi, Texas, in 1950 by Harmon Dobson and Paul Burton. Burger King began in 1953 in Jacksonville, Florida, as Insta-Burger King. The next year, it was taken over by Miami Franchisees David Edgerton and James McLamore, renaming it Burger King. White Castle was founded in 1921 in Wichita, Kansas, by Billy Ingram and Walter Anderson, known for small square burgers, also known as sliders. Jack in the Box was founded in 1951 in San Diego, California, by Robert O. Peterson.

Sonic Drive-In was founded in 1953 in Shawnee, Oklahoma by Troy Smith. Burger Chef was founded in 1954 in Indianapolis, Indiana, by Frank and Donald Thomas. Burger Chef was purchased in 1982 by the company that operates Hardee's, converting all store names to Hardee's. Steak 'N Shake was founded in 1934 in Normal, Illinois, by Gus Belt. Carl's Jr. was founded in 1941 in Delray Beach, Florida, by Carl Karcher. Wendy's was founded in 1969 in Columbus, Ohio, by Dave Thomas and named after his daughter.

The kids' meal debuted in 1973 at Burger Chef, known as the Funmeal. McDonald's added the Happy Meal to its menu in 1978. Other fast-food restaurant chains followed suit. Toys were added to the combo, in order to market children's meals. The chains today are using children's meals to influence healthier eating choices.

The other major business phenomenon of the 20th Century was mass media. In 1891, Thomas Edison was given a patent for the first motion picture camera. The first viewing palace for films was a peepshow in 1893. Movies used a film process developed by George Eastman in 1880. Edison built a movie studio in 1893 in New Jersey. Movies were introduced in European arcades in 1895. The first commercial motion picture exhibition was held in 1896 in New York. Edison developed sound with his motion picture, demonstrated in 1904.

In 1898, the first suggestions made that pictures with sound could be carried across large distances. Within three years, research was begun to carry the moving pictures to distant locations. This early version of television actually preceded the development of radio. In 1920, the first radio sets were sold by Westinghouse to promote its first station, 8XK in Pittsburgh, PA. In 1926, NBC Radio signed on the air. In 1926, Congress created the Federal Radio Commission, later the Federal Communications Commission, as the broadcasting regulatory entity. In 1927, CBS Radio signed on the air.

In 1927, the first television test pictures were sent. In 1928, the first American home got a TV set, to watch the first regularly scheduled TV programs, over WGY-TV and WRNY-TV. The first trans-oceanic TV signal was sent, from London to New York. In 1929, the first public demonstration of a color TV model was made. In 1930, the first closed-circuit TV projected on a big screen in a theatre. In 1931, CBS-TV and NBC-TV signed on the air. CBS' first station, W2XAB (later WCBS-TV) began regular daily programming. RCA and NBC put a TV transmitter atop the Empire State Building.

In 1938, NBC covered the first live, breaking TV news story (a fire). In 1939, NBC covered the opening of the World's Fair, as well as the first football game, baseball game and prize fight broadcasts. In 1940, the first basketball game and hockey match were broadcast, as was the first coverage of political conventions. In 1941, the first licensed commercial television station (WNBT-TV) went on the air. The first TV commercial cost sponsor Bulova Watches a total of nine dollars. In 1944, the first boxing and wrestling matches were broadcast. CBS began its first evening news show, hosted by Ned Calmer. NBC began its TV news show the next year. In 1945, the first public demonstration of a TV set in a department store was held, with 25,000 watching. At this point, nine commercial TV stations were in operation.

In 1946, audio tape introduced to American network radio. Bing Crosby brought the BASF process from Europe, so he could pre-tape his radio shows and spend more time on the golf course. Soon, most other network radio shows went to tape. This ultimately spelled the beginning of the end of network radio as a primary family entertainment medium.

On TV in 1946 was the first televised heavyweight boxing title championship and the first hour-long musical variety show broadcast by NBC (network consisting of three stations). In 1947, there were 44,000 TV sets in use and 40 million radios in use. That year marked the first mass production of television receivers.

In 1947, the Dumont Network signed on the air. It was conceived as a vehicle for selling Dumont TV sets. Named for founder Abner B. Dumont. Its flagship station was Channel 5, WABD in New York, and other affiliates provided programming to the network. That year also saw the first broadcast of a joint session of Congress. Also in 1947 was the first broadcast of a World Series baseball championship. CBS,

NBC and Dumont pooled their resources to jointly telecast to an audience of 4 million people.

In 1947, the first kinescopes were created. NBC and Eastman Kodak devised a process for recording programs off a TV monitor and distributing for later broadcast. Kinescopes paved the way for videotape and DVDs later. In 1948, there were one million TV sets in use, 36 TV stations in 19 cities, able to reach one-third of the U.S. population. That year, ABC-TV signed on the air.

In 1948, Columbia Records first issued long-playing record albums on the market. This changed the packaging and distribution of popular music, which gave the rise to a broader audience and music variety shows on television. "The Ed Sullivan Show/Toast of the Town" premiered on CBS. This became the longest-running variety show, lasting 1974 and syndicated ever since.

In 1948, the "Milton Berle Show/Texaco Star Theatre" premiered on NBC. Berle commanded the highest rating for a single time period, up to 92%. As a show of support, in 1951, NBC signed Berle to an exclusive 30-year contract, which it fully honored. The first Academy Awards ceremonies were broadcast on TV. As an equivalent venue for recognizing its own excellence, the Television Academy of Arts and Sciences was founded, subsequently bestowing its Emmy Awards. The first game show transitioned from radio to TV. It was "Winner Take All" on CBS, the first quiz show developed by Mark Goodson and Bill Todman, who subsequently produced the most game shows.

In 1949, Columbia Pictures was the first major Hollywood studio to enter TV production. Its Screen Gems subsidiary was prolific throughout the 1950s, 1960s and 1970s. RCA Victor Records first issued 45-RPM singles on the market. Laws were passed enabling TV aerials to be perched atop buildings to improve signals. In 1950, Revue Productions entered television, taking over Universal Studios in 1962 and becoming the most prolific supplier of filmed programming to television. The Korean War became the first living room war, via film footage sent back to networks.

In 1951, RCA unveiled the first community TV antenna system (forerunner of cable TV). Desilu Productions was formed. Its series, "I Love Lucy," was the first to be filmed in front of a live audience. A ratings hit, it set the pace for TV reruns. Desilu's prolific output over the next 16 years included "Our Miss Brooks," "December Bride," "The Lucy Show," "The Untouchables," "Star Trek," "Mannix" and "Mission: Impossible." "Hallmark Hall of Fame" premiered on NBC, with "Amahl and the Night Visitors" as its first show. This became the longest-running series of specials and cultural arts show.

In 1952, the coaxial cable was laid, facilitating national broadcast transmissions. 1953 witnessed the first live coast-to-coast broadcast: the inauguration of President Dwight D. Eisenhower, the first worldwide event coverage: the coronation of Queen Elizabeth, the highest rated TV event (the birth of Little Ricky on "I Love Lucy"), the first educational TV station (KUHT-TV, Houston, TX) signing on the air. Also in 1953, TV Guide began publication. RCA tested compatible color TV system on the air for the first time. Leonard Goldenson took over ABC-TV from previous owners, launching a long journey to make the fledgling network a contender to giants CBS and NBC. It took until 1976 for ABC to become #1 in the overall ratings. The network focused upon young viewers, who matured and remained loyal to the network of their youth.

1954 stands as television's Golden Year and the peak of its Golden Age. The first color TV show transmission was "Climax/Shower of Stars" on CBS. Walt Disney entered TV, hosting Disneyland and promoting his theme park concept. His first major mini-series hit was "Davy Crockett," launching a commercial merchandising tradition. In 1955, Warner Brothers and 20th Century-Fox both entered TV with episodic series production. In 1956, video tape was first used on television production. Originally, tape was used for commercials and portions of programs. By 1958, entire programs were taped and edited for later broadcast. This ultimately spelled the beginning of the end of live television (except for news shows). Desilu Productions acquired the RKO Pictures lot (later selling to Paramount in 1967). MGM entered TV with series based upon some of its movies: "Dr. Kildare," "The Thin Man," "Asphalt Jungle," "Northwest Passage."

In 1957, 40 million TV sets were in use. Jack Paar took over as host of "The Tonight Show" on NBC. The year saw the first coverage of the space exploration program and the entry of Dick Clark into the TV medium that he dominated for five decades. In 1958, the Dumont Network signed off the air, merging into ABC-TV. 1959 saw the Paola investigations into rock n' roll music, the recording industry and plugging of records on radio and television.

In 1960, 90% of all U.S. households had TV. An overhead blimp was utilized for the first time in live sports coverage. The year saw the first Olympics marathon coverage, originating from Rome. The Kennedy-Nixon debates set ratings and precedent for election coverage. JFK was the first TV era President. In 1962, Johnny Carson took over as host of "The Tonight Show" on NBC. Walter Cronkite took over as anchor of the CBS Evening News. 1963's major news event was the assassination of President John F. Kennedy. 1964's top ratings phenomenon was The Beatles on the "Ed Sullivan Show," signaling the major news and cultural icon: the British Invasion (rock music, fashions, fads). 1965 brought the advent of audio cassette tapes. In 1967, Super Bowl #1 was seen by 51 million viewers. The final episode of "The Fugitive" ranked next to the birth of Little Ricky as TV's highest ratings getter. National Educational Television hence became known as the Public Broadcasting System. In 1967, Ted Turner bought WTCG-TV, a UHF independent station in Atlanta and began programming TV series reruns, movies and sports. WTBS became the flagship for his broadcasting empire (CNN, TNT, etc.). 1968's major news events: assassinations of Martin Luther King and Robert F. Kennedy, plus rioting in the Chicago streets during the Democratic National Convention. 1968 saw the advent of eight-track tapes. 1969's major news event was the landing on the moon.

1970 was the last year for cigarette advertising on television. Satellite, cable and pay TV systems started their aggressive growth, in the beginning carrying clear reception for out-of-town channels. In 1971, the barter syndication strip series concept was introduced. 1972's major news event was tragedy at the Olympics games, as sports and news coverage melded. In 1974, Roone Arledge, head of ABC Sports, also took over as head of ABC News.

In 1976, the cable TV era began. Ted Turner's WTCG-TV in Atlanta became cable TV's first Superstation and changed its call letters to WTBS, the flagship for his broadcasting empire. Barbara Walters moved from NBC over to ABC, with her first stint was as co-host of the ABC Evening News with Harry Reasoner. In 1977, ABC-TV finally hit #1 overall in the ratings. The first home video cassette recorders went on the marketing, selling at $1,700 each. Blank video tapes were selling for $30 each. In 1978, Home Box Office premiered.

In 1980, the concept of videotape rentals was first introduced. The retail cost of VCRs went below $1,000 for the first time. Cable channels BET, Showtime and Cable News Network (CNN) premiered. In 1981 MTV and USA Network premiered. Classic television shows from the 1950s and 1960s began to be marketed on video cassette tapes. In 1982, A&E and TNN premiered. In 1983, the broadcast of the final episode of "Mash" became TV's highest ratings getter. It knocked the birth of Little Ricky and the final episode of "The Fugitive" down to second and third place. . In 1983, home shopping channels and The Disney Channel premiered. In 1985, the cost of blank videotapes dropped below $10 for the first time. VH-1 premiered.

In 1986, compact discs introduced as the newest technology for record albums, playing at 78 RPM (the original phonograph speed). CDs eclipsed vinyl records within the next five years and became the preferred source for music, over cassette tapes. This trend also spelled the beginning of the end for the Top 40 singles market. ABC cancelled "American Bandstand," ending its 39-year run on the network. In 1987, the Fox Network signed on the air.

In 1990, the retail cost of VCRs went below $250 and tapes below $5 for the first time. In 1992, Jay Leno took over as host of "The Tonight Show" on NBC. 1997 saw the advent of the Internet. In 2002, satellite radio was introduced.

In 1958, Congress founded the National Aeronautics and Space Administration to oversee space exploration. NASA sent up its first satellite that year. Manned space flights began in 1961, and they captivated the public. The space program galvanized the adventure of the unknown, the lessons from science and the overwhelming national pride. Astronauts were heroes, and the spaceflights were must-see television viewing.

The space program has brought modern life many inventions. There are 1,800 spin-offs in NASA's Technology Transfer Program, including CAT scanners, computer microchips, cordless tools, ear thermometers, freeze-dried food, insulation reflective techniques, invisible braces for teeth, enriched baby food, the joy stick, light-emitting diodes, memory foam, microwave ovens, scratch resistant lenses, shoe insoles, smoke detectors, solar energy, the swimsuit, powdered lubricants, water filters, space blankets, land mine removal, the soap soaker, flame resistant textiles, the ingestible thermometer pill, workout machines for conditioning, highway safety grooving, artificial limbs, pollution remediation, radial tires, ventricular assist devices, software catalogs and much more.

The 21st Century, in business and in lifestyles, is being dominated by technology, from cell phones to wi-fi, from the internet to social media and from modern adaptations of technologies from two earlier centuries.

Technology has influenced so many devices and niche industries, including aircraft navigation, alarm systems, analyzers, automated attendants, automobiles, broadband communications, cable fiber optics, call systems, cellular mobile station equipment, clocks, cloud storage, computers, converters, data management systems, digital test equipment, distributors, earth stations, educational and training systems, fiber optic tools, hardware, headsets, HVAC equipment, key systems, lighting systems, message systems, modems, monitoring systems, paging systems, power supplies, radio telephone equipment, railroad systems, receivers, revenue and billing systems, routers, security systems, semiconductors, signaling systems, storage systems, surge protectors, switches, telecommunications devices, teleconferencing, test equipment, towers, transformers, trucks, video games, video systems, wave guides, wireless equipment, work stations, dust busters, cochlear implants and much more.

Areas and industries benefiting from tech innovations include architecture, assistive technologies, banking and finance, construction, energy, healthcare, information technology, manufacturing, medicine, military, nursing, retail, risk management, science, speech and hearing, technology transfer, water treatment, weather forecasting and others.

There are seven levels of technology in business and corporate usage:

1. Basic Operations. Necessary equipment to do basic jobs. Telephones, word processors, fax machines, time-tracking mechanisms. Along with furniture and basic equipment, these are minimums for running a business.

2. Tools of the Trade. Contemporary technology, per area of departmental usage. Technology of the energy industry, for example, has customized design and usage. Every industry niche develops and perfects its own necessary-operations technology.

3. Accountability Systems. These include infrastructures which track, report, acknowledge and prioritize. Used primarily to crunch numbers, track dollars, count heads and generate reports.

4. Process Systems. An extension of industry-specific technology, it logs wells, charts flow of product through pipelines, projects demands and counts production statistics (per the example of the energy industry).

5. Meet the Marketplace. Technology of selling, marketing and serving clients. Databases, solicitation call sheets, customer tracking data, initiatives for follow-up, customer service data. Used to project markets, make sales and provide after-sale service.

6. Knowing Where Technology Ends. Understanding its true place in operations. Realistic appraisal of what it can and cannot do and how it supports core business operations.

7. Holistic Company Operations. Commitment to technology in terms of company functions. Greater commitment is given to people, philosophies of doing business, strategic planning, ethical operations and future-directed vision.

Management Styles

Organizations should coordinate management skills into its overall corporate strategy, in order to satisfy customer needs profitably, draw together the components for practical strategies and implement strategic requirements to impact the business. This is my review of how management styles have evolved.

In the period that predated scientific management, the Captain of Industry style prevailed. Prior to 1885, the kings of industry were rulers, as had been land barons of earlier years. Policies were dictated, and people complied. Some captains were notoriously ruthless. Others like Rockefeller, Carnegie and Ford channeled their wealth and power into giving back to the communities. It was an era of self-made millionaires and the people who toiled in their mills.

From 1885-1910, the labor movement gathered steam. Negotiations and collective bargaining focused on conditions for workers and physical plant environments. In this era, business fully segued from an agricultural-based economy to an industrial-based reality.

As a reaction to industrial reforms and the strength of unions, a Hard Nosed style of leadership was prominent from 1910-1939, management's attempt to take stronger hands, recapture some of the Captain of Industry style and build solidity into an economy plagued by the Depression. This is an important phase to remember because it is the mindset of addictive organizations.

The Human Relations style of management flourished from 1940-1964. Under it, people were managed. Processes were managed as collections of people. Employees began having greater says in the execution of policies. Yet, the rank and file employees at this point were not involved in creating policies, least of all strategies and methodologies.

Management by Objectives came into vogue in 1965 and was the prevailing leadership style until 1990. In this era, business started embracing formal planning. Other important components of business (training, marketing, research, team building and productivity) were all accomplished according to goals, objectives and tactics.

Most corporate leaders are two management styles behind. Those who matured in the era of the Human Relations style of management were still clinging to value systems of Hard Nosed. They were not just "old school." They went to the school that was torn down to build the old school.

Executives who were educated in the Management by Objectives era were still recalling value systems of their parents' generation before it. Baby boomers with a Depression-era frugality and value of tight resources are more likely to take a bean counter-focused approach to business. That's my concern that financial-only focus without regard to other corporate dynamics bespeaks of hostile takeovers, ill-advised rollups and corporate raider activity in search of acquiring existing books of business.

To follow through the premise, younger executives who were educated and came of age during the early years of Customer Focused Management had still not comprehended and embraced its tenets. As a result, the dot.com bust and subsequent financial scandals occurred. In a nutshell, the "new school" of managers did not think that corporate protocols and strategies related to them. The game was to just write the rules as they rolled along. Such thinking always invites disaster, as so many of their stockholders found out. Given that various management eras are still reflected in the new order of business, we must learn from each and move forward.

In 1991, Customer Focused Management became the standard. In a highly competitive business environment, every dynamic of a successful organization must be geared toward ultimate customers. Customer focused management goes far beyond just smiling, answering queries and communicating with buyers. It transcends service and quality. Every organization has customers, clients, stakeholders, financiers, volunteers, supporters or other categories of "affected constituencies."

Companies must change their focus from products and processes to the values shared with customers. Everyone with whom you conduct business is a customer or referral source of someone else. The service that we get from some people, we pass along to others. Customer service is a continuum of human behaviors, shared with those whom we meet.

Customers are the lifeblood of every business. Employees depend upon customers for their paychecks. Yet, you wouldn't know the correlation when poor customer service is rendered. Employees of many companies behave as though customers are a bother, do not heed their concerns and do not take suggestions for improvement.

There is no business that cannot undergo some improvement in its customer orientation. Being the recipient of bad service elsewhere must inspire us to do better for our own customers. The more that one sees poor customer service and customer neglect in other companies, we must avoid the pitfalls and traps in our own companies.

If problems are handled only through form letters, subordinates or call centers, then management is the real cause of the problem. Customer focused management begins and ends at top management. Management should speak personally with customers, to set a good example for employees. If management is complacent or non-participatory, then it will be reflected by behavior and actions of the employees.

Any company can benefit from having an advisory board, which is an objective and insightful source of sensitivity toward customer needs, interests and concerns. The successful business must put the customer into a co-destiny relationship. Customers want to build relationships, and it is the obligation of the business to prove that it is worthy.

Customer focused management is the antithesis to the traits of bad business, such as the failure to deliver what was promised, bait and switch advertising and a failure to handle mistakes and complaints in a timely, equitable and customer-friendly manner. Customer focused management is dedicated to providing members with an opportunity to identify, document and establish best practices through benchmarking to increase value, efficiencies and profits.

History and Heritage, Conclusion

The history and heritage of business was a series of processes, then methodologies, then formalized institutions and then quests to move to the next levels. The key stages were:

- Exploring.
- Colonizing the nation.
- Meeting basic needs of citizens.
- Automobiles.
- Pop culture.
- Technology inventions, development and usage.
- The consumer age.
- Development of service industries.
- Increased consumer discretionary spending.
- Responding to crises.
- Goods and services for human betterment.
- World leadership by business.
- Development and expansion of global markets.
- The transition of smoke stacks to high technology.
- Transition from an industrialized economy to an information based economy.

Business is at a most decisive crossroads. The rules have changed, always have and always will. A great many mosaics make up The Big Picture. Yet the wider perspective in business is rarely seen. Too many myopic niches dominate the view.

The potentiality of organizations is a progressive journey from information to insight. Foolhardiness is all being righteous about inconsequential things at the wrong times. People and organizations spend disproportionate amounts of time trying to behave like or look like someone else…or what they think others appear to be. Until one becomes one's own best role model, the futile trail will continue.

It's a whole new world. Pressures continue and accelerate for companies to stay in operation, become competitive, keep ahead of the marketplace and perform quality work. Businesses of all sizes are besieged with opportunities, competing information sources and large amounts of uncertainty. Most of the downfalls, trips, false starts and incorrect handling of situations are attributable to business' lack of focus on the macro and too much emphasis upon certain micros, to the exclusion of other dynamics.

Pictured are two of the earliest computer systems in the early 1950s. At left is the IBM 701 model, the company's first venture into mainframe computers. At right is the UNIVAC (Universal Automatic Computer).

Charles Lindbergh was welcomed to New York with a tickertape parade after his epic global air flight.

Henry Ford is pictured with his son Edsel Ford in an early automobile in 1907.
Ford Motor Company later produced the Edsel model from 1957-1959.

This is what urban sprawl looked like in 1952.
Motorists traded with "full-service" filling stations. Note two attendants, one
to fill the gasoline and another to check under the hood, tires and fluid levels.

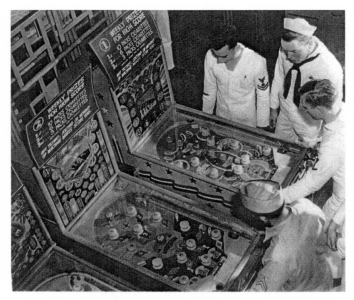

Pinball Machines have been a great source of entertainment since the 1930s. They appeared in arcades and expanded to restaurants, bars and other retail establishments. Their popularity spawned video games.

Dave Garroway is pictured during the premiere telecast of NBC-TV's "The Today Show," on Jan. 14, 1952. The graphics were low-tech, and there were two turntables on the set to play the music. This launched the tradition of morning TV shows.

Chapter 7

BUSINESS LEGENDS

Arthur Andersen became the youngest CPA (age 23) in Illinois. He founded his accounting firm in 1913. It expanded internationally into a major business services professional practice.

Walter Annenberg worked for his father's newspaper, The Philadelphia Inquirer and took over management of the business in 1942. He created other print media, including TV Guide in 1952 and Seventeen in 1954. He was the United States Ambassador to the United Kingdom from 1969-1974. He established the Annenberg School for Communication at the University of Pennsylvania and the University of Southern California. In 1989, he established the Annenberg Foundation.

Elizabeth Arden was born in Canada and pursued a nursing career. In 1908, she moved to New York and took a job as an assistant to a beauty stylist. Soon, she had her own salon on Fifth Avenue. Arden incorporated under her name, hired chemists to develop a facial cream and established a wholesale network to distribute her product. As years went by, she added beauty services and retreats.

Mary Kay Ash was born in Hot Wells, Texas. Her mother was trained as a nurse and later became a manager of a restaurant in Houston. Ash attended Dow Elementary School and Reagan High School in Houston, graduating in 1934. Ash married and had three children. While her husband served in World War II, she sold books door-to-door. Ash worked for Stanley Home Products. Frustrated when passed over for a promotion in favor of a man that she had trained, Ash retired in 1963 and intended to write a book to assist women in business.

The book turned into a business plan for her company, and in 1963, Ash started Mary Kay Cosmetics, with a storefront operation in Dallas. The company went public in 1968 and went private again in 1985. At the time of Ash's death in 2001, Mary Kay Cosmetics had 800,000 representatives in 37 countries, with total annual sales over $200 million. Mary Kay Ash authored three books, all of which became best-sellers.

John Jacob Astor was a fur trader and real estate developer. He gained entry to ports and bought surrounding properties, combining all of his holdings in 1808 as the American Fur Company. He loaned money to the government to finance westward exploration. When he died in 1848, Astor left much of his wealth to establish the New York Public Library.

Warren Avis founded a rent car company in Ypsilanti, MI, in 1948. Avis became the second largest rental car company in the U.S. by 1956, inspiring the advertising slogan, "When you're number two, you try harder." It also operates Budget Car Rental, Zipcar and other companies.

George Fisher Baker founded the First National Bank of New York City in 1863. Baker became one of the central figures in American finance. In 1908, he founded First Security Corporation. Among his philanthropy was a $6 million gift to Harvard University for the establishment of the Graduate School of Business.

George Ballas was the inventor of the Weed Eater, a string trimmer company founded in 1971. The idea for the Weed Eater trimmer came to him from the spinning nylon bristles of an automatic car wash. He thought that he could devise a similar technique to protect the bark on trees that he was trimming around. His company was bought by Emerson Electric and merged with Poulan, which was later purchased by Electrolux.

Phineas Taylor Barnum edited a newspaper and sold tickets at a Philadelphia theatre. He was taken with a show where a woman presented herself as the former nurse of George Washington. The show was phony, but he was intrigued with how far the public imagination could go. Barnum was convinced that there was no limit to the gullibility of the public. He purchased a museum of curiosities, brought singer Jenny Lind to the U.S. and served as the mayor of Bridgeport, CT. In 1871, he debuted The Greatest Show on Earth, partnering with his competitor James A. Bailey in 1881. He stated, "There's a sucker born every minute." The consummate promoter, P.T. Barnum always presented shows that were worth more than the price of admission.

Bernard Baruch entered business in 1889 and became a successful speculator on Wall Street. In 1916, he was appointed an advisor to President Woodrow Wilson on matters of conserving raw materials during World War I and at the Versailles peace conference. Baruch continued serving on economic commissions and in 1946 represented the U.S. on the Atomic Energy Commission. He advised every U.S. president from Wilson to Kennedy.

Eddie Bauer founded his first shop in Seattle in 1920 (when he was 21 years old), opening in the back of a hunting and fishing store. He expanded the line and renamed it "Eddie Bauer's Sport Shop." He developed heavy wool garments for outdoorsmen. He received more than 20 patents for clothing and outdoor equipment. In 1945, Bauer offered his first mail-order catalog. His principal business became manufacturing of clothing and catalog sales. In 1971, the company was sold to General Mills, who shifted the focus to casual clothing and expanded to 61 stores. Cross-branding with Ford Motor Company ensued. The Spiegel catalog company purchased Eddie Bauer from General Mills in 1988. Eddie Bauer Home was launched in 1991, selling furniture, décor, linens and tableware.

Leon L. Bean earned his first money at age nine, selling steel traps. He was an avid hunter and fisherman and in 1911 invented the waterproof boot. He prepared a mail-order circular, and by 1917 had enough money to build a boot factory. By 1834, the catalog grew to 52 pages. By 1937, sales surpassed $1 million.

David Belasco was a Broadway impresario. He managed Madison Square Garden, then the Lyceum, then became an independent producer. He elevated actors and playwrights to stardom, with the skill to draw crowds to the theatre that bore his name. Belasco was associated with more than 300 plays, known as the "bishop of Broadway."

Alexander Graham Bell trained as an instructor for the deaf. In 1874, he developed the "phonautograph," a combination of telegraphs with an electrical speaking device. By 1876, he perfected a system capable of producing intelligible human speech. In 1877, he formed the Bell Telephone Company, producing the device for the marketplace. He founded the Volta Laboratory, developing the "photophone," which transmitted speech by beams of light. Bell presided over the National Geographic Society, was a regent of the Smithsonian Institution and founded the Aerial Experiment Association.

Jeff Bezos was born in Albuquerque, NM, and raised in Houston, TX, where he attended River Oaks Elementary School. As a child, Bezos spent summers at his grandfather's South Texas ranch, where he developed talents in scientific pursuits. He graduated from Princeton University and founded Amazon.com in 1994. Bezos was named Time Magazine's Person of the Year in 1999. He founded Blue Origin, a human spaceflight company, in 2000.

William E. Boeing bought a shipyard in Seattle, WA, in 1910 and converted the property into his first airplane factory. The first planes produced were seaplanes. In 1917, the name was formalized as the Boeing Airplane Company. Planes produced during World War I became surplus after the war and were commissioned into commercial aircraft market. In 1925, Boeing built planes for the federal government to use on mail runs. Larger planes were built for commercial airlines. Boeing started producing jets for the military in the 1940s. It produced the first commercial jet airliner in 1958, with roll-out of the 737 model in 1967 and the 747 model in 1968. Boeing manufactures and customizes planes for companies worldwide.

Daniel Boone was born in Pennsylvania and visited the Kentucky wilderness in 1767. He led expeditions for hunting and trapping, then colonized settlements. He was influential in extending the new U.S. beyond the Allegheny Mountains, a frontier legend that inspired exploring and settlements.

Gail Borden came to Texas in 1835. He co-founded the Telegraph and Texas Register newspaper. In 1836, it moved to Harrisburg (which became Houston). The newspaper covered the fight for Texas independence, including events at the Alamo and San Jacinto. Borden sold the newspaper and went into politics, writing early drafts of the Texas Constitution. In 1851, he opened a factory in Galveston to produce meat biscuits (dehydrated beef). In 1856, he received a patent for his process of condensing milk by vacuum. With the founding of a milk company in

New York, the product improved and became successful. The milk is now called Eagle Brand.

Chef Boyardee is a line of canned Italian food products, introduced in 1928. Ettore Boiardi opened a restaurant in Cleveland, Ohio, in 1924. Customers began asking for his recipes. In 1928, he moved to Pennsylvania and opened a factory. The spelling was changed to help Americans pronounce his name.

Richard Branson started his first business in London in 1970, a student magazine that interviewed prominent personalities. He opened a retail record store ion 1971. Virgin Records was created in 1972, the name suggested to Branson because they were new at the record business. Virgin entered the airline industry, railroads, liquor, comic books, healthcare, energy and commercial space flight. Sir Richard Branson's Virgin Group comprises more than 400 companies.

Perry Brink founded an armored transportation service in Chicago, IL, in 1859, to guard money and valuables while in transit. Security services were added, for offices and homes, as well as logistics services. Brink's is headquartered in Richmond, VA, and has 650 branch offices in 150 countries.

William McLaren Bristol and John Ripley Myers founded Bristol-Myers in Clinton, NY, in 1887. They produced Sal Hepatica, a laxative mineral salt that became a best seller by 1903. Their Ipana toothpaste was the first to include a disinfectant, protecting against the infection of bleeding gums. In the 1930s, the company added Vitalis hair tonic for men and Mum deodorant. In 1959, Bristol-Myers purchased the Clairol Company, manufacturer of hair care products. In 1967, it acquired Mead-Johnson, producer of infant formulas. In the 1970s, the company introduced medicines. In 1989, Bristol-Myers merged with Squibb. In 1997, the company opened an expanded research campus in New Jersey.

Warren Buffett earned money as a child and showed early interest in the stock market and investing. He worked as an investment salesman, then as a securities analyst and stockbroker. He became a millionaire in 1962, due to partnerships. He took control of Berkshire Hathaway, a textile manufacturing company. He invested in a department store, The Washington Post, Capital Cities/ABC, Coca-Cola and many other industries.

Andrew Carnegie immigrated from Scotland to the U.S. when he was 13. He worked in factories and hit riches when a farm of his hit oil. He began consolidating industries, including oil companies, railroads, steamships, ironworks and steel mills (monopolizing the industry in 1880). He retired to Scotland and contributed $350 million of his wealth to a foundation to support worthwhile causes, peace and technology.

George Washington Carver was born into a slave family. He evolved into a distinguished chemist and botanist. He improved agricultural methods, changing soil-depleting farms to peanuts and sweet potatoes. His research inspired an agricultural revolution in the South.

Steve Chen, Chad Hurley and Jawed Karin founded YouTube, a video sharing website, in San Bruno, CA, in 2005. The original office was above a restaurant, and the first video posted was Karin at the San Diego Zoo. More than 100 million views per day have been realized, with videos uploaded by individuals and companies.

Harry Cohn and two partners founded the CBC Film Sales Corporation in 1919. Cohn took over and renamed it Columbia Pictures in 1934. Some of his studios most memorable films included "Mr. Smith Goes to Washington," "It Happened One Night," "Gilda," Three Stooges comedies, "Born Yesterday," "The Jolson Story" and "All the King's Men."

Samuel Colt worked in his father's textile factory and went to sea in 1830. He conceived the idea of a repeating firearm, utilizing a revolving set of chambers, each brought into alignment with a single barrel. To finance his gun prototypes, Colt toured as a demonstrator of laughing gas. He received the patent in 1836 and opened a factory to manufacture his guns. His other inventions included an underwater mine system for harbor defense, telegraphy and submarine cable. The westward expansion created demand for his guns, and Colt's firearms were essential in military service.

Christopher Columbus calculated that India was where the U.S. lies. He led expeditions to Iceland, the Madeiras and in 1492 took three ships from Spain to the New World. He discovered islands and established a colony. He returned to the Caribbean as the governor, followed by more exploratory voyages, including to Central America, an explorer of great vision and courage.

Ezra Cornell had a flair for things mechanical. He managed a flour mill and a plaster mill. He was associated with Samuel F.B. Morse, stringing together insulated wire along a series of poles, supervising the first telegraph line from Washington to Baltimore. He continued building telegraph lines, connecting major cities, a leader in unifying the Western Union Telegraph Company. With his wealth, he established a model farm, free public library and an agricultural college that evolved into Cornell University.

Stephen Covey is the author of such business classics as "The Seven Habits of Highly Effective People," "First Things First," "Principle-Centered Leadership," "The Seven Habits of Highly Effective Families," "The Eighth Habit" and "The Leader in Me." He was a prominent educator, businessman and speaker.

Philip B. Crosby has contributed to management theories and quality principles. He advocated four programs of doing things right the first time: the definition of quality being conformance to requirements, the system of quality being prevention, the performance standard being zero defects and the measurement of quality being the cost of non-conformance. He authored several books that are widely utilized by industry.

Jimmy Dean was a singer, recording artist and TV show host. His hit records included "Big Bad John," "P.T. 109," "Bumming Around," "I.O.U." and others. As an actor, he appeared on the "Daniel Boone" TV series and in the 1971 James Bond film "Diamonds Are Forever." In 1969, he founded the Jimmy Dean Sausage Company. His appearance in the TV commercials gave power to the food line. In 1984, the company was acquired by Consolidated Foods, Sara Lee Corporation. He remained the spokesperson for the product until 2004.

John Deere moved from Vermont to Illinois in 1836, opening a shop as a general repairman. He developed a steel blade made into a plow. In 1842, he built a factory, producing 100 plows the first year and 400 the next. He bought out other interests and was producing 2,400 in 1849. The catalog of products broadened to other agricultural implements, including tractors, combines, field sprayers, cotton pickers, seed drills, forage harvesters, bicycles, drivetrains and diesel engines.

Lee De Forest was an electrical engineer and inventor. His first patent was for an electrolytic detector that made possible the use of headphones with wireless receivers. In 1906, he invented the triode electron tube, with potential for relaying radio signals. His audion process evolved into radio. In 1919, De Forest developed a sound system for motion pictures. He made important contributions to the electric phonograph, television, radar and diathermy. He made and lost four fortunes in his life and remained committed to the educational potential for radio and TV.

Michael Dell bought his first calculator at age seven and his first computer at age 15, an Apple II, which he disassembled to see how it worked. He sold newspaper subscriptions, thus amassing an understanding of demographic data. While a student at the University of Texas at Austin, Dell started rebuilding computers and selling upgrade kits. In 1984, he opened a company to sell personal computers directly. In 1996, he started selling computers over the Internet. The Michael and Susan Dell Foundation support children's issues, medical education and family economic stability.

John DeLorean was born in Detroit, MI, where his father worked in factories. He studied industrial engineering. He attended the Chrysler Institute, with a master's degree in automotive engineering, working as an insurance salesman in order to improve his communication skills. He worked for Chrysler, then Packard and then General Motors as head of the Pontiac division. He was noted for birthing the Pontiac GTO, followed by the Firebird and the Grand Prix. After heading the Chevrolet division, he left GM in 1973 to found his own car company. The DeLorean hit the market in 1981.

William Edwards Deming was an electrical engineer and statistician who developed sampling techniques utilized by the U.S. Census Bureau. He championed the work of process control and worked with leaders of Japanese industry after World War II. He taught better design of products to achieve service, higher level of uniform product quality, improvement of product testing in the workplace and research centers, plus greater sales through side markets. Deming developed a system of quality management, encompassing four components: appreciating a system, understanding the variation, psychology and the theory of knowledge.

Walt Disney was one of the most creative pop culture figures of the 20th Century. He is profiled in the chapter "Icons and Legends for Children."

Peter Drucker was known as the "father of American business." In 1959, he coined the term "knowledge worker." In 1971 in California, he developed the nation's first MBA program for working professionals. His writings predicted many 20th Century business happenings: privatization and decentralization, the ascendency of Japan to world economic power status, the importance of marketing and the emergence of an information society powered by life-long learning. Drucker published 40 books. He demanded that public and private organizations operate ethically and decried managers who reap bonuses by laying off employees, declaring, "This is morally and socially unforgivable, and we will pay a heavy price for it." Other insights included: "A company should streamline bureaucracy. Managers should look for more efficient models for organizing work. Results are obtained by exploiting opportunities, not solving problems." He was accorded the Presidential Medal of Freedom in 2002.

E.I. Dupont de Nemours was a French chemist who migrated to the U.S. in 1800. In 1802, a company was founded near Wilmington, Delaware, to produce a superior gunpowder, utilizing investment capital and machinery from France. The firm acquired several other chemical companies. Dupont established one of the first research laboratories in the U.S., working on cellulose chemistry, lacquers and other non-explosive products. Dupont partnered with the automobile industry and developed polymers, synthetic rubber, Teflon, nylon, Dacron, Orlon, Mylar, Lycra, Tyvek, Nomex and many others. In 1981, Dupont acquired Conoco Inc., major oil and gas producing company. In 1999, Dupont sold its shares in Conoco, which merged with Phillips Petroleum Company.

Amelia Earhart was an Army nurse during World War I and a social worker in Boston before settling into a career in aviation. In 1928, she was the first woman to fly the Atlantic. In 1930-31, she was vice president of Luddington Airlines, an early carrier. In 1935, she made the first solo flight from Hawaii to the U.S. In 1937, while attempting a round-the-world flight, her aircraft was lost. Earhart has a firm place in air flight legend.

George Eastman opened a photography business at age 16 to support his family in Rochester, NY. He began the manufacture of photographic dry plates in 1878 and got a patent for roll film in 1884. He founded Eastman Kodak Company in 1892. He devised transparent film in 1889, which became an essential ingredient in the motion picture industry. His wealth went to establish health and educational institutions, including the Massachusetts Institute of Technology.

Thomas Alva Edison was perhaps America's most prolific inventor. He was home schooled and began inventing as a child. At age 21, he went to work in a stock brokerage firm and promptly made innovations to the ticker machines. He sold the rights to that process, setting himself up as a full-time inventor, wearing a chemist's white coat in the laboratory. Over the next five years, he averaged one invention per month. Entire industries evolved from his ideas, inventions and innovations.

In 1877, at age 30, Edison invented the phonograph unintentionally. At the time, Edison was trying to devise a high-speed telegraph machine as a counterpart to the telephone that Alexander Graham Bell had invented a year before.

For his contributions to the telephone, Edison had already become quite wealthy. Edison thought he heard sounds and sought out to track down the phenomena. It occurred to him that he could devise a low-cost machine that would record voices. On a metal cylinder, a needle would move. Once that apparatus was completed, Edison shouted a child's nursery rhyme into the mouthpiece, "Mary had a little lamb." He admittedly was shocked when it reproduced his voice.

Edison received his patent on the cylinder style phonograph in 1878. From 1879-1887, Edison dropped the idea of developing the phonograph and concentrated his energies on developing the electric light.

Meantime, a young German immigrant named Emile Berliner developed the gramophone, which played discs. It was patented in 1887 and involved the making of a reverse metal matrix from the original acid-etched recording. He then used the negative master to stamp positive duplicates. The record player became a huge success.

In 1888, Edison took note of Berliner's invention and retooled his cylinder technology for commercial recording. The first releases also recited poetry. The U.S. Marine Band recorded marches over and over again, as each consumer cylinder was a master. Only the wealthy could afford cylinders, priced in 1890 at $10 each. The machine on which they played sold for $200.

By the end of the 19th Century, Berliner's record machine process was out-distancing Edison's cylinder machine. This was similar to the manner in which VHS tapes out-distanced beta-max tapes in the early 1980s, becoming the dominant technology. By 1900, Edison had gotten into the commercial recording business but kept putting out cylinders until 1911, well past the time that Berliner's phonograph record had become the industry standard. The cylinders had more disc space to contain longer performances, but the phonograph records were the preferred medium. In 1919, experimentation began on electrical recording and reproduction. Until then, the phonographs were cranked by hand. Those developments came from companies other than Edison.

On Nov. 1, 1929, the Edison Company announced that they would cease the production of phonographs and records. The announced reason was so that they could concentrate on the manufacture of radios and dictating machines, which is what Edison's talking horn started out to be in the first place. Thomas Alva Edison was then 82 years old, and had long since ceased to be active in the business.

The two oldest record companies, Columbia (founded in 1898) and RCA Victor (founded in 1901) are still with us today. The two oldest record companies developed the next technologies as alternatives to the breakable 78RPM recordings. Though both companies started research and development in 1931, Columbia introduced the long-playing record (LP) in 1948, and RCA Victor introduced the 45RPM single in 1949.

The fortunes and electrical recording techniques of Columbia, RCA Victor, Brunswick and others had years earlier shoved Edison's recording empire into nostalgia. One can still find Edison cylinders in antique shops. The genius (Thomas Alva Edison) died in 1931. By that time, the recording industry had left its infancy and was experiencing the growing pains of youth. Edison saw it all and fathered it all, the industry that he started back in 1877.

By the way, the compact disc (CD) is an updated version of Emile Berliner's phonograph record, developed in 1877. CD's were developed by Sony and Philips in the late 1970s. Both companies started the research independently of each other but, learning from Edison's demise, combined as a joint effort in 1979. CDs had their first commercial releases in 1982. Both the original record and CD play at the same speed, 78RPM.

Albert Einstein was a German born physicist who formulated in 1905 and announced in 1915 his Theory of Relativity. The theory explains the behavior of objects in space and time, and it can be used to predict everything from the existence of black holes, to light bending due to gravity, to the behavior of the planet Mercury in its orbit.

In the 100 years since, relativity has many spin-off technologies and benefits to modern life: Global Positioning System, electromagnets, gold's yellow color, gold's ability to not corrode easily, mercury as a liquid, old TV sets with cathode ray tube screens, lighting systems and nuclear plants.

Marshall Field moved to Chicago in 1856 and worked as a traveling salesman and clerk for a wholesale house. He then partnered in and managed other stores, the result being Marshall Field and Company in 1881. It manufactured items and sold them under the company name. By 1895, the store was grossing $40 million per year. He donated to the University of Chicago and the 1893 Chicago Exposition. His descendants continued running the retail chain and owned three Chicago newspapers.

Malcolm Forbes took over the publishing of Forbes Magazine in 1957. The magazine was founded by his father B.C. Forbes in 1917. Malcolm was a proponent of capitalism and free market trade. The magazine diversified into real estate sales and a second publication, Egg, covering New York nightlife.

Henry Ford epitomized the American myth. He was born into a farming family in Michigan, was mechanically proficient as a child and became a machinist. In 1891, he moved to Detroit, as an engineer with the Edison company. Experiments with engines led in 1896 to his first automobile. In 1899, he founded Detroit Automobile Company. In 1903, he founded the Ford Motor Company, introducing the Model N. In 1908, he introduced the popularly priced Model T. In 1913, to meet growing production schedules, Ford introduced the continuously moving assembly line. In 1915, Ford doubled his workers' pay. In 1941, Ford became the last automaker to unionize.

Benjamin Franklin was a printer, author, inventor, scientist, diplomat and statesman. His most notable scientific work was on the nature of electricity. His career of unparalleled diversity marks Franklin as one of history's top legends.

Robert Fulton had a flair for all things mechanical. He was a gunsmith, designed a paddlewheel boat, was a jeweler painter and miniaturist. He designed a steamboat for use on the Hudson River, in 1806, steaming up the river from New York to Albany. Fulton oversaw the construction of other steamboats and the organization of passenger and freight lines.

John Kenneth Galbraith was an instructor at Harvard and professor of economics at Princeton University. He directed economic policy bureaus for the U.S. government. In the 1950's, he published a series of landmark books, "American Capitalism," "The Great Crash," "The Affluent Society" and "The New Industrial State." He traced the historical shift of economic power from landowners to capitalists to a managerial and technical elite structure that he saw as common to all industrial nations.

George Gallup was head of research for the Young and Rubicam Advertising Agency in New York. In 1935, he founded the American Institute of Public Opinion and originated the Gallup Polls as statistical surveys of public reactions to every potential issue in news and radio-TV programming. The polls were published regularly in hundreds of newspapers, to high fanfare. Gallup advocated the need for change in education that would stress discovery and self-learning. He wanted to create a more informed public that would make wiser choices.

Bill Gates was in the eighth grade when he bought a computer terminal and a block time for use by the school's students. He wrote his first computer program on a GE system. He Wrote the school's computer system to schedule classes. While studying at Harvard, he and Paul Allen established their own computer software company, Microsoft, with its first office in Albuquerque, NM. The company moved to Bellevue, WA, in 1979. Microsoft launch its retail version of Windows in 1985. He topped the Forbes list of wealthiest people several times. The Bill and Melinda Gates Foundation has brought philanthropy, compassion and vision to countless global initiatives.

J. Paul Getty drilled his first oil site and made his first million in 1916. Getty diversified the holdings and grew the companies, incorporating into Getty Oil in 1967. Forbes Magazine said in 1957 that Getty was the richest man in America.

King C. Gillette founded his company as a razor manufacturer in Boston, MA, in 1901. The first safety razor with a disposable blade was introduced in 1903. The twist-to-open model was introduced ion 1934. The adjustable razor was introduced in 1958, the super razor in 1966 and Trac II in 1971, the Mach3 Turbo in 2001. One of the most memorable advertising campaigns was Gillette's "Look Sharp, Feel Sharp, Be Sharp" in the 1950s and 1960s. The company merged into Procter & Gamble in 2005.

Adam Gimbel founded a general store in Vincennes, IN, in 1887, moving to Milwaukee, WI. He acquired a second store in Philadelphia, PA, then a third in New York City in 1910. Gimbel's became the leading rival to Macy's. Gimbel's went public in 1922 and bought an upscale chain from Horace Saks, known as Saks Fifth Avenue. The Slinky toy made its debut at Gimbel's, rolling down the escalator. The Gimbel's chain closed in 1986.

George W. Goethels was an engineer employed on several civic works projects. In 1907, he was commissioned by President Theodore Roosevelt to head construction of the Panama Canal. Goethels supervised 30,000 employees of various nations. The Canal opened in 1914 and stimulated global trade. Goethels consulted other public programs, including the Port of New York Authority.

Leonard Goldenson captained the rescue of the ABC network, the merger of the United Paramount Theatres with ABC and the steady building of the TV and radio networks to #1 status. His experiences are chronicled in the excellent autobiographical book, "Beating the Odds."

Samuel Gompers was the most influential labor leader in American history. His American Federation of Labor provided response to the needs of industrialized workers, improving conditions without political agendas. He ran the AFL for 40 years, using strikes and boycotts in the mix with consensus negotiations.

Charles Goodyear ran a retail store, selling hardware and farm implements. In 1830, the India rubber industry came into being. Goodyear sought to manufacture rubber products of superior quality. About 1838, he acquired a patent for a process where sulfur could eliminate the stickiness of rubber. By 1844, he perfected the vulcanization process. Goodyear exhibited rubber goods at expositions in London and Paris in the 1850's. After Goodyear's death, the rubber industry grew and prospered.

Berry Gordy was an assembly line worker at Ford's plant in Detroit, which inspired his musical career. He also wrote songs for friend Jackie Wilson. In 1959, Gordy founded his own record company, following Ford's lead to create a mass production system for hit records. Hitsville USA produced the Motown Sound, which revolutionized pop music and radio listening in the 1960's and 1970's. The Motown Sound featured a dynamic roster of artists, including Diana Ross & the Supremes, Marvin Gaye, The Four Tops, Smokey Robinson & the Miracles, Mary Wells, Junior Walker & the All-Stars, Stevie Wonder, Michael Jackson, The Temptations, Martha & the Vandellas, The Marvelettes and many more. Gordy hoped that his stable of stars would headline New York's Copacabana Nightclub, and all achieved much more stellar fame, influence and respect. The Motown Sound inspired soul music, broadened the radio airplay configuration and inspired generations of soul superstars, songwriters and music producers.

Max Gotchman opened a chain of Army surplus stores in 1937 in San Antonio, TX, and Austin, TX. It evolved into Academy Super Surplus and later Academy Sports & Outdoors. It is the fourth largest chain of retail sporting goods stores.

Katherine Graham became publisher of The Washington Post in 1967. She became the first female Fortune 500 CEO in 1972. She had Benjamin Bradlee as editor and sought financial counsel from Warren Buffett. Graham presided over the Post in the Watergate era. Coverage of the event was driven by the paper, and it affected every fabric of American life.

Merv Griffin started as a singer on the radio at age 19. Bandleader Freddy Martin heard him and hired Griffin to be the lead singer with the group for four years. Griffin's biggest hit with the Martin band was "I've Got a Lovely Bunch of Cocoanuts." Griffin continued to sing and then got hired to host TV game shows. From 1958-19062, he hosted "Play Your Hunch" on NBC-TV. In 1965, he began hosting a TV talk show, which ran for 21 years. Griffin created and produced other shows, notably "Jeopardy," "Dance Fever," "Headline Chasers" and "Wheel of Fortune." Griffin sold his TV production company for $250 million, which he later invested in hotels (Beverly Hilton and Resorts Hotel and Casino in Atlantic City, Paradise Island Resort and Casino).

William Randolph Hearst was born into a wealthy California family. He persuaded his father, who had acquired the San Francisco Examiner for a bad debt, to let him take over its operation. Hearst made the paper a success and then bought the New York Morning Journal. He instituted several circulation building features, including color comics, sensational crime reporting and society gossip. Hearst added newspapers, plus the magazines Harper's Bazaar and Cosmopolitan to his publishing empire. He also owned radio stations, movie studios, a castle in Wales and real estate holdings in New York, California and Mexico.

Hugh Hefner studied psychology after a hitch in the Army. He worked as personnel manager, department store advertising copywriter and editor at Esquire Magazine. With $10,000 capital, he founded Playboy Magazine, which debuted in 1953 with Marilyn Monroe on the cover. Features on the good life were complimented by glorious nude photo spreads. In 1965, he purchased the Palmolive Building in Chicago and turned it into Playboy corporate headquarters. He built the Playboy mansion and a chain of nightclubs, all extending the philosophy and lifestyle of the magazine. In 1968, Playboy was the nation's 12th highest circulated magazine.

John D. Hertz began his career as a reporter for a newspaper in Chicago. In 1904, he took a job selling cars, although he could not drive. He saw a solution for the inventory of trade-in cars, as a taxicab company. He founded the Yellow Cab Company in Chicago in 1915, followed by a cab manufacturing company in 1920. He acquired a rental car business in 1924, renaming it the Hertz Drive-

Ur-Self Corporation. In 1933, Hertz bought an interest in the Lehman Brothers investment bank. The Hertz Corporation went public in 1953.

George A. Hormel worked in a Chicago slaughterhouse and as a traveling buyer of wool and hyde materials. He settled in Austin, MN, and opened a meat packing company in 1891. With the introduction of refrigerated cars, Hormel grew the territories for his meat products. The company was incorporated in 1901. Hormel added dry sausages to the product line in 1915, chicken products in 1928, chili in 1936, Spam in 1937, Little Sizzlers sausages in 1961 and Cure 81 hams in 1963.

Howard Hughes was one of the most flamboyant and colorful entrepreneurs the world has ever known. Like his father, he enjoyed tinkering with mechanical things and as a youth built a shortwave radio set and started the Radio Relay League for amateurs. In 1919, Hughes was paralyzed for a short time by an unexplained illness, developing a lifetime phobic regard for his health.

On a visit to Harvard, his father took him on an airplane ride, an experience that stimulated a life-long love of aviation. Howard spent time with his uncle Rupert, a writer for Samuel Goldwyn's movie studios, also sparking a future career interest. Howard was attending classes at Rice Institute when his father died in 1924, the elder Hughes died. At age 18, Howard received access to a large part of the family estate and dropped out of Rice. Through the decision by a Houston judge, who had been a friend of his father's, Howard was granted legal adulthood on Dec. 26, 1924, and took control of the tool company.

After a summer of tinkering with a steam-powered car, Howard and wife Ella headed for Hollywood. Howard sought to make movies. He hired Noah Dietrich to head his movie subsidiary of the Hughes Tool and Lewis Milestone as director. Hughes worked next on his epic movie "Hell's Angels," a story about air warfare in World War I. He wrote the script and directed it himself. He acquired 87 World War I airplanes, hired ace pilots, took flying lessons and obtained a pilot's license. During production, he crashed and injured his face. Since talkies had become popular, Hughes added dialogue scenes to "Hell's Angels" that included actress Jean Harlow. Released in 1930, it was the most expensive movie to that date. It was a box-office smash, making Hughes accepted by the Hollywood establishment. He went on to produce "Scarface" (1932) and "The Outlaw" (1941).

In 1932, Hughes acquired a military plane and formed the Hughes Aircraft Company as a division of Hughes Tool Company. He personally test-flew experimental planes. He set a new land-speed record of 352 miles per hour with his H-1 (the Winged Bullet). He converted a special Lockheed 14 for an around-the-world flight, studying weather patterns. He invested in military aircraft. Hughes Aircraft won a contract to build a flying boat, the "Spruce Goose," which he flew.

In 1948, Howard Hughes purchased the movie studio RKO, and in 1955 he sold it to the General Tire Company for profit. Hughes also invested in Trans World Airlines, and in 1956 pushed the company into the jet age by purchasing 63 jets. In 1953, he founded the Hughes Medical Institute in Delaware, designated as the main recipient of his will.

In 1967, Hughes began buying properties to build a business empire in Nevada. In 1970, he took over Air West. In 1972, he sold Hughes Tool Company stock to the public and renamed his holdings company Summa Corporation. This ended his role as a businessman and entrepreneur. In poor health, he went to Panama, Canada, London and Acapulco. He boarded a plane to check into a Houston hospital on April 5, 1976, but died on the way.

Joseph and William Hunt founded the Hunt Bros. Fruit Packing Company in Sebastopol, CA, in 1888. Focused on canning the products of California's fruit and vegetable industries, they grew to shipping 100,000,000 cans per year in 1941. The company was taken over in 1943, and the focus was on canned tomato products. The Wesson Oil and Snowdrift companies merged with Hunt's in 1968. The next merger was with McCall Corporation and Canada Dry. The conglomerate merged with Beatrice Foods in 1983. Hunt's brands were sold to ConAgra Foods in 1990.

Colis P. Huntington was a peddler and opened a store in New York. In 1849, he moved to California, taking his store to sell to those participating in the Gold Rush. In 1860, he financed the survey for a railroad route across the Sierra Nevada Mountains. His Central Pacific Railroad Line was completed and joined with the Union Pacific in 1869 at Promontory Point, Utah. In 1884, the lines merged with the Southern Pacific. He invested in other railroads and steamship companies.

Lee Iacocca began his career as an engineer at Ford Motor Company in 1946. He served in sales and marketing roles and was brought to the Dearborn headquarters and moved up the ranks. In 1960, he was named vice president and general manager of the Ford Division. He championed design and introduction of the Ford Mustang, Ford Escort and models of Lincoln and Mercury. He left Ford in 1978 and was recruited to Chrysler Corporation. Iacocca went to Congress and negotiated a bailout for Chrysler, working over the next years to turn the company around and repay the loan. New models released included the Dodge Aries and Plymouth Reliant. In 1987, he engineered the acquisition of AMC, including the Jeep lines. He retired as chairman and CEO of Chrysler in 1992.

Steve Jobs was 13 when he called on Bill Hewlett of Hewlett-Packard, asking for parts for an electronics school project. Hewlett gave him a job, working on the assembly line. While at Homestead High School, he met Steve Wozniak, a fellow electronics aficionado. Jobs worked at Atari and began attending meetings of the Homebrew Computer Club with Wozniak in 1975. Wozniak invented the Apple I computer in 1976. Jobs, Wozniak and Ronald Wayne formed Apple Computer Corporation in the garage of Jobs' home in Los Altos, CA. Apple II was introduced in 1977. Jobs became one of the youngest people to reach the Forbes list of America's richest people. The Macintosh was introduced in 1984. Jobs left Apple and founded NeXT Inc. in 1985. Jobs funded a company in 1986 that later became Pixar. In 1997, Apple bought NeXT, and Jobs came back as CEO. He shepherded company innovations, such as iTunes, the iPhone, Mac OS X and the Apple Stores.

Jesse Jones established his own business, the South Texas Lumber Company. He expanded into real estate, commercial buildings and banking. Within a few years, he was the largest developer in the area and responsible for most of Houston's major construction. He owned 100 buildings in Houston and built structures in Fort Worth, Dallas and New York City.

In 1908, he purchased part of the Houston Chronicle. In 1908, he organized and became chairman of the Texas Trust Company and was active in most of the banking and real estate activities of the city. By 1912, he was president of the National Bank of Commerce and was an original stockholder in Humble Oil & Refining Company. As chairman of the Houston harbor board, he raised money for the Houston Ship Channel.

During World War I, President Woodrow Wilson asked Jesse Jones to become the director general of military relief for the American Red Cross. He remained in this position until he returned to Houston in 1919. He became sole owner of the Houston Chronicle in 1926.

President Herbert Hoover appointed Jones to the board of the Reconstruction Finance Corporation, a new government entity established to combat the Great

Depression. President Franklin D. Roosevelt appointed Jones as chairman of the RFC, a position he held from 1933 until 1939. In this capacity, Jones became one of the most powerful men in America. He helped prevent the nationwide failure of farms, banks, railroads, and many other businesses. The RFC became the leading financial institution in America and the primary investor in the economy. The agency also facilitated a broadening of Texas industry from agriculture and oil into steel and chemicals. In 1940, Jones was offered the post of Secretary of Commerce.

Will Keith Kellogg started by selling brooms, then moved to Battle Creek, MI, to help his brother run a sanitarium. As part of the diet for patients, the Kellogg brothers pioneered in making flaked cereal. In 1897, Will and John founded the Sanitas Company, commercially producing whole grain cereals. In 1906, he founded the Battle Creek Toasted Corn Flake Company, later becoming the Kellogg Company. In 1930, he formed the M.K. Kellogg Foundation.

Sebastian S. Kresge was a salesman whose territory included several of the Woolworth stores. He decided to open his own 5-cent and 10-cent store, in 1897 in Memphis, TN, with a second added in Detroit. In 1912, the S.S. Kresge Corporation was chartered, with 85 stores. In 1962, the chain opened the first Kmart store in Garden City, MI, expanded to department store status. In 1977, S.S. Kresge Corporation changed its name to Kmart Corporation.

Jack LaLanne became committed to nutrition, exercise and healthy lifestyle at an early age. In 1936, he opened the first health and fitness club in the U.S., located in Oakland, CA, providing exercise and weight training and giving nutritional advice. He designed the first leg extension machines. His health spa chain expanded to 200+ by the 1980s. He began his TV show in 1953, and it ran for 34 years. In 1959, LaLanne recorded the first fitness record album. He published several books and workout videos. This spawned many aspects of the fitness industry, including the workout programs by Jane Fonda, Richard Simmons and others.

William Hesketh Lever and James Darcy Lever were running a grocery store when they entered the soap industry, founding Lever Brothers in England in 1885. The first product was Sunlight Soap, later joined by Lux, Lifebuoy and Vim. Lever House was built in 1950 in New York City, serving as the American headquarters of the company.

John L. Lewis was born into a mining family in Iowa and, in 1919, became president of the United Mine Workers. In 1935, Lewis and other union leaders organized the Congress of Industrial Organizations (CIO). As a labor organizer over a 50-year period, he was one of the most powerful men in the U.S.

John Edmund Liggett started working in his grandfather's snuff shop in St. Louis, MO, in 1844. The company was J.E. Liggett and Brother in 1858, creating its own blended cigarettes in 1869. In 1873, Liggett partnered with George Smith Myers, incorporating as the Liggett & Myers Tobacco Company. Chewing tobacco was manufactured in 1875 and cigarettes introduced in 1883. Following Liggett's death in 1897, L&M merged into the American Tobacco Company. Chesterfield was introduced in 1912, L&M filters in 1953, Lark in 1963, Eve in 1970.

Henry Luce was a reporter with the Chicago Daily News and the Baltimore News. In 1922, he and partner Britten Hadden formed Time Magazine, reworking articles from newspapers and including commentaries, forming the first news magazine. Luce carried on after Hadden's 1929 death, steering time and adding other magazines to the empire: Fortune in 1930, Life in 1936 and Sports Illustrated in 1954. His wife, Clare Boothe Luce, wrote plays and served in Congress.

Roland Hussey Macy worked on a whaling ship and in 1843 opened the first dry goods store. The first Macy's was established in Haverhill, MA, in 1851 to serve mill industry workers. In 1858, Macy moved the store to New York City, north of where the other dry goods stores were located. The store expanded into neighboring storefronts, offering more departments. After R.H. Macy died in 1877, ownership passed to family and other partners. In 1902, the flagship store moved to the corner of 34th Street and Broadway, a department store expanded to a full block. The building and the Macy character were in the 1947 movie classic "Miracle on 34th Street." In 1978, the building was added to the roster of National Historic Landmarks. In 1983, Macy's expanded beyond the New York area, merging in 1994 with Federated Stores and in 2006 acquiring the May Stores.

Herbert Marcus, his sister Carrie and her husband A.L. Neiman founded a department store with women's clothing in Dallas, TX, Neiman-Marcus, in 1907. The store premiered the first annual fashion show in the U.S. in 1927. Men's clothing was added in 1929. Stanley Marcus joined the store in 1927 and became the CEO in 1950. He was responsible for massive expansion and innovations such as the Distinguished Service in Fashion Award, the first haute couture boutique to introduce weekly fashion shows, the first to host concurrent art exhibitions, the

International Fortnight celebrations, his and hers gifts, holiday catalog and more. Stanley Marcus stood as a beacon for women's fashions globally.

Louis B. Mayer was co-founder and head of production for MGM Studios. He was known as the King of Hollywood, reigning at MGM from 1924-1951. MGM was known for big, prestigious pictures, including "Wizard of Oz," "The Great Ziegfeld," "The Human Comedy," "On the Town," "Meet Me in St. Louis," "Tale of Two Cities," "Ninotchka," "The Philadelphia Story," "National Velvet," "An American in Paris," "Singing in the Rain," "The Women," "Babes in Arms," "Lassie Come Home," "Boys Town," "Captains Courageous," "Dr. Jekyll & Mr. Hide," "Waterloo Bridge" and many more.

Oscar Mayer was a German immigrant who worked at a meat market in Detroit, MI. In 1883, he and his brother leased a market and sold bratwurst and liverwurst. In 1904, the company began branding products for wider distribution. In 1919, the company opened a processing plant in Madison, WI. In 1981, the company was acquired by General Foods and later by Kraft Foods.

William James Mayo and Charles Horace Mayo were physicians in Minnesota. The brothers visited medical centers to keep abreast of medical and surgical techniques. As their proficiency advanced, so did their practice and reputation. A group practice began in 1889 evolved into the Mayo Clinic. In 1915, they established the Mayo Foundation for Medical Education and Research.

Cyrus McCornick invented the mechanical reaper in 1831 and began manufacturing that agricultural equipment in 1844.

John G. McCrory opened his first 5-cent and 10-cent store in Scottdale, PA, in 1882. One of his early investors was Sebastian S. Kresge, whose Kresge chain of stores evolved into Kmart. At its peak, McCrory's operated 1,300 stores under its own name, as well as such names as J.J. Newberry, TG&Y, G.C. Murphy and H.L. Green.

Marshall McLuhan was a philosopher of communications theory. He coined the slogans "the medium is the message" and "the global village." He predicted the worldwide web 30 years before it was invented.

Andrew Mellon operated a lumber company and entered the family banking business. Within 10 years, he ran the financial institution and started backing companies that became industrial giants (Alcoa, Gulf Oil, Union Steel). In 1902, the banking house became Mellon National Bank. In 1921, President Warren

G. Harding appointed Mellon as Secretary of the Treasury. In 1932, President Herbert Hoover named him Ambassador to Great Britain. In 1937, he donated his art collection to the federal government, with funds to establish the National Gallery of Art.

Ward Melville created the Thom McAn brand of shoes, opening the first retail store in New York in 1922. The name was inspired by a Scottish golfer, Thomas McCann. By the late 1960s, Thom McAn was the largest shoe retailer, with 1,400 stores. The chain closed stores and began providing the shoes to other chains, notable K-Mart and Wal-Mart.

Karl Menninger, M.D., founded the Menninger Institute for psychiatric research in Topeka, KS, in 1920. In 1941, he founded the Menninger Foundation to provide clinics for research, professional education and diagnosis and treatment programs on the relation of psychiatry to law, religion, industry and education.

J.P. Morgan was the dean of American financiers. He founded his banking house in 1895, a syndicate to bail out the national treasury during a gold-reserve depletion crisis. Morgan bought out several steel companies and named the roll-up U.S. Steel in 1901. His financial empire also included railroads, International Harvester, General Electric, AT&T, marine companies and many others.

Philip Morris worked in his family's tobacco shop in London, England. By 1854, he began making his own cigarettes. After Philip died in 1873, his brother Leopold Morris carried on the trade. Philip Morris Ltd. Was incorporated ion 1902. PM began advertising Marlboros in 1924. The company made its first cigarettes at a Richmond, VA, factory in 1929. The company made several acquisitions, including Miller Brewing Company, General Foods and Kraft Foods.

Samuel F.B. Morse was an artist and opened a studio in Boston, MA, in 1815. While on a voyage to Europe for art studies in 1832, a conversation on discoveries in electromagnetism inspired in him an invention for the transmission of information. While still onboard the ship, he drafted sketches for a telegraph. By 1838, Morse had a working model for translating letters into dots and dashes. In 1843, Congress appropriated funds to build the first telegraph line. In 1844, Morse tapped the first message, "What hath God wrought."

Rupert Murdoch took charge of his family's newspaper chain in Australia when he was 21. He bought newspapers in New Zealand and Canada, plus an Australian record company. In 1968, he bought the Sun newspaper and later Sky Television in the U.K. Murdock entered the U.S. media market in 1973, purchasing the San Antonio Express-News. He purchased the New York Post in 1976 and became a naturalized U.S. citizen in 1985. Murdoch bought six TV stations owned by Metromedia, becoming the basis of the Fox Network in 1986.

Earl Nightingale started working in the radio industry, which led to his work as a motivational speaker. In 1956, he recorded "The Strangest Secret," a record album, which became the first spoken word LP to go gold. In 1960, he recorded a condensed version of the book "Think and Grow Rich" by Napoleon Hill. He hosted "Our Changing World," a syndicated radio program. He co-founded the Nightingale-Conant Corporation, with Lloyd Conant, to produce motivational records, cassette tapes and CDs. Nightingale is a member of the National Radio Hall of Fame.

Larry Page and Sergey Brin were Ph.D. students and teamed on a research project at Stanford University in 1996. They studied search engines and how they ranked websites. They created Page Rank and incorporated their company Google in 1998. By 2011, the number of visitors to Google surpassed one billion per month.

William S. Paley took a chain of 16 radio stations and grew it into the Columbia Broadcasting System in 1927. Paley grasped the potential of radio, with great programming essential to advertising sales and revenue. He created a major news division that coincided with World War II. CBS was known as the "tiffany network" for its quality in every programming real. CBS excelled in phonograph records with its Columbia label, developing the LP in 1948. CBS expanded into television. In 1976, Paley founded the Museum of Broadcasting.

James Cash Penney began working for the Golden Rule chain of stores in the Midwest in 1898. The owners offered Penny a partnership in a store in Wyoming in 1902. He opened two more stores and bought out the owners in 1907. By 1913, there were 34 stores, he incorporated as J.C. Penny Company and moved the headquarters to Salt Lake City, UT. The number of stores reached 1,400 by 1929. Penney was involved in founding the University of Miami and created the James C. Penney Foundation in 1954.

Henry Ross Perot started worked from 1957-1962 as a salesman for IBM. He founded Electronic Data Systems in Dallas, TX, in 1962. EDS received contracts from corporations and government and went public in 1968, was acquired by

General Motors in 1984. He founded Perot Systems Corporation in Plano, TX, in 1988, later acquired by Dell.

Tom Peters has served as a management consultant, as an Organizational Effectiveness practice leader. In 1982, he published "In Search of Excellence." Other books have included "The Little Big Things," "Thriving on Chaos," "The Pursuit of Wow" and "Reimagine, Business Excellence in a Disruptive Age."

Charles Alfred Pillsbury and his uncle founded the C.A. Pillsbury Company in 1872, processing grain and flour. By 1889, Pillsbury had five mills along the Mississippi River. In 1949, the Pillsbury Bake-Off began. In the 1950s, the company introduced packaged baking dough, with the popular advertising campaign "nothing says loving like something from the oven, and Pillsbury says it best." In the 1960s, Pillsbury began manufacturing artificial sweetener, along with drink products.

Charles William Post worked in the agricultural machinery business, inventing and patenting a plow, harrow and hay stacking machine. In 1895, he founded the Postum Cereal Company. He introduced Grape-Nuts in 1897, corn flakes in 1904 and Post Toasties in 1908. Post also invested heavily in real estate development. Much of his wealth went to Long Island University, which named the C.W. Post Campus in his honor.

Ronald M. Popeil went to work in 1952 at his family's manufacturing company in Chicago. He sold his father's inventions to department stores, including the Chop-O-Matic and Veg-O-Matic. Since he could not carry enough demonstration equipment to all stores, young Ron filmed demonstrations. The next leap was to television, and the infomercial was born. He was known for using the phrases "slice and dice," "set it and forget it"," "slice a tomato so thin it only has one side" and "but wait there's more." In 1964, he formed his own company Ronco, to market his father's products and those of others. Ronco got into the production of record albums, compilations of hits from other labels. In 1993, Ron Popeil was awarded the Nobel Prize in Consumer Engineering for redefining the industrial revolution with his devices.

William Procter (a candle maker) and James Gamble (a soap maker) moved from the U.K. to Cincinnati, OH. Procter & Gamble was founded in 1837. During the Civil War, P&G had contracts to provide candles and soap to the troops. In 1882, the floating soap Ivory was introduced. Other products created were Crisco oil in 1911, Tide detergent in 1946, Prell shampoo in 1947, Crest toothpaste in 1955, Downy fabric softener in 1960, Pampers in 1961 and Olestra in 1996. Through acquisitions, other products added to the P&G line included Charmin, Folgers Coffee, Pepto-Bismol, Old Spice aftershave, Noxzema creams, Max Factor cosmetics and Iams pet foods.

Joseph Pulitzer came to America in 1865, without any money. He went to work for newspapers and in 1880 bought the St. Louis Post Dispatch. His papers covered sensationalism and controversy. He bought the New York World, endowed the Columbia School of Journalism and created the Pulitzer Prize for excellence in drama, music, literature and newspapers.

George Pullman left school to work as a clerk and apprentice to a cabinetmaker. In 1855, he worked on streets and buildings in Chicago, earning money to realize his dream of becoming an inventor and designer. In 1858, he contracted with the Chicago and Alton Railroad to remodel day coaches into sleeping cars. In 1859, he moved to Colorado and operated a store, while developing plans for the Pullman cars. In 1864, he got patents for upper and lower berths and in 1867 became president of the Pullman Palace Car Company. He also owned Eagle Wire Works and was president of the Metropolitan Elevated Railroad in New York.

Walter Reed was a physician in the U.S. Army Medical Corps. He conducted research into fevers and epidemics. The hospital in Washington, D.C., is named in his honor.

Eliphalet Remington forged his first rifle barrel while working as a blacksmith. He founded a factory to make firearms in Ilion, NY, in 1816. The business expanded in 1856 to the manufacture of agricultural equipment. In 1873, Remington started production on the first typewriter and hence remained an industry leader in both firearms and typewriters.

Richard Joshua Reynolds started working on his family's tobacco farm. In 1874, he started his own tobacco business at a railroad hub, Winston-Salem, NC. In 1913, Reynolds introduced the packaged cigarette, Camel. In 1919, nephew Richard Reynolds founded a company to supply tin foil for the packaging of cigarettes. It evolved into the Reynolds Aluminum Company, with Reynolds Wrap introduced in 1947. That company had bought the maker Eskimo Pies (foil wrapped) in 1924.

Anthony Robbins began his career by promoting seminars for Jim Rohn. Robbins launched his own work as a self-help coach and produced his first infomercial "Personal Power" in 1988. He incorporated neuro-linguistic programming, fie walking and board breaking into his motivational talks. He began the Leadership Academy in 1997, with other books including "Unlimited Power," "Awaken the Giant Within" and "Money: Master the Game." Robbins has inspired leadership education and the work of other speakers.

John D. Rockefeller went to work in a mercantile firm in Cleveland, OH, in 1855. In 1859, he founded his first business as a commodity trading operation. In 1863, he and partners organized a company to build an oil refinery. In 1870, through mergers, he formed Standard Oil of Ohio. By 1875, Rockefeller controlled large refineries in New York and Pennsylvania. By 1878, he dominated the entire industry, with the Standard Oil Trust formed in 1882. He established the Rockefeller Institute for Medical Research in 1901, the General Education Board in 1902, the Rockefeller Foundation in 1913 and the Laura Spelman Rockefeller Memorial Foundation in 1918. During the Depression, Rockefeller went out on the streets of New York, handing out dimes to the less fortunate.

George W. Romney grew up on a potato farm in Oakley, ID. He worked in wheat and sugar beet fields at age 11. He worked in construction in Salt Lake City, UT, at age 14, later serving as a Mormon missionary. He worked for a U.S. senator in Washington and operated a dairy bar in nearby Rosslyn, VA. He worked for Alcoa as a lobbyist. In 1937-38, Romney was president of the Washington Trade Association Executives. He moved to Detroit, MI, and managed the Automobile Manufacturers Association. In 1948, he joined Nash-Kelvinator and championed the development of the Rambler. Nash merged with the Hudson Motor Co. and became American Motors Corporation in 1954, with Romney as AMC's first president and chairman. As the Big Three automakers introduced large gas guzzling cars, AMC specialized in smaller economy cars. Romney was dubbed "a folk hero of the American auto industry." He stepped down from AMC to run for Governor of Michigan and was elected. Romney sought the Republican Presidential nomination but was defeated by Richard Nixon. Once Nixon became President of the U.S., he appointed Romney as Secretary of Housing and Urban Development, holding the post until 1973. Romney then became chairman of the National Center for Voluntary Action, 1973-1990.

Harland Sanders began selling fried chicken in 1930 at his roadside restaurant in Corbin, Kentucky, the location being a former Shell filling station. In 1936, he was bestowed the title of Kentucky colonel by Governor Ruby Laffoon. The original recipe was finalized in 1940. Sanders was re-commissioned a colonel in 1950 and began to dress the part.

Sanders opened his first franchise in 1952 in South Salt Lake, Utah. Franchisee Pete Harman commissioned the renaming of the company to Kentucky Fried Chicken and introduced the bucket in 1957. This author met Sanders when he opened his fourth franchise in 1959 in Austin, Texas. The KFC chain grew, challenging the dominance of hamburgers in the fast-food industry. Sanders sold the company in 1964 but remained a spokesperson for the company until his death in 1979. The company changed hands and was acquired in 1988 by PepsiCo, which also operates Pizza Hut and Taco Bell.

David Sarnoff moved from Russia to the U.S. when he was nine. He studied engineering and began work in 1906 on wireless communications services. In 1913, he joined the Marconi Radio Company as chief inspector and rose through the ranks to management. Marconi was merged with Radio Corporation of America in 1919. Sarnoff was elected general manager of RCA in 1921, executive vice president in 1929, president in 1930 and chairman of the board in 1947. RCA was the leading manufacturer of radio sets in the 1920s, and Sarnoff championed the founding of the National Broadcasting Company to provide programming. Then came television, and RCA pioneered in the manufacture of color TV sets.

Brothers Conrad and Marcel Schlumberger founded an oil well services company in France in 1926. The company recorded the first electrical resistivity well log in 1927. Schlumberger supplies the petroleum industry with such services as seismic acquisition and processing, formation evaluation, well testing and directional drilling, well cementing and stimulation, artificial lift, well completions, flow assurance and consulting and information management. The company is involved in the groundwater extraction and carbon capture and storage industries.

Howard Schultz began his career as a salesman for Xerox. In 1979, he became general manager for a coffee maker company. He visited a client of the coffee maker, a shop called Starbuck's. He was impressed with the company's knowledge of coffee and vowed to work further with them. Schultz later joined Starbuck's as director of marketing. On a trip to Italy, he saw coffee shops on every corner, as meeting places of preferred destination. Schultz persuaded the Starbuck's owners to broaden the menu and convert to the café concept. The owners decided to focus on Peet's coffee and tea, selling Starbuck's to Schultz. At one time, Schultz was owner of the Seattle Super Sonics basketball team.

Charles Schwab launched an investment newsletter in 1963. In 1971, his first incorporated to offer traditional brokerage services, as well as publishing the newsletter. Schwab opened his first branch office in 1975 and began offering seminars to clients in 1977. He opened the first 24-hour quotation service in 1980 and joined the New York Stock Exchange in 1981.

Richard W. Sears and Alvah C. Roebuck started in 1888 by reselling watches purchased in quantity. The company was renamed Sears, Roebuck and Company and began diversifying into non-watch lines. By 1894, their mail-order catalog had grown to 322 pages, including sewing machines, bicycles, sporting goods, automobiles and more. By 1895, the company had $800,000 in sales and a 532-page catalog. In 1906, Sears opened its catalog plant and the Sears Merchandise Building Tower in Chicago. In 1933, Sears released the first of its Christmas catalogs. The first retail store opened in 1925, which spawned a national chain. Sears began diversifying, adding Allstate Insurance in 1931 and Homart Development Company in 1959 for the building and leasing of malls. Sears established such major brands as Kenmore, Silvertone, Craftsman, DieHard, Toughskins and Supertone.

Peter Senge holds degrees in Aerospace engineering and social systems modeling. He chairs the Society for Organizational Learning and wrote the book "The Fifth Discipline," championing learning organizations.

Isaac M. Singer ran away from home at age 12 and became a machine shop apprentice. In 1851, he studied a sewing machine and in 11 days built an improved model that enabled uninterrupted sewing and made it possible to stitch anywhere on the material. By 1860, the Singer Sewing Machine Company became the leader in the industry. When Singer died in 1875, the sewing machine helped with domestic chores and built a major clothing industry.

Aaron Spelling was the longest running and most successful producer of TV series. Raised in Dallas, he went to Hollywood to be a scriptwriter. As an actor, he appeared on such shows as "I Love Lucy," "Soldiers of Fortune," "Alfred Hitchcock Presents" and "Gunsmoke." He wrote screenplays for many shows and evolved into a producer. Spelling's first shows were "Zane Gray Theatre," "Johnny Ringo," "The

Dick Powell Show," "Burke's Law" and "Honey West." Then came "The Love Boat," "Mod Squad," "Guns of Will Sonnett," "Charlie's Angels," "Starsky & Hutch," "Fantasy Island," "Dynasty," "Melrose Place," "Beverly Hills 90210," "Charmed" and many made-for-TV movies.

Edward R. Squibb taught anatomy in college and was a surgeon in the U.S. Navy. While at sea, he determined that many of the drugs supplied were of inferior quality. In 1851, he gained permission to establish a laboratory in the Brooklyn Naval hospital to produce chemicals and drugs for the armed forces. In 1859, he built a laboratory to commercialize the drugs. He drafted the model for the first pure food and drug laws in New York. In 1892, his sons entered the business. The company grew into one of the largest pharmaceutical houses.

John Studebaker taught his five sons to make wagons in Ohio. Sons Clement and Henry became blacksmiths in South Bend, IN, in 1852, making metal parts and complete wagons. They built wagons for settlers going westward, the military and fancy carriages. In 1875, brother Jacob started running the carriage factory. Studebaker designed the carriages pulled by the Budweiser Clydesdales in 1900. Next generations of Studebakers joined the company, which began making automobiles in 1902. An assembly line plant was built in Hamilton, Ontario, Canada, in 1941. Studebaker merged with Packard in 1950. In the 1960s, Studebaker diversified by manufacturing appliances, auto parts and missile components.

David Susskind began his career as a press agent for Warner Bros. studio, then as an agent for Music Corporation of America. He then formed Talent Associates, producing plays, movies and television shows. In 1958, he launched "Open End," a talk show on the public TV station in New York. It was retitled "The David Susskind Show" in 1966, syndicated nationally and covered a wide range of topical subjects. Talent Associates produced such TV series as "Mr. Peepers" and "Get Smart," such TV specials as "Death of a Salesman" and "The Glass Menagerie" and such movies as "Loving Couples" and "A Raisin in the Sun."

Peter Thiel founded PayPal, an online funds transfer system, with Max Levchin in 1996. He was the first outside investor in Facebook in 2004. He launched Clarium Capital, a global macro hedge fund, in 2005.

Ted Turner was manager of an advertising agency in Macon, GA. Turner sold several radio stations and in 1967 bought a TV station in Atlanta, WJRJ, Channel 17. He changed the call letters to WTCG ("Watch This Channel Grow"). He ran off-network reruns and Atlanta Braves telecasts. In 1976, he struck a deal to beam his channel on cable systems nationally. Channel 17 became the Super Station and in 1978 changed its call letters to WTBS. In 1976, Turner bought the Atlanta Braves and the Atlanta Hawks. He founded Cable News Network in 1980, Turner Network Television in 1988, the Cartoon Network in 1992 and Turner Classic Movies in 1994. Turner Broadcasting System merged with Time Warner in 1996, that company merged with AOL in 2001.

William Underwood opened a food packing company in 1822. The original products were placed in glass jars, including pickled vegetables and mustards. By 1836, he shifted packing to cans coated with tin. These cans were valuable for settlers moving west and for military troops during the Civil War. Canned products expanded to include seafood, vegetables and meats, the most popular being Underwood Deviled Ham (developed in 1868).

Cornelius Vanderbilt was a pioneer capitalist. In 1810, at age 16, he operated a ferry for passengers and freight in New York. During the war of 1812, he was authorized to transport provisions to regiments around New York. It evolved into a fleet of carriers worldwide, which gave him the nickname Commodore. He then sought mail, freight and passenger service routes. By 1846, he was a millionaire. He invested in railroads, operating cross-country. In 1862, he purchased the New York and Harlem Railroad, using it to initiate streetcar service. By 1874, he controlled the New York Central, with the largest aggregate of miles of track (14,000). By 1877, his wealth was $100 million. His endowment went to Vanderbilt University in Nashville, TN.

Sam Walton became the youngest Eagle Scout in Missouri's history. He worked for J.C. Penny Co. as a management trainee, did military service in World War II and then took over management of a variety store. He established a chain of Ben Franklin stores, having 15 of them by 1962 and the Walton's store in Bentonville, AR. The first Wal-Mart superstore was opened in 1962 in Rogers, AR. When he died in 1992, the chain included 1,960 Wal-Mart and Sam's stores. In 1998, Walton was named by Time Magazine as one of the 100 most influential people of the 20th Century.

John Wanamaker started working as a delivery boy at age 14 and entered the men's clothing business at 18. In 1861, with Nathan Brown, he founded Brown and Wanamaker, which became the leading men's clothier in the U.S. within

10 years. In 1875, he opened a dry goods and clothing business, inviting other merchants to sublet from him. In 1896, he purchased A.T. Stewart in New York and broadened the department store chain. In 1918, Wanamaker's stores piped music to each other, this innovation giving birth to commercial radio.

Montgomery Ward worked for various dry goods stores. While working for a St. Louis wholesale house, he became acquainted with the situations of farmers who found it difficult to find goods at fair prices. He figured a strategy to acquire goods wholesale and offer by mail at small markups, thus eliminating the expense of running a retail operation. In 1872, he opened a mail-order dry goods business in Chicago, the first one-page catalog offering 30 items. The business and the catalog continued to grow. In 1900, the company relocated to the Ward Tower in Chicago. His fortune was distributed to various charities, notably Northwestern University.

Fred Waring led a famous singing group, The Royal Pennsylvanians. His chorale appeared in concert and recorded throughout the 1930s, 1940s and 1950s. Inventor Frederick Jacob Osius had a patent for an electric blender and went to Waring in 1937 for financial backing. Waring put the blender on the market, to great success. The Waring Blender became widely used in hospitals for specific diets of patients and was used by Dr. Jonas Salk in his work in developing the polio vaccine.

Harry, Albert, Sam and Jack Warner founded Warner Bros. Pictures in Hollywood in 1923. Their first films were silent. They introduced sound to the movies with "Don Juan" in 1926 and "The Jazz Singer" in 1927. Memorable Warner Bros. films included "Casablanca," "Mildred Pierce," "Jezebel," "The Maltese Falcon," "The Wild Bunch," "A Star is Born," "Now Voyager," "Hondo," "Little Caesar," "The Public Enemy," "Key Largo," "Captain Blood," "Dirty Harry," "The Big Sleep," "The Treasure of Sierra Madre" and "Gold Diggers of 1933."

Booker T. Washington was born on a plantation and, at age 16, walked 500 miles to enroll in the Hampton Normal and Agricultural Institute. In 1881, he was asked to head the Tuskegee Institute, inspiring many blacks the virtues of hard work, perseverance, honesty and thrift. He counseled compliant productivity and championed many causes for human rights, education and work opportunities.

Lew Wasserman began working as an usher at a theatre in Cleveland, OH, then became a booking agent and serving six decades as an influential talent agent. He headed Music Corporation of America, representing actors, musicians and instituting the system of stars getting pieces of film profits. In 1962, he purchased Universal Pictures and Decca Records, running the combined company as MCA until 1990.

Thomas John Watson went to work at the National; Cash Register Company in 1899, serving as business manager and sales manager. In 1914, he formed Computer Tabulating Recording Company, which in 1924 became International Business Machines. He inspired constant reminder of duty to his employees, thus the IBM slogans "serve and sell," "make things happen," "be better than average" and "think." His company inspired the Second Industrial Revolution, where computers and other cybernetic devices performed business tasks.

Noah Webster was teaching and grew dissatisfied with textbooks available to children. This led him to write "The American Spelling Book" in 1783, followed by a grammar book in 1784 and a reader in 1785. He lobbied for national copyright laws. In 1793, he founded a newspaper. After 20 years of work, his "American Dictionary of the English Language" was published in 1828. Five years later, he published an authorized English language version of the Bible. For generations, his speller was used to teach children to read.

Jack Welch earned degrees in chemical engineering and joined General Electric in 1960. He moved up the ladder and in 1981 became the company's youngest chairman and CEO. He sought to streamline GE, fostering a small company environment in a large corporation. He championed quality programs, informality at work and accountability management. He has continued teaching and inspiring other leaders through programs, books and speeches. He instilled an organizational behavior called "boundarylessness," which removes barrier between traditional functions and inspires good ideas from wherever they emanate.

George Westinghouse was granted the first patent at age 19, and there were 400 others. His early inventions were designed for usage on railroads, with the major development being the air brake in 1869. He founded the Westinghouse Air Brake Company in 1872. The Westinghouse Electric Company was founded in 1886 to produce dynamos, transformers and motors for power systems. In 1893, Westinghouse supplied lighting for the World's Columbian Exposition in Chicago. Westinghouse products covered the consumer landscape in the 20th Century.

Eli Whitney went to work in his father's shop, repairing violins and manufacturing nails and hatpins. He met a woman and her plantation manager, learning from them to need in the South for a device to separate short staple upland cotton from its seeds. In 1793, he then built a hand-operated cotton gin, perfecting it to clean 50 pounds of cotton per day. His factory built the first milling machine. By 1795, U.S. exports of cotton were 40 times greater than what they had been before invention of the cotton gin.

Frank W. Woolworth went to work as a store clerk. In 1873, he convinced his boss that a bargain counter he had seen in another store would work well in theirs. Overstocked and damaged goods were priced five cents. In 1879, Woolworth began a store of his own in Utica, NY, with a variety of goods priced at a nickel. He opened another in Lancaster, PA, offering goods up to 10 cents. Other stores were opened in Buffalo, Erie and Scranton. He rolled those and other acquisitions into the F.W. Woolworth Company in 1912. The Woolworth Building was opened in New York in 1913, then the city's tallest structure. By 1919, Woolworth had more than 1,000 stores. In the 1960s, the chain broadened into department stores, renamed Woolco.

Frank Lloyd Wright was an architect who designed more than 1,000 buildings in a career spanning 1888-1959. He advocated buildings designed around human lifestyles, using the terms "organic architecture" and "the architecture of democracy." His commissions were worldwide, changing notions of spaces in which people live and work.

Darryl F. Zanuck co-founded 20th Century-Fox Pictures in Hollywood in 1933. He remained as head of production for the studio until 1956, returning again in 1962. His legacy of great films included "The Grapes of Wrath," "Gentleman's Agreement," "All About Eve," "Miracle on 34th Street," "The Snake Pit," "Tobacco Road," "Laura," "Twelve O'Clock High," "The Ox-Bow Incident" and many more.

Florenz Ziegfeld was a showman who began his Ziegfeld Follies in New York in 1907 and produced annually for 24 years. The extravaganzas featured songs, sketches, dancing numbers and total showmanship. His stars included Fanny Brice, Will Rogers, Eddie Cantor, Nora Bayes, W.C. Fields, Ruth Etting and many more. Ziegfeld built his own theatre in 1927 and staged such Broadway musicals as "Rio Rita" and "Show Boat."

Zig Ziglar worked as a salesman for several companies, moving to Dallas, TX, in 1968 to be training director for the Automotive Performance company. For the next 20 years, he presented motivational seminars worldwide. He was a prominent sales trainer and author, spawning an industry in motivational programs. His son Tom has continued the Ziglar legacy with motivational programs in all business settings.

Mark Zuckerberg wrote a program called Facemash, while a student at Harvard University in 2003. Facemash attracted 450 viewers during its first hours online, as a website for students to communicate with each other. It evolved into Facebook, opened to public access in 2006. By 2010, it had 500 million users, making it the largest social network site.

Business Narrative by the Author

From history, I've learned that there's nothing more permanent than change. For everything that changes, many things remain the same. The art of living well is to meld the changeable dynamics with the constants and the traditions. The periodic reshuffling of priorities, opportunities and potential outcomes represents business planning at its best.

One learns three times more from failure than from success. By studying and reflecting upon the events of the past and the shortcomings of others, then we create strategies for meeting the challenges of the future.

In business, we must learn lessons from the corporate crises, the also-rans and the conditions which controlled the history. Some of those lessons that we could well learn came from these watershed events:

- The Civil War. This is a classic and tragic case of two sides fighting for causes and not fully understanding the other side's motivations. The South saw slavery as an economic factor and the only system of labor management they had ever known. The North saw opportunities to champion humanity issues, underlying the threat of insurgence within our own nation. Neither side fully articulated its issues, nor sought to negotiate before hostilities broke out. This war caused severe rifts in U.S. society for another 100 years.
- America's shift from an agricultural to an industrial economy.
- Prohibition. Take something away from consumers, and say that the action is in their best interest. They'll want the commodity even more. The great lengths that people went to getting their liquor fixes enabled organized

crime to gain major footholds in America. The legislation that created Prohibition was wrong, and that action by a few spawned the gangster era, which became big business in America. Congress finally recounted after untellable damage was done.

- The Great Depression. Economics are a series of ebbs and flows. Failure to anticipate and to prepare for the next drop and to expect that the good times will never cease is foolhardy. Failure to exercise crisis management after the crash and to restore stability in judicious ways caused the Depression to drag on. It was a World War that finally pulled America out of its greatest economic slump. Lessons from the Great Depression should have been applied during the high-riding days of technology stocks and a stock market that over-hyped so much. The dot.com bust and corporate debacles could have been avoided if lessons from the Great Depression had been learned, updated and utilized.
- Diversity in the workplace.
- Shift from an industrial to an information economy.
- Watergate, bringing about more accountability by the public sector.
- The Dot.Com Bust. Analogies from the Great Depression to the dot.com crash were many. Too many tech companies did not feel as though corporate protocols of the older companies applied to them. Shortcuts were taken. The media unfairly crowned superficial darlings, such as Enron. Regulators had relaxed standards. Common practice in investment communities was to over-hype stock potential, without seeing who was truly at the switches of these companies. Had the scandals not triggered public outcry when they did, this chain of events could have led to another Great Depression.
- Corporate scandals, bringing about reforms, ethics and higher corporate accountability.

Two early titans of American business,
Cornelius Vanderbilt (left) and John D. Rockefeller (right).

Pictured is Alexander Graham Bell (left), working with
Thomas Watson in 1887 on telephone inventions.

Pictured is David Sarnoff in 1912, working as a telegraph operator in Massachusetts. He went on to run the NBC radio and TV network for many years.

Howard Hughes was an industrialist, aviator and movie studio owner.

*Pictured are two giants in the restaurant chain industry.
At left is Ray Kroc of McDonald's. At right is Colonel
Harland Sanders, founder of Kentucky Fried Chicken.*

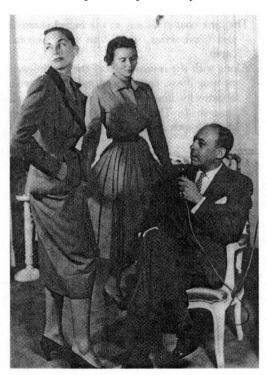

Stanley Marcus is pictured with models in a high-fashion show.

When he was an executive with Ford, Lee Iacocca championed the design and production of the Mustang.

Chapter 8

STORIES AND STRATEGIES
OF THE BUSINESS LEGENDS

How Companies Got Their Names

Companies are named for the simplest of purposes, often for ease and recognition factor. Companies should create monikers that let customers clearly know what they do, or at least make the public curious to learn more.

Good company names ring true to company values, offer something for the marketplace to aspire and differentiate each company from the others. The best company names are clear and direct, without trite jargon. Business is a mirror of life and offers opportunities to free enterprise. Many of the most respected corporate names have clarity and long shelf lives. Often, the great names ring new meanings into old words, phrases and ideas.

Here are examples of how memorable company names (and strategies) evolved:

3M stems from the company's original name, Minnesota Mining and Manufacturing Company.

7-Eleven. Convenience stores, originally called U-Totem, renamed in 1946 to reflect their newly extended hours, 7:00 a.m.-11:00 p.m.

Adobe was named after the Creek that ran behind co-founder John Warnock's house.

Amazon symbolizes a larger volume of potential sales than with a single bookstore.

Arby's stands for the initials of its founders, the Raffel brothers.

Arm and Hammer represents the strength of the Vulcan, the Roman god of fire and metal working, adopted from the Vulcan Spice Mills.

Atari was adapted from a Japanese word when the player's pieces are in danger of being captured in the game Go.

Audi was adapted from the Latin for the last name of its founder, August Horch.

Bridgestone was named after founder Sojiro Ishibashi. His last names translates to "bridge of stone."

Canon was named after Kwanon, the first camera produced by Precision Optimal Instruments Laboratories.

Coca-Cola was named for the cola leaves and kola nuts, which were originally used in the flavoring of the soft drink.

Comcast comes from the words "commercial" and "broadcast."

ConocoPhillips is shortened from the merger of the Continental Oil Company and Phillips Petroleum Company.

CVS originally stood for Customer Value Stores.

Ebay was originally part of the Echo Bay Technology Group. EchoBay.com was taken by a mining company. Thus, the shortened designation to Ebay.

Hasbro is short for the name of its founders, brothers Henry and Halel Hassenfeld.

H&R Block was founded by Henry W. Bloch and Richard Bloch, who changed the spelling in order to avoid mispronunciation.

IBM stems from the company's original name, International Business Machines.

Ikea a composite of the first letters in the Swedish founder's name plus the first letters of names of the property and village in which he grew up: Ingvar Kamprad Elmtaryd Agunnaryd.

Intel. Robert Noyce and Gordon Moore initially incorporated their company as NM Electronics. Intel came by using the initial syllables from INTegrated Electronics.

JVC stands for the Japan Victor Corporation.

Kia translates as "rising from Asia" in Hanji.

Lego comes from the Danish "leg godt," which means "play well."

Mattel comes from the names of its founders, Harold Matson and Elliot Handler. Mattel's Barbie Doll was named after Handler's daughter.

Nabisco is shortened from the original name, National Biscuit Company.

Nikon was shortened from the original Japanese name Nippon Kogaku, which means Japanese Optical.

Nintendo comes from the Japanese name Nintendou, which means "entrusted heavens."

Nissan was abbreviated from the original name Nippon Sangyo, which means "Japan Industries."

Nokia was founded as a wood pulp mill that later produced rubber products in the city of Nokia, Finland.

QVC stands for quality, value and convenience.

Pepsi Cola was named from the digestive enzyme pepsin.

Reebock is named after an African antelope, the rhebock.

SEGA started as Service Games of Japan, which began by importing pinball machines to American military bases in Japan.

Sharp was named for the company's first product, the ever-sharp pencil.

Skype was originally Sky-Peer-to-Peer, shortened to Skyper, then to Skype.

Sony came from the Latin word "sonus," meaning sound. It was chosen in order to be easily pronounced in multiple languages.

Sprint was an acronym for the Southern Pacific Railroad Internal Communications.

Starbuck's was inspired by a character in "Moby Dick," the book written by Herman Melville.

Taco Bell was named in honor of founder Glen Bell.

Verizon is a combination of the Latin word veritas (truth) and horizon.

Virgin Records was the name suggested to founder Richard Branson because they were new at the record business.

Volkswagen. Ferdinand Porsche wanted to produce a car that was affordable, the Kraft-Durch-Freude-Wagen (German phrase for people's car).

Walmart was a modification of the name for Sam Walton's Five and Dime stores, expanded into supercenters.

Wendy's was named Dave Thomas after his daughter Melinda, who used Wendy as a nickname.

Here are the characteristics of good company names and, thus, company philosophy:

- Focus upon the customer.
- Honor the employees.
- Show business as a process, not a quick fix.
- Portray their company as a contributor, not a savior.
- Clearly defines their niche.
- Say things that inspire you to think.
- Compatible with other communications.
- Remain consistent with their products, services and track record.

The Colonel and Me. The Value of Life-Long Mentoring.

The year was 1959. I was a young disc jockey at a radio station in Austin, TX.

Colonel Harland Sanders entered my life. I was 11. He was 65. I only met him once. Yet, he influenced my life. I later reorganized his company. The Colonel had just founded a fast food empire called Kentucky Fried Chicken. He was heralded as an entrepreneur who was also a senior citizen.

My entertainment mentors were Cactus Pryor and Bob Gooding. The 24-year-old newscaster at the radio station was Bill Moyers, who told me that I must think like a world-class visionary, grow into the role and not just remain a radio DJ.

In 1959, radio stations used to do live remotes from advertisers' locations. The first which I attended was at the Armstrong-Johnson Ford dealership. The second was at what was the fourth KFC franchise to open in the United States. It occupied one counter at 2-J's Hamburgers, an established Austin restaurant, owned and operated by Ralph Moreland.

There I was on live radio, interviewing Colonel Sanders about his new business enterprise. Rather than discussing the taste of the food, I asked about his desired legacy and the Big Picture goals of the organization. Already thinking like a visionary then, I asked the bigger questions.

The KFC empire grew, and a burgeoning fast food industry engulfed it. There became too many competitors, too much franchising, too much hype and just as many who exited the industry as quickly as they entered it.

Fast forward 20 years to 1979. I was retained to come in and analyze the strategy and structure of the KFC Corporation. That's what I do for businesses of all sizes. I come in after the wrong consultants have given bad advice, after knee-jerk reactions to changing business climates had taken tolls on existing market players.

By 1979, there were other players dominating the fried chicken niche. Nationally, there were Popeye's and Church's. Locally, we had Frenchy's and Hartz. And then there were the players in the burger wars, who were adding chicken items to their menus.

Over at KFC, the Colonel had sold his interest to a corporation and remained on the payroll as a commercial spokesman. Colonel Sanders died in 1979. Meetings commenced at headquarters about the future direction of the company and the product. The corporate owner was a liquor company. Its CEO (John Y. Brown, later to become Governor of Kentucky) asked me to envision the overall future of the fried chicken industry, not just the KFC "brand."

I commissioned focus groups. I opined that we needed to go after minority consumers and aggressively build stores in inner-city neighborhoods. To test the premise, I staged a focus group dinner meeting at a prominent inner-city church, eliciting ideas and insights. One resulting project was "KFC Kalendar," an advertising campaign that showcased community events and public service announcements to diverse communities. I wrote editions of the Kalendar for radio and newspapers. Its recognition and success evolved into the national ad campaign: "We Do Chicken Right."

KFC was a watershed in my career (at that point 21 years long). It influenced what I've preached for the last 30+ years: determine who your stakeholders are.

Learn all that you can about your customers, their customers and those affected by them. Extend your business model beyond what it once was and into new sectors. The branding does not drive the strategy but instead is a sub-sub-sub set of Big Picture strategy, which must drive all business disciplines.

Here is some closing wisdom, connecting back to 1959. I juxtapose my advice to some of the records that we were playing on the radio when doing that live remote from the grand opening of that early KFC franchise. These insights still hold impact on the business culture of today. These come from the Golden Oldies music of that era:

- "Did he ever return? No, he never returned. Yet his fate is still unlearned. He may ride forever through the streets of Boston. He's the man who never returned." Song by the Kingston Trio. (Pursuing the same strategies, year after year, yields you the same predictable outcomes and shortcomings.)

- "And they call it puppy love." Song by Paul Anka. (Living in a fantasy without viewing the realities of the marketplace sets companies up for failure.)

- "Higher than the highest mountain, and deeper than the deepest sea. Softer than the gentle breezes, and strongest than the wide oak tree. Faithful as a morning sunrise, and sacred as a love can be. That's how I will love you. Oh darling, endlessly." Song by Brook Benton. (An empowered workforce must support the corporate objective, and the art with which it does spells success.)

- "I told her that I was a flop with chicks. I'd been that way since 1956. She looked at my palm and she made a magic sign. She said what you need is Love Potion Number Nine." Song by The Clovers. (Research tells us that only 2% of all consultants are real advisers. Most are vendors who prescribe what kool-aid that they're selling. Business coaches and their ilk are to be avoided.)

- "Who walked in with Mary Jane, lipstick all a mess. Were you smooching my best friend, if the answer's yes. Bet your bottom dollar, you and I are through. Cause lipstick on your collar told a tale on you." Song by Connie Francis. (Ethics cannot be edicted from afar. The ethical conduct of business has a direct relationship on the ability to grow and prosper.)

- "Hold me tight and don't let go. Thunder, lightning, wind and rain. This feeling's killing me. I won't stop for a million bucks. If it wasn't for having you, I'd be barking in Harlem too. Don't let go." Song by Roy Hamilton. (Sustainability of a growth strategy breeds steady, measured success.)
- "When you're near me, my head go goes all around. My love comes tumbling down. You've got what it takes to set my soul on fire. You've got what it takes for me. Song by Marv Johnson. (66.7% of all businesses cannot grow any further. Learn when enough growth is enough.)
- "Venus, goddess of love that you are. Surely, the things I ask cannot be too great a great task." Song by Frankie Avalon. (Building corporate cultures and successful businesses means making and sticking to commitments.)
- "Here I stand in my world of dreams. You don't know how much I care. You don't know the torch I bear. You don't know how much I care. Yes and here I stand." Song by Wade Flemons. (Corporate cultures depend upon real-time conditions, projected outcomes and policies that promote steady growth.)

Flip Sides, Second Acts and Successful Careers

It used to be said that people have three careers in them. Those who are particularly successful have many more. It's all about evolving. What we start out as is different from what we progress into, both for companies and individuals.

Have you ever had reunion business relationships? It's amazing how the circumstances change things the next time around. The people who denied your friend requests on Linkedin are now pursuing you as a celebrity on Facebook. As they know and trust you, they want to associate with you. It's all perspective and the building of a multi-tiered Body of Work, stellar reputation and track record.

One of the great music figures was Burt Bacharach. His role model was George Gershwin. Bacharach started his music writing career by taking "work for hire," tailoring songs to particular performers. He wrote a lot of flip sides to hit records and was recognized as a consistent hit maker. The Bacharach repertoire expanded, and he developed his signature musical style, along with lyricists such as Hal David.

That is the way that I am with business wisdom. I continually dust off old chestnuts and reapply them for clients, in my books, through my speeches and in sharing with mentees. The case studies become the substance of what we provide future clients. We benefit from going back and learning from our own early Body of Work, assuming that we strategized our career to be a long-term thing, as Burt Bacharach did.

Some of the most creative professionals work behind the scenes and then later get accorded star status. Many character actors who subsequently became stars included Humphrey Bogart, Edmond O'Brien, Anne Bancroft, Anthony Hopkins, Angela Lansbury, Jack Elam, Ruth Gordon, Wallace Beery, Christopher Walken, Cloris Leachman, Karl Malden, William Conrad, Madeline Kahn, Jack Klugman, Ward Bond, William Frawley, Shelley Duvall, Edward Everett Horton, Thelma Ritter, Tilda Swinton, Thomas Mitchell, Eddie Albert and James Woods. They worked continuously and played every kind of role. Well-trained and experienced actors carried plays and films.

In the music world, singers front the bands. Talented people write the songs, design the arrangements and conduct the bands. One of the great men of music was Nelson Riddle. His expertise became the signature recording styles of Nat King Cole, Frank Sinatra and others. Sometimes, Riddle had hit records with his own band, including 1956's "Lisbon Antigua" (#1 on the charts) and the theme songs to TV's "Route 66" and "The Untouchables." In 1979, I emceed a music symposium with Riddle as the guest. I produced a documentary of his music. While it was playing for the audience, I noticed Riddle's hand behind the skirted table, conducting my documentary in time to the music.

Another favorite of mine is Perry Botkin Jr. The public does not recognize his name, but you liked his recordings over the years. His father (Perry Botkin Sr.) was a guitar player and bandleader who worked with Bing Crosby and other greats of the 1930s, 40s and 50s. Botkin Sr. played the guitar cues for the "Beverly Hillbillies" TV show in the 1960's. Enter Perry Jr. into music. He was a masterful arranger and orchestral conductor. He was to 1960s and 70s music what Nelson Riddle was in the 1940s and 50s. Botkin Jr. provided lush arrangements for easy listening singers such as Ed Ames, Carly Simon, Sammy Davis Jr., Vikki Carr and The Lettermen. He conducted the Capitol house orchestra, the Hollyridge Strings. One of the most popular Christmas records is "Feliz Navidad" by Jose Feliciano, and that's Botkin's arrangement.

Then, there are the second bananas. The greatest art in building successful companies is to select, nurture and support good #2 people and beyond. I call that strategy "the Ed McMahon syndrome."

Everything we are in business stems from what we've been taught or not taught to date. A career is all about devoting resources to amplifying talents and abilities, with relevancy toward a viable end result. Failure to prepare for the future spells certain death for businesses and industries in which they function.

These are the marks of building upon early business activity and moving forward to the next plateaus:

- Personal abilities, talents and working style.
- Resources being developed.
- Relationships and interaction with other people
- Ability to rise above circumstances beyond your control.
- Timing. Things that were not achievable in early careers are now yours to master.

A rich and sustaining Body of Work results from a greater business commitment and heightened self-awareness. None of us can escape those pervasive influences that have affected our lives, including music and the messages contained in songs. Like sponges, we absorbed the information, giving us views of life that have helped mold our business and personal relationships.

Take-Away Business Narratives by the Author

Given the history and heritage of business, I offer the following take-away ideas to put business into perspective.

The biggest problem with business, in a one-sentence capsule, is: People exhibit misplaced priorities and impatience, seeking profit and power, possessing unrealistic views of purpose, and not fully willing to do the things necessary to sustain orderly growth and long-term success.

What organizations and individuals started out to become and what we've evolved into being are decidedly different things. The path toward progress takes many turns, expected and unexpected. How we evolve reflects the teachings, experiences and instincts that are not part of formal education.

Take ownership of planning programs, rather than abdicate them to human resources or accounting people. Predict the biggest crises that can beset your company. 85% of the time, you'll prevent them from occurring. Challenge yourself to succeed by taking a Big Picture look, while others are still thinking and acting small-time. Your biggest resource is a wide scope and the daring to visualize success and then all of its components.

An Institutional Review is a look at activities that contribute to an organization's success and well-being. This transcends a traditional audit and identifies factors that already contribute well to the organization, rather than simply looking for ways to cut, curtail or penalize. It is more than just trimming the fat and criticizing incorrect activities in the organizational structure. This review is the basis for most elements that will appear in a strategic plan, including the organization's strengths, weaknesses, opportunities, threats, actions, challenges, teamwork, change management, commitment, future trends and external forces.

Finely develop skills in every aspect of the organization, beyond the scope of professional training. Amplify upon philosophies of others. Mentoring, creating and leading have become the primary emphasis for your career. Never stop paying dues, learning and growing professionally. Develop and share own philosophies. Long-term track record, unlike anything accomplished by any other individual, contributing toward organizational philosophy, purpose, vision, quality of life, ethics, long-term growth.

Niche consultants place emphasis in the areas where they have training, expertise and staff support for implementation...and will market their services accordingly. An accounting firm may suggest that an economic forecast is a full-scope business plan (which it is not). A trainer may recommend courses for human behavior, believing that these constitute a Visioning process (of which they are a small part). Marketers might contend that the latest advertising campaign is equivalent to re-engineering the client company (though the two concepts are light years apart). Niche consultants believe these things to be true, within their frames of reference. They sell what they need to sell, rather than what the client really needs. Let the buyer beware.

No entity can operate without affecting or being affected by its communities. Business must behave like a guest in its communities, never failing to give potlache or return courtesies. Community acceptance for one project does not mean than the job of community relations has been completed. It is not "insurance" that can be bought overnight. It is tied to the bottom line and must be treated accordingly, with the resources and expertise to do it effectively. It is a bond of trust that, if violated, will haunt the business. If steadily built, the trust can be exponentially parlayed into successful long-term business relationships.

The hot new idea is to focus on depth-and-substance…not on flash-and-sizzle. Those who proclaim that hot ideas make good coaches, then they are vendors selling flavors of the month…not seasoned business advisors. If coaching is based only on hot ideas, it is nothing more than hucksterism. Coaching must be a thorough process of guiding the client through the levels of accomplishment.

Customer Focused Management is a concept that goes far beyond just smiling, answering queries and communicating with buyers. It transcends customer service training. In today's highly competitive business environment, every dynamic of a successful organization must be toward ultimate customers. Companies must change their focus from products and processes toward the values they share with customers. Customer Focused Management goes beyond just the dynamics of service and quality.

One learns three times more from failure than success. One learns three times more clearly when witnessing and analyzing the failures of others they know or have followed. History teaches us about cycles, trends, misapplications of resources, wrong approaches and vacuums of thought. People must apply history to their own lives-situations. If we document our own successes, then these case studies will make us more successful in the future.

There comes a point when the pieces fit. One becomes fully actualized and is able to approach their life's Body of Work. That moment comes after years of trial and error, experiences, insights, successes and failures. As one matures, survives, life becomes a giant reflection. We appreciate the journey because we understand it much better. We know where we've gone because we know the twists and turns in the road there. Nobody, including ourselves, could have predicted every curve along the way.

Success and failure: it's a matter of perspectives. Out of every 10 transactions in our lives, five will be unqualified successes. One will be a failure. Two will depend upon the circumstances. If approached responsibly, they will become successful. If approached irresponsibly, they will turn into failures. Two will either be successful or will fail, based strictly upon the person's attitude. A 90% success rate for a person with a good attitude and responsible behavior is unbeatable. There is no such thing as perfection. Continuous quality improvement means we benchmark accomplishments and set the next reach a little further.

Professionals who succeed the most are the products of mentoring. The mentor is a resource for business trends, societal issues and opportunities. The mentor becomes a role model, offering insights about their own life-career. This reflection shows the mentee levels of thinking and perception that were not previously available. The mentor is an advocate for progress and change. Such work empowers the mentee to hear, accept, believe and get results. The sharing of trust and ideas leads to developing business philosophies.

Visioning is the process where good ideas become something more. It is a catalyst toward long-term evaluation, planning and implementation. It is a vantage point by which forward-thinking organizations ask: What will we look like in the future? What do we want to become? How will we evolve? Vision is a realistic picture of what is possible.

Lessons Learned, Quotes from Business Legends

"An organization's ability to learn, and translate that learning into action rapidly, is the ultimate competitive advantage." Jack Welch

"Being the richest man in the cemetery doesn't matter to me. Going to bed at night saying we've done something wonderful, that's what matters to me. It's not the customers' job to know what they want." Steve Jobs

"If you can dream it, then you can achieve it. You will get all you want in life if you help enough other people get what they want." If you learn from defeat, you haven't really lost. Life has many different chapters; One bad chapter doesn't mean it's the end of the book." Zig Ziglar

"It is not the strongest of the species that survives, nor the most intelligent, but the one most responsive to change." Charles Darwin

"Many of life's failures are people who did not realize how close they were to success when they gave up." Thomas Edison

"We are all faced with a series of great opportunities brilliantly disguised as impossible situations." Charles R. Swindoll

"The best way to predict the future is to invent it." Alan Kay

"A leader is a person you will follow to a place you wouldn't go by yourself. Speed is useful only if you are running in the right direction." Joel Barker

"The minute you're satisfied with where you are, you aren't there anymore." Tony Gwynn

"Individuals and organizations that are good react quickly to change. Individuals and organizations that are great create change." Robert Kriegel

"The customer rarely buys what the business thinks it sells him." Peter Drucker

Chapter 9
NON-PROFIT LEGENDS

S ociety has cared for and protected citizens. Non-profit organizations and non-governmental agencies have legacies of service to causes.

Categories of non-profit organizations that have served our communities include associations, advocacy groups, schools, colleges, universities, churches, arts groups, community coalitions, healthcare providers, foundations, drug abuse agencies, literacy agencies, school support entities, community umbrella organizations, fund raising entities, leadership organizations, youth organizations and many more.

These are some of those who have brought meaningful differences in peoples' lives.

The American Association of Retired Persons (AARP) was founded by Dr. Ethel Percy Andrus in Ojai, California, in 1958. Its programs include advocacy, lobbying and services to persons over the age of 50. Its motto is "to serve, not to be served."

The American Foundation for the Blind was organized in Vinton, Iowa, in 1921. It has advocated legislation and access to help persons with vision loss. It is the largest producer of braille writers and talking books. Helen Keller dedicated her life to working with AFB. The Foundation works with technology companies, making products more accessible by those with vision limitations.

The American Red Cross began during the Civil War, when Clara Barton took care of wounded soldiers. She recognized the need for medical nursing, supplies at the battlefronts and the need for morale boosts. The international Red Cross organization started in 1863 and encouraged Ms. Barton to create the American chapter. In 1881, she obtained formal recognition and served as its president until 1904. The organization's activities extended to floods, famines, fires and other disasters.

The Anti-Defamation League was founded by the Independent Order of B'Nai B'rith in 1913. Its goals and programs strive to fight anti-semitism, bigotry, terrorism, persecution and discrimination. It defends civil rights and democratic ideals.

The Better Business Bureau was founded in 1912. Its goals are to advance marketplace trust, expose frauds, promote business efficiencies, encourage ethical conduct of business and celebrate excellent customer service. It has educational programs, rating system, dispute resolution, professional development and awards recognition through its chapters.

Big Brothers and Big Sisters started in 1902 when Ernest Coulter, a clerk in New York Children's Court, befriended kids in need of positive influences. It was chartered in 1904, with each of 39 volunteers agreeing to befriend one child each. In 1934, President and Mrs. Franklin D. Roosevelt became patrons of the Big Brothers and Big Sisters Foundation. In 1958, the Big Brothers Association was charted by Congress. In 1970, Big Sisters International was incorporated. In 1977, both organizations merged.

Blood banks take donations from individuals, storing the blood for future transfusions, in order to save lives. John Braxton Hicks first experimented with chemical methods of preventing coagulation of blood in the 1890s. The first transfusion was performed by Dr. Albert Hustin and Dr. Luis Agote in 1914. The British Red Cross established the first blood donor service in 1921. One of the first blood banks was founded in Barcelona, Spain, in 1936. Dr. Bernard Fanfus began the first hospital blood bank in Chicago, IL, in 1937. The Blood for Britain campaign in 1940 took collections in the U.S. and provided them to the U.K. The plastic bag for blood collection was introduced in 1950. Collection and distribution programs now exist in every community around the world.

Boy Scouts was founded in 1907 in England by Robert Baden Powell. The American scouting program was founded in 1910. Its purpose was to "teach patriotism, courage, self-reliance and kindred values." Learning for Life is a school and work-site subsidiary program of BSA.

Boys' Club was founded in 1860 in Hartford, Connecticut. In 1906, dozens of independent organizations joined as Federated Boys' Clubs. In 1990, they became Boys and Girls Clubs of America, providing after-school programs via 4,000 member clubs. This is the official charity of Major League Baseball. A former club member, actor Denzel Washington, has been the organization's spokesperson since 1993.

Camp Fire Girls was formed in 1912, as girls in Thetford, Vermont, watched males participate in outdoor activities through the Boy Scouts. The organization tried to merge with the Girl Scouts but continued as an independent entity. During World War I, Camp Fire Girls sold Liberty Bonds. They planted millions of trees and supported orphans. The name was changed to Camp Fire Boys and Girls in 1975, then in 2012 to Camp Fire.

CARE was founded 1945 as the Cooperative for Assistance and Relief Everywhere. It is a non-partisan non-government agency. It began by sending CARE packages to countries in Europe who were torn by war. CARE expanded the globe, assisting areas in need with food, supplies and diplomatic service. CARE has helped construct schools and provided philanthropic services across the globe.

The Children's Defense Fund is a child advocacy and research group, founded in 1973 by Marian Wright Edelman. It provides a voice for children who cannot vote, lobby or speak for themselves, fostering youth leadership programs.

Children's Miracle Network Hospitals was founded by Marie Osmond and her family, John Schneider, Joe Lake and Mick Shannon in Salt Lake City, Utah, in 1983. It raises funds for 170 children's hospitals in the U.S. and Canada, plus medical research and public education on children's health issues.

The Corporation for Public Broadcasting was created by act of Congress in 1967. It funds and advances the work of the Public Broadcasting Service (PBS) and National Public Radio (NPR).

Cystic Fibrosis Foundation was organized in Philadelphia, Pennsylvania, in 1955. It awards research grants for studying cystic fibrosis, a genetic disorder that affects the lungs, pancreas, liver, kidneys and intestine.

Disabled American Veterans was founded by Robert Marx in Cincinnati, Ohio, in 1921. Marx had been injured during his World War I service. A women's auxiliary was formed in 1922. DAV was given a federal charter in 1932. DAV provides benefits assistance, outreach, research and advocacy.

Easter Seals was founded in 1919 as the National Society for Crippled Children. The organization assists children and adults with physical and mental disabilities, plus special needs. Services include medical rehabilitation, residential, job training and employment, child care, adult day care, camping, recreation and substance abuse programs.

Girl Scouts were founded in 1912 by Juliette Gordon Low. That first chapter in Savannah, Georgia, has grown to 3.6 million members throughout the U.S. In 1917, a troop in Oklahoma began selling cookies at their local high school. In 1922, Girl Scouts of the USA recommended cookie sales, and a chapter in Philadelphia organized the first drive. Since then, each council has operated its own sales of cookies each year to raise funds in support of programs.

Habitat For Humanity was founded in Americus, Georgia, in 1976. It has assisted more than four million people in the construction, rehabilitation and preservation of more than 800,000 homes. It is the largest non-profit building organization. Programs include A Brush with Kindness, mortgage assistance, Global Village Trips, RV Care-A-Vanners, Women Build, youth programs, recovery efforts along the Gulf Coast and Haiti, Collegiate Challenge and AmeriCorps Build-a-Thon.

Junior Achievement was founded in 1919 by Horace Moses, Theodore Vail and Winthrop Crane, in Springfield, Massachusetts. It works with local business in delivering programs on entrepreneurship, financial literacy and work readiness. In 1975, JA introduced its in-school program, Project Business.

The John F. Kennedy Center for the Performing Arts opened in 1971 and presents theatre, dance, ballet, orchestral, chamber, folk, jazz and pop concerts. It is the busiest performing arts complex in the U.S. A major event is Kennedy Center Honors, held each December.

The League of Women Voters was founded in 1920 by Carrie Chapman Catt, during a meeting of the National American Woman Suffrage Association. It hosts forums, debates and policy institutes nationally to inform voters on the candidates and issues in election cycles.

Leukemia & Lymphoma Society was founded in 1949 by Rudolph and Antoinette de Villiers in White Plains, New York. It is a voluntary health organization dedicated to funding blood cancer research, education and patient services.

Little League Baseball was founded in 1939 in Williamsport, Pennsylvania. It organizes sports programs nationally and hosts the Little League World Series each August in Williamsport.

Make a Wish Foundation was founded in 1980 in Phoenix, Arizona. It arranges experiences for children aged 3-17 with life-threatening conditions, referred by physicians. Wishes are granted through 61 chapters. Professional wrestler John Cena holds the record for the most wishes granted (450), followed by Justin Bieber and the National Women's Collegiate Fraternity Chi Omega.

March of Dimes Foundation was launched in 1938 by President Franklin D. Roosevelt to combat polio. It works to improve the health of mothers and babies.

Multiple Sclerosis Society was founded in 1946. It supports research, professional education and treatment in the area of multiple sclerosis, a disease in which insulating covers of nerve cells in the brain and spinal cord are damaged.

Muscular Dystrophy Association was founded in 1950. Comedian Jerry Lewis hosted its first fund raising telethon, and it has remained an annual event each Labor Day. MDA combats muscular dystrophy and diseases of the nervous system by funding research, treatment and patient education.

NAACP was founded in 1909 by Moorfield Storey, Mary White Ovington and W.E.B. Du Bois in Baltimore, Maryland. It has addressed segregation, disfranchisement, social barriers, desegregation, civil rights, equal employment opportunities and educational initiatives, building coalitions worldwide.

The Partnership for a Drug-Free America was founded in New York City in 1985. It was a consortium of advertising agencies who produced public service messages discouraging drug use. It coordinated campaigns with the federal government in its efforts to stem the spread of illegal drugs.

The Salvation Army was founded in 1865 by William Booth in England to respond to conditions stemming from the industrial society. In 1880, the U.S. branch was formed by George Railton. The Army has worked to serve those most in need, combatting forces of evil.

Society for Prevention of Cruelty to Animals (SPCA) was founded in London, England, in 1824. It is a global animal welfare organization, operating programs on animal welfare, assisting in cruelty to animal cases and finding new homes for unwanted animals.

St. Jude Children's Research Hospital, a pediatric treatment and research center, was founded in Memphis, Tennessee, in 1962 by entertainer Danny Thomas, with help from Lemuel Diggs and Anthony Abraham. It was named after Thomas' patron saint, St. Jude Thaddeus but is non-denominational and open to all. The institution has advanced successes in cancer treatment, pediatric brain tumor treatment and survival from lymphoblastic leukemia. Danny's daughter Marlo is the national spokesperson for St. Jude's, which opened the Marlo Thomas Center for Global Education and Collaboration in 2014.

Sunshine Kids was founded by Rhonda Tomasco in Houston, Texas, in 1982. It offers programs for children who are undergoing cancer treatment at hospitals across the U.S. It hosts hospital parties, community events, letter signings and other signs of encouragement to children.

Thousand Points of Light was a program during the Presidency of George H.W. Bush. It recognized citizens and companies for community good deeds and stewardship. It has 250 affiliates in 22 countries.

UNICEF was founded in 1946 as the United Nations Children's Fund, providing food and healthcare services to war-torn countries. The organization is known for its "Trick Or Treat" program, where children collect money for humanitarian service. Programs support children's rights, corporate responsibility and food distribution. I worked with two of UNICEF's goodwill ambassadors: Vincent Price (on the Campaign for Child Survival) and Audrey Hepburn (on (hunger and literacy initiatives).

The United Way was founded as Community Chest in Cleveland, Ohio, in 1913. There were 1,000 Community Chest organizations in 1948, when they were combined to form the United Foundation. The name United Way was adopted in 1963, modified to United Way of America in 1970. It is an umbrella organization, providing funding and support to thousands of non-profit organizations nationally.

YMCA was founded in 1844 in London, England, by George Williams, to provide healthy activities for men in cities. By 1851, the Young Men's Christian Association had spread throughout Europe and to the United States. Continued growth saw sports activities, fitness programs and activities geared at the entire family. In 1977, the YMCA was immortalized in a popular record by The Village People, with its accompanying dance becoming a craze that is still shared.

YWCA was founded in 1855 in London, England, by Mary Jane Kennaird and Emma Roberts. YWCA USA was founded in 1858 and now has 300 associations serving 2.6 million people. Programs include health, fitness, aquatics, career nourishment, early childhood education, housing and shelter, economic empowerment and leadership development.

Humanitarian Legends

James Earl Carter was President of the U.S. from 1977-1981, the only U.S. president who once lived in public assistance housing. He was a peanut farmer and Governor of Georgia prior to becoming President. In 1982, he established the Carter Center as the basis for advancing human rights. He has conducted peace negotiations, has monitored 96 elections in 38 nations and has fostered programs to reduce disease in under-developed nations. He has been a major proponent of Habitat For Humanity. In 2002, he received the Nobel Peace Prize for his work "to find peaceful solutions to international conflicts, to advance democracy and human rights, and to promote economic and social development."

Edith Cavell (1865-1915) was the first nurse in World War I. She was executed as a spy for having helped Allied soldiers to escape Belgium. On her last night, she wrote fellow nurses, "I have told you that devotion will give you real happiness, and the thought that you have done, before God and yourselves, your whole duty and with a good heart will be your greatest support in the hard moments of life and in the face of death."

Winston Churchill (1874-1965) was a British statesman, intellectual orator, diplomat to the world and one of the greatest leaders of the 20th Century. He served as Prime Minister in the United Kingdom from 1940-1945 and from 1951-1955. In 1948, he warned of an "Iron Curtain" of Soviet influence and promoted European unity. Churchill had a strong relationship with the U.S. From 1939-1945, he and President Franklin D. Roosevelt exchanged 1,700 letters and telegrams and met to discuss world affairs 11 times. In 1963, President John F. Kennedy, authorized by Congress, proclaimed Churchill an Honorary Citizen of the U.S.

Marie Curie (1867-1934) was the first woman to win a Nobel Prize and the first person to win it twice. She was a physicist and chemist who conducted pioneering research on radioactivity (a term that she created). Other research covered radioactive isotopes and the discovery of two elements, polonium and radium. She founded the Curie Institutes in Paris, France, and Warsaw, Poland.

Albert Einstein (1879-1955) was the leading physicist of his era and the most celebrated scientist of the 20th Century. He espoused positions on pacifism and advocated international cooperation.

Elizabeth Fry (1780-1845) campaigned for better conditions in prisons and established charities for the poor and homeless.

Mahatma Gandhi (1868-1948) led the independence movement in India. He sought to unite different religious traditions, as well as improving conditions in the Indian caste system and rights for women. He advocated achieving equity through non-violent methods.

Bob Geldof is a rock star, leader of the group The Boomtown Rats. He was the driving force behind "Band Aid" in 1984. It was a record featuring the talents of most major British rock stars, to raise funds to assist famine relief in Ethiopia. The song was titled "Do They Know It's Christmas?" Geldof was one of the organizers of the Live Aid concert, a 16-hour extravaganza to raise money and awareness for Africa. He became involved in the work of non-governmental organizations and was the leading spokesperson on Third World debt and relief.

Inspired by the work of Geldof and Band Aid, a group of American recording artists organized by Michael Jackson and Lionel Richie created USA for Africa. A total of 47 top stars recorded the song "We Are the World." That hit record raised funds for relief of famine and disease in Africa. Hands Across America, a benefit concert followed. The record and concert raised more than $100 million for the humanitarian efforts.

Also inspired by Live Aid and USA for Africa was Farm Aid, organized in 1985 by Willie Nelson, John Mellencamp and Neil Young. Farm Aid concerts have continued every year since 1985.

These charity concerts and campaigns were in the tradition of others: John Lennon's 1969 Give Peace a Chance and George Harrison's 1972 Concert for Bangladesh. Entertainers appeared on fund-raising telethons following such events as Sept. 11, 2001, Hurricane Katrina and Hurricane Sandy.

Jane Goodall is a humanitarian and environmentalist who has devoted years to studying behaviors of chimpanzees in their native habitat. Observed Ms. Goodall, ""Chimpanzees have given me so much. The long hours spent with them in the forest have enriched my life beyond measure. What I have learned from them has shaped my understanding of human behavior, of our place in nature."

Billy Graham began his ministry in 1947 and has conducted 400+ crusades in 185 countries and territories on six continents. He hosted "Hour of Decision," a weekly radio program, for 50 years. Graham integrated his revivals in 1953. He invited Martin Luther King to jointly preach with him at a 1957 event in New York City. Graham later bailed Dr. King out of jail, after being arrested during demonstrations. Billy Graham has been a spiritual adviser to several U.S. Presidents.

Audrey Hepburn (1929-1993) was a popular film star who won an Oscar as Best Actress in 1953's "Roman Holiday." Her string of memorable films included "Breakfast at Tiffany's," "Sabrina," "War and Peace," "My Fair Lady" and "Wait Until Dark." She is one of the few entertainers who won Oscar, Emmy, Grammy and Tony Awards. She worked for many years with UNICEF, beginning in 1954, in service to children and families in the developing world. She fulfilled field missions in Ethiopia, Turkey, Honduras, El Salvador, Guatemala, Vietnam, Somalia, Mexico and other countries. In 1992, she was accorded the Presidential Medal of Freedom for her work with UNICEF. Observed Miss Hepburn, ""Taking care of children has nothing to do with politics. Anyone who doesn't believe in miracles is not a realist. I have seen the miracle of water which UNICEF has helped to make a reality. Where for centuries young girls and women had to walk for miles to get water, now they have clean drinking water near their homes. Water is life, and clean water now means health for the children of this village."

Ima Hogg (1882-1975) was a philanthropist and patron of the arts. She helped found the Houston Symphony Orchestra in 1913. In 1929, she founded the

Houston Child Guidance Center, an agency to provide therapy and counseling for disturbed children and their families. In 1940, she established the Hogg Foundation for Mental Health. In 1960 she served on a committee appointed by President Dwight D. Eisenhower for the planning of the National Cultural Center (now the Kennedy Center) in Washington, D.C. In 1962, at the request of Jacqueline Kennedy, Ima Hogg served on an advisory panel to aid in the search for historic furniture for the White House. In 1969 Miss Ima, Oveta Culp Hobby and Lady Bird Johnson became the first three women members of the Academy of Texas, an organization founded to honor persons who "enrich, enlarge, or enlighten" knowledge in any field.

Jesse Jackson is a minister, human rights advocate and community champion. He was the founder of organizations that merged to form Rainbow/PUSH. While attending North Carolina A&T University, he was a football quarterback and was elected student body president. He worked in the civil rights movement, working for Dr. Martin Luther King Jr., and was ordained a minister in 1968. Jackson worked with the Southern Christian Leadership Conference and built coalitions to address diversity in economic terms. People United to Serve Humanity began in 1971, and the Rainbow Coalition was founded in 1984. He was involved in the national political discourse, running twice for President in primaries.

Lady Bird Johnson (1912-2007) was the First Lady of the U.S. from 1963-1969. She was born Claudia Alta Taylor and became a strong supporter of the environment. She married Lyndon Baines Johnson in 1934 and supported his political activities, including service in the U.S. House of Representatives, U.S. Senate, as Vice President and as President of the U.S. Mrs. Johnson supported many causes, and environmental initiatives became her worldwide legacy. Gerald Ford awarded her the Presidential Medal of Freedom in 1977. Mrs. Johnson and actress Helen Hayes founded the National Wildflower Research Center in 1982. Her books include "A White House Diary" and "Wildflowers Across America."

Helen Keller (1880-1968) was deaf and blind from the age of two. She overcame her two disabilities, as portrayed in the Broadway show and film, "The Miracle Worker." Keller became an author, activist and campaigner for deaf and blind charities.

Martin Luther King (1929-1968) was a minister and civil rights activist. He sought to end discrimination and racism through non-violent methods. His work focused on abolishing racial segregation. Dr. King led the Montgomery Bus Boycott in 1955 and the 1963 March on Washington, which culminated in the "I Have A Dream" speech. He was influential as a speaker, organizer, leader and beacon for change. Dr. King's birthday is a U.S. national holiday.

Nelson Mandela (1918-2013) was incarcerated for 27 years for his efforts to abolish racial segregation in South Africa. He is regarded for his human rights work. Mandela spent his youth working with the African National Congress, which advocated a non-violent approach to changing the apartheid laws in the country. In 1956, he was charged with treason for his efforts. Though he was meant to serve a life sentence for an array of unjust charges, Mandela was released in 1990 and became President in 1994. His efforts served as inspiration for human rights advocates worldwide.

Mother Teresa (1910-1977) devoted her life to serving the poor and neglected in society. She was born in Albania and lived in India, with a worldwide mission. A Roman Catholic nun, Mother Teresa became involved in humanitarianism after reading about missionaries in Bengal. She founded and worked for the Missionaries of Charity in Calcutta, India. The Missionaries of Charity now number 600, reaches 133 countries and cares for refugees, sick and orphaned children, the aged, AIDS victims and the mentally ill.

Florence Nightingale (1820-1910) was a nurse who helped improve hospital practices which improved patient survival rates.

George Orwell (1903-1950) was a campaigning writer who warned about the dangers of totalitarian states. His novels "Animal Farm" and "1984" are symbols of revolutions which go wrong.

Rosa Parks (1913-2005) was a civil rights activist who refused to give up her seat on a bus, thus launching a campaign to end segregation.

Abbe Pierre (1912-2007) championed conditions for the homeless, founding shelters. His impassioned pleas included, "My friends, help me, A woman has just frozen to death at three this morning, on the pavement of the Boulevard Sebastopol, clutching the document by which she was expelled from her home the day before." In his later years, Pierre was voted France's most popular man.

Princess Diana of Wales (1961-1997) was active in various charities seeking improvements in human welfare, from AIDS to a campaign to prevent landmines.

She visited terminally ill people across the world and championed animal welfare programs. Other causes that Princess Diana supported included Help the Aged, the Trust for Sick Children, the youth branch of the British Red Cross, Chester Childbirth Appeal, National Hospital for Neurology and Neurosurgery, Dove House, Meningitis Trust, Welsh National Opera, Preschool Playgroups Association, Royal School for the Blind, Malcolm Sargent Cancer Fund for Children, the Guinness Trust, Birthright, Variety Club, National Children's Orchestra, Royal Brompton Hospital and Eureka.

Oral Roberts (1918-2009) was a well-known religious leader, the first to practice television evangelism, beginning in 1954. He founded Oral Roberts University in Tulsa, OK, in 1963. He founded Golden Eagle Broadcasting in 1996, a satellite television network known for Christian and family programming.

Eleanor Roosevelt (1884-1962) was First Lady of the United States from 1933-1945. She was a delegate to the United Nations and helped write the Universal Declaration of Human Rights. She championed a variety of non-partisan public works.

Jonas Salk (1914-1995) was a medical researcher and virologist. He discovered and developed the first effective polio vaccine. His books included "Man Unfolding," "Survival of the Wisest," "World Population and Human Values" and "Anatomy of Reality: Merging of Intuition and Reason." His last years were spent in researching a vaccine for HIV.

Albert Schweitzer (1875-1965) was a physician, music scholar, theologian and medical missionary in Africa. Dr. Schweitzer won the Nobel Prize in 1952.

Harriet Beecher Stowe (1811-1896) wrote "Uncle Tom's Cabin," which helped challenge public attitudes toward slavery. She lived in Hartford, CT, next door to author Mark Twain.

Harriet Tubman (1822-1913) was born into slavery. One door, she went to the store top buy supplies and met another slave who had left the fields without permission. His overseer caught them, and she was injured in the event. Tubman and her brothers escaped slavery in 1949. Though warned not to assist others in escaping difficult plights, she developed the Underground Railway. In later years, she promoted giving women the right to vote. Her pioneering activism has been widely celebrated. In 2014, the asteroid Tubman was named in her honor.

Booker T. Washington (1856-1915) was from the last generation of African Americans who was born into slavery and ascended to stellar plateau as a leading educator. Poverty necessitated him starting to work at age nine, in a salt furnace and coal mine. He attended the Normal and Agricultural Institute in Hampton, VA, later returning as a faculty member. In 1881, he was named president of the Tuskegee Institute in Alabama. He was a strong believer in industrial training for blacks. He established the National Negro Business League. His books included "Up From Slavery" and "My Larger Education."

William Wilberforce (1759-1833) was the leading figure in a campaign to end slavery in Britain. He supported social reforms, including animal welfare. He stated, ""If to be feelingly alive to the sufferings of my fellow-creatures is to be a fanatic, I am one of the most incurable fanatics ever permitted to be at large."

Potlache

Potlache is the ultimate catalyst toward community stewardship. The word "potlache" is a native American expression, meaning "to give." For American Indians, the potlache was an immensely important winter ceremony featuring dancing, food and gift giving. Potlache ceremonies were held to observe major life events. The native Americans would exchange gifts and properties to show wealth and status. Instead of the guests bringing gifts to the family, the family gave gifts to the guests.

Colonists settled and started doing things their own way, without first investigating local customs. They alienated many of the natives. Thus, the cultural differences widened. The more diverse we become, the more we really need to learn from and about others. The practice of doing so creates an understanding that spawns better loyalty.

When one gives ceremonial gifts, one gets extra value because of the spirit of the action. The more you give, the more you ultimately get back in return. Reciprocation becomes an esteemed social ceremony. It elevates the givers to higher levels of esteem in the eyes of the recipients.

Potlache is a higher level of understanding of a company that breeds loyalty and longer-term support. It leads to increased quality, better resource management, higher employee productivity, reduced operating costs, improved cash management, better management overall and enhanced customer loyalty and retention.

Categories of Non-Profit Organizations

Non-profit organizations are the backbone of modern society. Every individual and business should support one or many. All of us are recipients of their services, community goodwill and worthwhile objectives.

I have worked with more than 1,500 non-profit, public sector, and non-governmental entities over many decades. I interfaced with many on behalf of corporate clients. I conducted independent performance reviews of many. I served on boards of directors, search committees, awards panels, review boards and task forces for many. I have spoken at conferences, strategic planning retreats, symposia, workshops and board meetings for hundreds.

Non-profit organizations face many challenges beyond the scope of just providing core services. In the process of growth, membership, fund-raising, community relations, administrative and accountability activities, it is vital for each organization to ascertain its niche, constituent base, purpose and long-term potentiality.

I put together this analysis of non-profit organizations, having advised and worked with several hundred of them, at all sizes and stages of growth. This examination of the varying levels of non-profit organizations is for the purpose of pinpointing those unique probabilities, challenges and opportunities for the successful conduct of business.

1. Limited scope

Characteristics:

- Prompted by an impetus to form. Seemed like a good idea at the time.
- Often cater to the egos of founders.
- Not adept at fund-raising, marketing, board recruitment or volunteer retention.
- Fail to build support outside own nucleus.
- Entirely inner-focused.
- Limited impact and probably not long-lasting.

Fund Raising:

- Often exist hand-to-mouth.
- Individual-based.
- Little or no corporate support.

- Doesn't quite look good enough on paper to get second glances from funders.

Public Awareness:

- Very little.
- Leaders don't really understand the value and, thus, don't prioritize.
- No cohesive image. They view one article or one mention as a savior.

Board:

- Sparse, not a full working board.
- Gets whomever is available or most committed.
- No rules and responsibilities.
- Little accountability by board members, thus little productivity.
- High turnover.

Management:

- Volunteer.
- Inexperienced at non-profit organization administration.
- Cannot afford full-time staff.
- Non-centralized, often at odds with board members.

External Support:

- Little, outside board and contributors.
- Have not or will not build pockets of political and community support.
- Have not collaborated with other organizations toward common goals.

Non-Profit Standing:

- Not accorded foundation or corporate certification status.
- Never considered for important grants.
- Organization will always be in a tailspin, from crisis to crisis.

Examples:

- Small cottage foundations.
- Support mechanisms for persons afflicted with certain diseases.

2. Niche-cause

Characteristics:

- Organization has gone past the startup category (#1) and aspires to grow.
- Most remain true to mission and not seeking uncontrollable growth.
- Defined constituencies...don't presume to serve everybody.

Fund Raising:

- Have a few angels.
- Still not on the radar for foundations and corporate givers.
- May look good on paper, but need track record in order to attract major funding.

Public Awareness:

- Caught in a mindset that one article will magically do it all for the organization.
- Unsophisticated about value, usage and methodologies of public awareness.
- Differing viewpoints on this issue cause dissension among leaders.

Board:

- Junior executives on the boards, often their first board roles-responsibilities.
- No board development provided.
- Board routinely turns over, with little consistency.
- Those who control board often push own agendas.

Management:

- Part-time or single-staff. Might share executive director with other groups.
- Volunteers still handle most of the work.
- Scenario 1: executive director not the leader, takes assignments from the board.
- Scenario 2: executive director runs the show, keeping board members at bay.

External Support:

- Organization is inner-focused and does not reach to outside constituencies.
- Collaborate only when circumstances force the practice.
- Non-Profit Standing:
- Not yet on the active radars of foundations or corporations.
- About half grow to the next level. The others wither or merge with other groups.

Examples:

- Child care councils, literacy provider agencies.

3. Advocacy

Characteristics:

- Growth is beyond geographical boundaries.
- Have multiple services, targeting defined, similar or related constituencies.
- Continue to develop additional services.

Fund Raising:

- Beginning to get attention for foundation grants, mostly the smaller ones.
- Beginning to attract corporate support, mostly in-kind services and volunteerism.
- Starting to amass good case studies, cases for support and grant proposal skills.

Public Awareness:

- Sometimes in the news but don't fully capitalize upon image opportunities.
- Think they cannot afford to market.

Board:

- These recruit members to serve, knowing they're the keys to successful growth.
- Mid-managers from business and advocate volunteers comprise the boards.
- Advocates and corporate volunteers often at odds about control of organization.

Management:

- Professional, full-time.
- Multiple professionals, with balanced staff.

External Support:

- Regular foundation bases of support.
- Often considered as viable organization for future foundation support.
- Beginning to receive public sector funding too.

Non-Profit Standing:

- Learn the difference between a hobbyist stance and a professional organization.
- Take steps to refine itself and become a longtime entity.

Examples:

- Small disease-oriented organizations
- School support-reform groups
- Small theatre groups

4. Emerging

Characteristics:

- These are the ones to watch. Many will have staying power.
- Some know their niche, refine their focus and stay lean.
- Others target strategically how they will grow.

Fund Raising:

- Beginning to attract family, estate and trust contributors.
- Maintain a small cadre of loyal benefactors.

Public Awareness:

- Image, name recognition and publicity become the primary focus.
- Services and community presence must have a distinct "point of difference."
- Continued refinement of branding and public perceptions will facilitate the future.

Board:

- Highly committed volunteers, some elected and some appointed.
- Cliques and issue-oriented contingencies vie for board control.
- Term-limited spots, with design for regular board turnover to bring in fresh faces.

Management:

- Have a professional management team.

External Support:

- Strong, loyal and renewable.

Non-Profit Standing:

- Have received good reviews and favorable ratings.
- Begin collaborating with other non-profit organizations.

- May be seen as umbrella organizations to other supporting constituencies.

Examples:

- Mid-sized provider organizations
- Niche-focused and small universities
- Mid-sized trade associations
- Leadership organizations

5. Midstream

Characteristics:

- Have proved themselves to go the distance.
- They plan, evaluate and function in a business-like manner.
- Generally well respected and maintain high levels of community involvement.

Fund Raising:

- Lots of ongoing special events.
- Regular corporate contributors.
- Regularly attract family, estate and trust contributors.

Public Awareness:

- High profile, out of necessity…more often for events than for programs.

Board:

- All elected, with prestige attached to selections.
- Board members get training and development on how to be most effective.

Management:

- Stable professional management team.
- Members are active, working closely with staff.

External Support:

- Strong, loyal and renewable.
- Possess skill at finding new pockets of funding, corporate support and grants.

Non-Profit Standing:

- Regularly partner with other public sector and non-profit entities.
- Examples:

- Mid-sized universities,
- Large trade associations
- Muscular Dystrophy Association, Cystic Fibrosis, Multiple Sclerosis, etc.
- Mid-sized theatre groups, school boards

6. Mainstream

Characteristics:

- These are the ones that other non-profits look to as role models.
- They continually must evolve to next levels, never resting on well-earned laurels.

Fund Raising:

- Leadership knows that development is the lifeblood of the organization.
- One or two major annual events, plus secondary campaigns.
- Many individual and family givers.
- Many grants as source of support for defined projects, institutes and initiatives.

Public Awareness:

- Maintain a high profile, out of necessity, most often for programs and services.

Board:

- Upper management from corporations enthusiastically volunteer to serve.
- Board development is required and encouraged.

Management:

- Stable professional management team.
- Members are active, working closely with staff.

External Support:

- Strong, loyal and renewable.

Non-Profit Standing:

- Regularly audited, scrutinized and accountable for all actions.
- High goodwill, consistency and reputability based.

Examples:

- Major universities.
- Major theatre groups.

- Public television and radio.
- American Heart Association, American Cancer Society, etc.

7. Premium

Characteristics:

- These are the ones that other non-profits look to as role models.
- They continually must evolve to next levels, never resting on well-earned laurels.

Fund Raising:

- Development is a key responsibility for most of the leadership.
- Corporate culture revolves around fund-raising campaigns and giving issues.
- Have regular pockets of support, annual drives and secondary-support events.

Public Awareness:

- High profile, by design and out of necessity.

Board:

- Top echelon of community and business leaders jockey for seats on boards.
- Every board member has a job description, applicable skills and accountability.
- Board development is a primary activity, and board members continually evolve.

Management:

- Have a stable professional management team.
- Members are active, working closely with staff.

External Support:

- Strong, loyal and renewable.

Non-Profit Standing:

- Regularly audited, scrutinized and accountable for all actions.
- Highly goodwill, consistency and reputability based.

Examples:

- United Way, American Red Cross, etc.
- Major arts groups (opera, ballet, symphony).
- Tradition-tier universities.

Billy Graham is pictured with Texas Governor John Connally in 1963. Rev. Graham led the prayer breakfast and invocation at Connally's first inauguration.

Author Hank Moore is pictured with Audrey Hepburn. Photo taken in 1990.

Author Hank Moore is pictured with
Lady Bird Johnson. Photo taken in 1993.

Martin Luther King traveled the world in pursuit of peace initiatives. This
photo of Dr. King and his wife, Coretta Scott King, is from a 1959 mission
to India, meeting with followers of Mahatma Gandhi.

Chapter 10
QUESTIONS

Glimpses into Futurism via golden oldie music archives.

S ome people ask too many questions. Most don't ask enough of the right ones. Some seek true answers. Some try to glean keen insights between the lines of the answers.

The best way to build a business or a career is to investigate the facts, uncover the needs and get others to articulate what they would consider good solutions. Wise businesses employ research and customer relations techniques to stay ahead of the curve. Understanding what is being said enables further research and, with the facts in place, comes strategized organizational growth.

These are ways in which people and organizations pose questions:

? Obtain information.
? Cast aspersions.

184

? Clear up rumors.

? Create rumors.

? Asking for the sake of asking.

? Brainstorm for ideas.

? Determine problems and bottlenecks.

? Find out more.

? Avoid finding out more, by asking non-essential or masked questions.

? Ascertain about a person, their opinions and their personality.

? Justify a budget for investigating, probing or reviewing.

? Use the questioning process to further positive objectives, such as organizational vision, change management and quality processes.

? Use the questioning process to further hidden agendas or gloss over ? Asking to make points (either directly or nebulously).

For an "outside-the-box" reflection through everyone's memory base (the entertainment genre), here are some of life's most probing question, taken from the lexicons of pop music:

Are

"Are the stars out tonight? I don't know if it's cloudy or bright. Cause I only have eyes for you, dear." Written by Harry Warren & Al Dubin (1933)

"Are you sincere when you say 'I love you?' Are you sincere when you say 'I'll be true?' Do you mean every word that my ears have heard? Are really mine every day, all the time? I'd like to know which way to go, will our love grow? Are you sincere?" Andy Williams (words-music by Wayne Walker) (1958)

"Are you lonesome tonight? Do you miss me tonight? Are you sorry we drifted apart? Does your memory stray to a bright summer day? Is your heart filled with pain? Shall I come back again?1920s song by Ray Turk & Lou Handman (later revived by Elvis Presley)

"I hear the music coming out of your radio. Are you there with another girl?" Burt Bacharach & Hal David (1965)

"Are you from Dixie? Cause I'm from Dixie too." song hit of 1916

"Are you ready to sit by the throne? Are you ready not to be alone? Somebody's coming to take you home." Pacific Gas & Electric (1970)

"Aren't you glad you're you?" Bing Crosby (1946)

Can

"Can we talk?" Joan Rivers (gag line to comedy routines)

"Can you tell me why? You in your false securities tear up my life, condemning me. Never give in. Tell me why?" Bronski Beat (1994)

"Can I do this? I don't know, can you?" Pee Wee Herman (frequent gag line on the oxymoron of someone asking permission to do something vs. the capability to do it)

"I swear the day is going to come so soon. The truth is going to burst a lot of balloons. Mister, can't you see?" Buffy Sainte-Marie (1972)

"Look into my eyes. Can't you see they're open wide? Everybody's got their history, on every page a mystery. You can read my diary you're in every line. Would I lie to you baby?" Charles & Eddie (1992)

"Can you find it in your heart? Forgive me, I was thoughtless and acted badly. Can't we make another start? I'm repenting, and your arms alone can save me. Must you tell me that it's over? Think it over." Tony Bennett (composed by Stillman & Allen)

"Can't you see that she's mine? Don't you know I love her so? I don't care what the people say. I'm going to keep on holding her hand." Dave Clark Five (1964)

Did

"Did you ever see a dream walking? Well, I did." song hit of 1933

"Did you ever have to make up your mind? It's not often easy and not often kind. Did you ever have to finally decide? Say yes to one and let the other one ride? There's so many changes and tears you must hide." John Sebastian & the Lovin' Spoonful (1965)

"Didn't I blow your mind this time? Well, didn't I?" The Delfonics (1968)

Do

"Do you want to dance and hold my hand? Tell me that I'm your man? Do you want to dance under the moonlight? Squeeze me all through the night?" Bobby Freeman (1958)

"Do you love me, really love me, now that I can dance?" The Contours (1962)

"Do you know the way to San Jose? In a week or two, they'll make you a star. And all the stars that ever were are parking cars and pumping gas." Dionne Warwick, written by Burt Bacharach & Hal David (1968)

"Do you believe in magic in a young girl's heart? How the music can free her whenever it starts? Believe in the magic that can set you free. If you believe like I believe." John Sebastian & the Lovin' Spoonful (1965)

"Listen. Do you want to know a secret? Do you promise not to tell? Closer, let me whisper in your ear. I'm in love with you." The Beatles (1964)

"Don't look back 'cause you know what you might see. Look into the wall of my mind's eye. I think I know but I don't know why the questions are the answers you might need. Do you know what I mean?" Oasis (1997)

"Do you love as good as you look?" The Bellamy Brothers (1981)

"Do you know what it means to miss New Orleans? I know I'm not wrong. The feelings get stronger, the longer I'm away." Louis Armstrong (1956)

"Do you really want to hurt me? Do you really want to make me cry? That's a step a step too far. Give me time to realize my crime." Culture Club (1983)

"Do you see what I see? A star dancing in the night, with a tail as big as a kite. Do you hear what I hear? A song high above the tree, with a voice as big as the sea. Do you know what I know? A child shivers in the cold. Let us bring him silver and gold." Christmas song

Does

"Does anybody really know what time it is? Does anybody really care? If so, I can't imagine why." Chicago (1970)

"Does your chewing gum lose its flavor on the bedpost overnight? If your mother says don't chew it, do you swallow it in spite? If only I could know the answer to my question. Is it yes or is it no?" 1924 song, revived by Lonnie Donnegan (1961)

"Does my ring hurt your finger?" Charley Pride (1967)

Don't

"Don't it make you want to go home? All God's children get weary when they're wrong. It's been a long time. Now the grass don't grow and the river don't flow like it did in my childhood days." Joe South (1970)

"Don't you want me baby? You know I can't believe it when I hear that you won't see me. It's much too late to find you think you've changed your mind. You'd better change it back or we will both be sorry." The Human League (1982)

For

"For whom the bell tolls? It tolls for thee" Ernest Hemingway

Has

"Five foot two, eyes of blue. But oh, what that five foot can do. Has anybody seen my gal?" song hit of 1926 (recorded by Gene Austin, Art Landry, Ernie Golden)

Have

"Have you ever been lonely? Have you ever been blue?" Ted Lewis (1933)

"I want to know, have you ever seen the rain coming down on a sunny day?" Creedence Clearwater Revival (1970)

"Have I told you lately that I love you? Well darling, I'm telling you now." Gene Autry

"Have you heard who's kissing her now? Do you think she's blue? Did she say we're through? Has she found someone new? Have you seen the way she looks now? Does she act the same when she hears my name? Does she say who's to blame?" song hit for Joni James

How

"How can I be sure, in a world that's constantly changing?" The Rascals (1967)

"How can people be so heartless? How can people be so cruel? How can people have no feelings? How can they ignore their friends? Easy to be hard. Easy to be cold." song by Gerome Ragni, James Rado and Galt MacDermot, from the Broadway musical "Hair" (1968)

"How much do I love you? I'll tell you no lie. How deep is the Ocean? How high is the sky? How many times a day do I think of you? How far would I travel to be where you are? How far is a journey from here to a star?" song by Irving Berlin

"How will I know if he really loves me? Tell me, is it real love? How will I know if he's thinking of me? If he loves me. f he loves me not." Whitney Houston (1986)

"How'd we ever get this way? But now it's just a memory. Why does it do as it does? Time and time again, I wonder how it all began." Andy Kim (1968)

"How many times must a man turn his head and pretend he just doesn't see? The answer, my friend, is blowing in the wind." Bob Dylan (1962)

"How can you mend a broken heart? How can you stop the rain from falling down? How can you stop the sun from shining? What makes the world go round? How can you mend this broken man? How can a loser ever win?" The Bee Gees (1971)

"How much is that doggie in the window, the one with the waggily tail? I do hope that doggie's for sale." Patti Page (1953)

"How important can it be? So the story got around? But it happened all so long ago. Why get lost in yesterday? The important thing is here and now. I have grown so much wiser now. Even foolish hearts can learn." 1955 song recorded by Joni James

"How can you expect to be taken seriously? How am I gonna get through? What have I done to deserve this?" The Pet Shop Boys (1990)

"How'd you like to spoon with me?" song hit of 1906

"Somewhere there's music, I'll paint the tune. Somewhere there's heaven, it's where you are. How high the moon?" recorded by Les Paul & Mary Ford

"How ya gonna keep 'em down on the farm, after they've seen Paree?" song hit of 1919

If

"If I fell in love with you, would you promise to be true? And help me understand? If I give my heart to you, I must be sure." The Beatles (1964)

"If you leave me now? You'll take away the biggest part of me. Baby, please don't go. You'll take away the very heart of me. How could we let it slip away? How could we end it all this way?" Chicago (1976)

"If I give my heart to you, will you handle it with care? Will you always treat me tenderly and in every way be fair? Will you swear that you'll be true to me, by the light that shines above? Think it over and be sure. When you promise all those things to me, then I'll give my heart to you." Doris Day (1954) (composed by Crane/Jacobs/Brewster)

Is

"Is there still room for me beneath the old apple tree?" song hit of 1916

"Is everybody happy?" signature greeting of bandleader Ted Lewis in the 1930s and 1940s

"Is you is, or is you ain't my baby? The way you've been acting lately makes me doubt. Is my baby still my baby too?" Buster Brown (1960)

"Is that all there is to a fire, the circus, to love, to life? If that's all there is, my friend, then, let's keep dancing, break out the booze and have a ball." Peggy Lee (1969)

"Is there any chance that you and I can start all over? Do you still have faith in our romance? Is there any chance that you might forgive? Will you say that you'll try?" Marty Robbins (1960)

Isn't

"Isn't it romantic?" song classic from the 1920s

"Isn't it bliss? Aren't we a pair? You here at last on the ground, me in mid-air. Send in the clowns. Don't bother, they're here." Song from "A Little Night Music" (1973)

"Isn't it a pity? Isn't it a shame? Forgetting to give back. Their eyes can't hope to see the beauty that surrounds them." George Harrison (1970)

"Isn't it about time?" Stephen Stills (1973)

"Isn't this a lovely day to be caught in the rain? You were going on your way. Now you've got to remain. Long as I can be with you, it's a lovely day." Irving Berlin (1935)

May

"May I speak with you? May I bring you joy? Girl, I've been searching for someone like you." Maurice Williams & the Zodiaks (1959)

Shall

"Shall we dance? On a bright cloud of music, shall we fly? Shall we still be together, with our arms around each other? And shall you be my new romance?" Richard Rodgers & Oscar Hammerstein, from "The King & I" (1951)

What

"What would you do if I sang out of tune? Would you stand up and walk out on me?" The Beatles (1967)

"Say, kids, what time is it? It's Howdy Doody Time. It's time to start the show. So, kids, let's go." Buffalo Bob Smith (1947)

"What child is this?" traditional Christmas song

"What is my life without you by my side? What I feel, I can't say. What I know, I can't do. Then I'll try my best to make everything succeed." George Harrison (1970)

"What in the world's come over you? Seems like we never get along. Could you ever change your mind? If you do, I'll still be here, longing, waiting for you." Jack Scott (1960)

"What becomes of the brokenhearted? Who has love that's now departed? But for me they come tumbling down. I know I've got to find some kind of peace of mind. I'll be searching everywhere just to find someone to care." Jimmy Ruffin (1966)

"Baby, what'd I say? See the girl with the diamond ring? She knows how to shake that thing. See the girl with the red dress on? She can dance all night long." Ray Charles (1959)

"What do you get when you fall in love? A guy with a pin to burst your bubble. So, for at least until tomorrow, I'll never fall in love again." Burt Bacharach & Hal David (1969)

"What am I living for, if not for you? Nobody else will do." Chuck Willis (1958)

"What now my love, now that you left me? How can I live through another day? Watching my dreams turning to ashes. What now my love, now it's over? I feel the world closing in on me." 1966 song hit by Sonny & Cher, others

"What kind of fool am I, who never fell in love? What kind of man is this, an empty shell? What kind of cloud am I? What do I know of life? Why can't I fall in love like any other man? And maybe then I'll know what kind of fool I am." Anthony Newley (1962)

"What is love? Five feet of heaven in a pony tail...the cutest pony tail that sways with a wiggle when she walks." The Playmates (1958)

"What are you doing the rest of your life? I have one request…that you spend it with me." Michel Legrand, Alan & Marilyn Bergman (1969)

"What do I have to do to get the message through? How can I prove that I really love you? Don't tell me that it's no use. Love's always been my excuse." Kylie Minogue (1987)

"What'll I do when you are far away? What'll I do, with just a photograph to tell my troubles to? When I'm alone with only dreams of you that won't come true, what'll I do?" song by Irving Berlin

"What kind of girl do you think I am?" Loretta Lynn (1967)

"What is this thing called love? Just who can solve its mystery? Why should it make a fool of me?" song by Cole Porter

What's

"What's up doc?" Bugs Bunny (signature comical question in cartoons)

"What's this whole world coming to? Things just ain't the same. Anytime the hunter gets captured by the game." Smokey Robinson (1967)

"What's he doing in my world? If he's not more than just a friend, then why were you kissing him? Did you tell him that you're my girl? If your love is really true, tell him I won't make for two." Eddy Arnold (1965)

"What's new, pussycat? I've got flowers and lots of hours to spend with you. You're so thrilling, and I'm so willing to care for you." Burt Bacharach & Hal David (1965)

"What's your name? Is it Mary or Sue? Do I stand a chance with you? It's so hard to find a personality with charms like yours for me. Ooh wee." Don & Juan (1962)

"What's love got to do, got to do with it? What's love but a second hand emotion? Who needs a heart when a heart can be broken? What's love but a sweet old fashioned notion?" Tina Turner (1984)

"What's new? How is the world treating you? How did that romance come through? Seeing you is grand. Pardon my asking, what's new? I still love you so." Johnny Burke & Bob Haggart, recorded 1929 by Bing Crosby, 1983 by Linda Ronstadt

When

"When will I see you again? When will we share precious moments? Will I have to wait forever? Will I have to suffer the whole night through? Are we in love, or are we just friends? Is this my beginning, or is it the end?" The Three Degrees (1974)

"When you smile at me, well, I know our love will always be. If you will, I know all will be fine. When will you be mine?" Kalin Twins (1958) (composed by Jack Reardon & Paul Evans)

"I've been cheated. I've been mistreated. When will I be loved? I've been turned down. I've been pushed round. I've been made blue. I've been lied to. When will I be loved?" The Everly Brothers (1960) (recorded 1975 by Linda Ronstadt)

Where

"Where have all the flowers gone? Long time passing, long time ago. When will they ever learn?" Pete Seeger (1962)

"Where's the playground, Susie? You're the one who's supposed to know her way around. The carousel has stopped us here. What merry-go-round can you ride without me? How can you stand?" Glen Campbell (1969) (composed by Jim Webb)

"Where do I go? Follow the river. Is there an answer that tells me why I live and die?" by Gerome Ragni, James Rado, Galt MacDermot from the Broadway musical "Hair" (1968)

"Where are you? Where have you gone without me? I thought you cared about me. What had we to gain? When I gave you my love, was it all in vain? Where's my heart? Where is the dream we started? I can't believe we're parted. Where are you?"Frank Sinatra

"Where is the love?" Donny Hathaway & Roberta Flack (1972)

"Where do I begin to tell the story of how great a love can be? Where do I start? There'll never be another love, another time. She fills my heart with very special things." Carl Sigman & Francis Lai (theme from "Love Story") (1970)

Which

"Which way are you going, Billy? Can I go too? I have nothing to show, if you should go away." The Poppy Family (Terry & Susan Jacks) (1970)

Who

"Who can I turn to, when nobody needs me? My heart wants to know, and so I must go where destiny leads me. Maybe tomorrow I'll find what I'm after. Who can I turn to, if you turn away?" Anthony Newley (1962)

"I long to wake up in the morning and find everything has changed. And all the people I need don't wear a frown. Maybe I'm reaching far too high. For I have something else entirely free. To question such good fortune, who am I?" Petula Clark (1967)

"Who put the bomp in the bop shoo bop shoo bop? Who put the ram in the rama lama ding dong? Who was that man? I'd like to shake his hand, for making my baby fall in love with me." Barry Mann (1961)

"Tell me, who wrote the Book of Love? I've got to know the answer. Was it someone from above? Oh, I wonder, wonder who wrote the Book of Love?)The Monotones (1958)

"Who are you? I really want to know." Peter Townshend & The Who (1978)

"Who will the next fool be?" Bobby Bland (1962)

"Who can explain it? Who can tell you why? Fools give you reasons. Wise men never try." Richard Rodgers & Oscar Hammerstein, from "South Pacific"

"Who's sorry now? Who's sad and blue? Who's crying too? Not like I cried over you. You had your way. Now you must pay." Connie Francis (1957)

"Who do you think you are, to take such advantage of me?" Bo Donaldson & the Heywoods (1974)

"Who's making love to your old lady, while you're out making love?" Johnnie Taylor (1968)

"Trying to find the sun. And I wonder, still I wonder, who'll stop the rain?" Creedence Clearwater Revival (1970)

"Who's zooming who?" Aretha Franklin (1985)

"Who's afraid of the big bad wolf?" Three Little Pigs, Disney cartoon classic (1933)

"Who stole my heart away? Who makes me dream all daydreams that I know will never come true? Who makes my happiness true? Should I answer yes?" song written by Otto Harbach, Oscar Hammerstein and Jerome Kern (1925)

Why

"Why do birds sing so gay? Why does the rain fall from up above? Why does my heart skip this crazy beat? Why do fools fall in love? Why do they fall in love?" Frankie Lymon & the Teenagers (1955)

"Why, oh why, do I love Paris? Because my love is near." song by Cole Porter

"Why does the sun go on shining? Why does the sea rush to shore? Why do the birds go on singing? Why do the stars glow above? Don't they know it's the end of the world? It ended when you said goodbye." Skeeter Davis (1963)

"Why can't we be friends? I've seen you around for a long, long time. The color of your skin doesn't matter to me, as long as we can live in harmony. Sometimes I don't speak right, but I know what I'm talking about." War (1975)

"You had plenty of money in 1922. You let other women make a fool of you. Why don't you do right, like some other men do? Get out of here and get me some money too." Benny Goodman (1943)

"Each night I ask the stars up above, why must I be a teenager in love?" Dion & the Belmonts (1959)

"Why don't you believe me? It's you I adore. Can I promise more? How else can I tell you? What more can I do? I love only you." Joni James (1952)

"If you let me make love to you, then why can't I touch you? From the very first moment I saw you, it's been a different world. My missing links and little kinks have now been found. But you're still the same, like a frozen flame. It sure seems a shame." C.C. Courtney (from the Broadway musical "Salvation")

"Why don't you love me like you used to do? How come you treat me like a worn out shoe? I'm the same old trouble that you've always been through. How come you find so many faults with me? What makes you treat me like a piece of clay?" Hank Williams (1950)

Will

"Is this a lasting treasure, or just a moment's pleasure? But will my heart be broken when the night meets the morning sun? Will you still love me tomorrow?" Carole King (1961)

"Will I find my love today? Will I see her smiling face in some quiet magic place? How I wonder where we'll meet. Will she come my way?

Will we share a smile, a tear?" Johnny Mathis (song composed by Fogarty & Shaw) (1957)

"What will I be? Will I be pretty? Will I be rich? Will we have rainbows day after day? Que sera sera, whatever will be will be." Doris Day (1956) (composed by Livingston & Evans)

Would

"Would you lay with me in a field of stone?" Tanya Tucker (1974)

"Would you like to swing on a star? Carry moonbeams home in a jar? And be better off than you are? Are would rather be a pig? If you don't care a feather or a fig, you may grow up to be a pig." Bing Crosby (1944)

Wouldn't

"Wouldn't anybody like to meet a sweet old fashioned girl?" Teresa Brewer (1956)

"Wouldn't it be nice if we were older? Wouldn't it be nice to live in the kind of world where we belong? Happy times together, we'd be spending. Maybe if we think and wish and hope and pray, it might come true." The Beach Boys (1966)

When you ask questions, you get answers. Sometimes, the answers are factual. Others offer reflections into how people think or feel. Still other answers contain nuggets of gold, those insights that can transform your organization into a valued success. In business, we call that Organizational Vision.

To get the best answers, one must ask the best questions, think beyond the obvious and stretch the idea process. An extended version of this concept is called a Focus Group, gleaning insights from stakeholders, prospects and target constituencies. People directly involved in the decision process may brainstorm and obtain new ideas via a Think Tank.

Answers to Questions, Statements and Affirmations

"Hey life, look at me. I can see through reality. Now I see life for what it is. It's not a dream. It's not a bliss. It happened to me, and it can happen to you." "The Happening" (1967) sung by Diana Ross & the Supremes

"Question me an answer right away. Then, I will answer with a question, clear and bright, day and night." Burt Bacharach & Hal David, from the musical "Lost Horizon" (1972)

"What goes up must come down. Spinning wheel must go round." Blood, Sweat & Tears (1969)

"If I loved you, time and again I'd want to say all that I want you to know. Longing to tell you but afraid and shy. I'd let my golden chances pass me by." Richard Rodgers & Oscar Hammerstein, from "Carousel" (1946)

"While you see a chance, take it." Steve Winwood (1981)

"How sweet it is!" Jackie Gleason (signature exclamation from his TV shows)

"How sweet it is to be loved by you." Marvin Gaye (1965)

"When I fall in love, it will be forever." 1930s song

"What you see is what you get." Flip Wilson (from his "Geraldine" comedy routines)

"Whatever Lola wants, Lola gets." From 1955 Broadway musical "Damn Yankees"

"When you wish upon a star. Makes no difference who you are. Your dreams will come true." Jiminy Cricket, in the Disney movie classic "Pinnochio" (1941)

"I've looked at life from both sides now. Those bright illusions I recall. I really don't know life at all." Judy Collins (1968)

"War is not the answer. Only love can conquer hate. You've got to find a way to bring some understanding today. Talk to me so you can see what's going on." Marvin Gaye (1971)

"Don't make me over. Now that I'd do anything for you. Don't pick on the things I say, the things I do. I'll always be by your side, whenever you're wrong or right. Accept me for what I am. Accept me for the things that I do." Burt Bacharach & Hal David (1962)

"Imagine there's no heaven. It's easy if you try. No help below us. Above us only sky. Imagine all the people living for today." John Lennon (1971)

"You must remember this. A kiss is just a kiss. A sigh is just a sigh. The fundamental things apply as time goes by." Herman Hupfield (song popularized in "Casablanca")

"The day would surely have to break. It would not be new, if not for you." Bob Dylan

"If I ruled the world, every day would be the first day of spring. Every heart would have a new song to sing. Every man would be as free as a bird. Every voice would be a voice to be heard." Leslie Bricusse & C. Ornandel (from the Broadway musical "Pickwick") (1964)

"There ain't no good guys. There ain't no bad guys. There's only you and me, and we just disagree." Dave Mason (1978)

"When my bankroll is getting small, I think of when I had none at all. And I fall asleep, counting my blessings." song by Irving Berlin

"Life goes on, after the thrill of living is gone." John Mellencamp, (1982)

"When it's time to change, you've got to rearrange." The Brady Bunch (1972)

"When there's a smile in your heart, there's no better time to start." Peter Pan

"Longer than always is a long, long time." "More" (from "Mondo Cane") (1963)

"When you move real slow, it seems like mo'." Curtis Mayfield (1963)

"I was so much older then. I'm younger than that now." Bob Dylan

"It's your thing, Do what you want to do." The Isley Brothers (1969)

"Kicks just keep getting harder to find. And all your kicks aren't bringing you peace of mind. Before you find out it's too late, you better get straight." Paul Revere & the Raiders (1966)

"And in the end, the love you take is equal to the love you make." The Beatles (1969)

Questions for Business

When the forces of change and the resistors of progress clash, who usually prevails?

How much have you or your company changed within the last year? How? In what ways? If not, are you proud of staying the same?

Don't you know that those who steadfastly rebuke change become social-business dinosaurs?

To what do you ascribe the success of your competition?

How will you establish a Point of Difference for your company?

What constitutes a leader? What leadership qualities were you taught? What weren't you taught?

What things are executives not taught on the way up?

Why do executives fail to go the distance and fall from the ladder?

How much do you study forces outside your organization that could affect your livelihood?

How loyal are your present employees?

What are the costs of replacing and training workers?

Wouldn't it be nice if people would focus more upon the positives than the negatives?

How might you showcase and benchmark your accomplishments?

If problems outweigh accomplishments, how will you turn that tide?

Have you attended a management training program during the past year?

Might some fresh approaches work for your business?

Where do you expect to be in another 10 years?

If you don't plan for the future, what will likely happen?

What expertise do consultants have, outside of their core business experience?

When was the last time that you failed? What did you learn from it?

Isn't success a natural outgrowth of failure?

When was the last time that you were successful at something? Why?

What are the most important things that you learned in life?

Who were your teachers and mentors? What did they teach you that you use now?

How long can band-aid surgery be applied to an organization and really stick?

Shouldn't Strategic Planning be conducted to assure long-term business success?

What valuable lessons did you learn from competitors, colleagues and consultants?

How many successes were attributable to you?

If the ideas were not yours, whose brain power enabled your company to succeed?

Have you thanked your business collaborators lately? If not, when?

Are there plans for crisis management or preparedness?

Isn't change wonderful?

Who is directly responsible for your failures and successes?

How far behind the trends can a company stay?

Where are the bright young professionals of tomorrow coming from?

How are you insuring that new talents will be trained properly and allowed to blossom?

Who is really in charge of your organization? Who runs what?

Have you been taught ways to manage change, rather than becoming a victim of it?

When the organization does not progressively grow, who are the losers?

What are the costs of an non-empowered and undereducated workforce?

How does a company on the downslide patch its problems?

How many companies have you seen fail because they did all the wrong things?

What pro-active things are you doing? With whom? For what goals?

Chapter 11

YOU MUST REMEMBER THIS: QUOTES FROM THE ICONS AND LEGENDS

Business Strategies by the Author, Paralleling the Quotes.

This is a compendium section, containing quotes and extrapolations into business culture from history's biggest names, including Thomas Jefferson, William Shakespeare, Yogi Berra, Albert Einstein, John F. Kennedy, Bob Dylan, Thomas Payne, Franklin Roosevelt, John Steinbeck, Proverbs, Winston Churchill, Henry Kissinger, etc. Quotes are broad-based, for maximum appeal.

This section offers the quotes for motivation. It also functions as a "PDR of business," a wide-scope view of Big Picture strategies, methodologies and recommendations. It also contains sage advice that the leadership quote books do not encompass.

Quotes and analysis are applicable to stages in the evolution of a business, leadership development and mentoring. This is a creative way of re-treading old knowledge to enable executives to master change, rather than feel as they're victims of it.

Adversity, Enemies, Competitors

"A man cannot be too careful in the choice of his enemies." Oscar Wilde

"Under conditions of tyranny, it is easier to act than to think." Hannah Arendt

"All men would be tyrants if they could." Daniel Defoe, 18th Century English writer

"Truth forever on the scaffold. Wrong forever on the throne." James Russell Lowell

"Any excuse will serve a tyrant." Aesop

"Better a thousand enemies outside the house than one inside." Arabic proverb

"Even a paranoid can have enemies." Henry Kissinger (1977)

"If you have no enemies, then fortune has not smiled upon you." William Shakespeare

Adversity, Enemies, Competitors

Every business and community is at a crossroads. There exist two options:

1. Each organization can be seen and known as a dynamic community that addresses its problems and moves forward in a heroic fashion, as a role model to the rest of the world.
2. Or, organizations can bury their heads in the sand and hope media attention dies down, thus becoming a generic tagline for troubled business waters.

Undoubtedly, most of us want to choose option one and seek complex answers for the judicious practices of moving forward.

Volatile business contractions, uneasy economic climate, plant explosions, health care crises, hostile corporate takeovers, governmental shakeups, and financial failings are crises that upset the routine of business life. Some jolting incident puts every organization into a reaction mode. The consequences of miscommunication in a crisis can be devastating to all involved.

We learn a lot from our competitors, including those whom we respect and those in whom we do not put much stock. They are our competitors for many reasons. The ideal planning process looks squarely at the marketplaces and analyzes why all players succeed and fail. These nuggets of wisdom serve as basis for our own future successes.

Age, Longevity, Wisdom

"Life begins at 40." Sophie Tucker

"It is never too late to learn. There's many a good tune played on an old fiddle. An adult is one who has ceased to grow vertically but not horizontally. You've reached middle age when all you exercise is caution." Proverbs

"The only thing I regret about my past life is the length of it. If I had my past life over again, I'd make all the same mistakes, only sooner." Tallulah Bankhead, actress

"Man arrives as a novice at each age of his life." Nicolas Chamfort, 18th Century French writer

"Middle age is youth without its levity and age without decay." Writer Daniel Defoe

"Youth is a blunder, manhood a struggle, old age a regret." Benjamin Disreali, statesman

"Middle age is when your age starts to show around the middle." Bob Hope

"At 20 years of age, the will reigns; at 30, the wit; and at 40, the judgment." Benjamin Franklin

"The four stages of man are infancy, childhood, adolescence and obsolescence." Art Linkletter

"All that the young can do for the old is to shock them and keep them up to date." George Bernard Shaw

Age, Longevity, Wisdom

Everything we are in business stems from what we've been taught or not taught to date. A career is all about devoting resources to amplifying talents and abilities, with relevancy toward a viable end result.

Amassing a Body of Knowledge is a long and enjoyable process. It is the first step toward a career-life Strategy, which evolves into a Vision. A Mission Statement is 1% of a Strategic Plan, which is 20% of a Visioning Program.

Most of us learned about business (which is a compendium of life relationships) "in the streets." Today's business leaders entered and pursued careers without a strategic plan or service manual. Professionals pursue many approaches to garnering information and, ultimately, to unlocking the answers that inevitably lie within. Methods include seminars, books, consultations, professional association involvement, training, organizational development, executive roundtables, civic activities and much more.

Failure to prepare for the future spells certain death for businesses and industries in which they function. The same analogies apply to personal lives, careers and Body of Work. Greater business awareness and heightened self-awareness are compatible and part of a holistic journey of growth. None of us can escape those pervasive influences that have affected our lives. Like sponges, we absorbed information and perceptions of life that have helped mold our business and personal relationships.

Appearances, Image

"All that glitters is not gold. Men should be what they seem. Through tattered clothes, small vices do appear. Robes and furred gowns hide all." William Shakespeare

"Handsome is as handsome does. Fine feathers make fine birds. A man need not look in your mouth to know how old you are. Never judge from appearances. You can't tell a book by its cover. Vice is often clothed in virtue's habit. Appearances are deceptive." Proverbs

"At 50, everyone has the face he deserves." George Orwell, 20th Century novelist

"Things are entirely what they appear to be, and behind them, there is nothing." Jean-Paul Sartre

"The world is governed more by appearances than realities, so that it is fully as necessary to seem to know something as to know it." Daniel Webster (1782-1852)

"Beware so long as you live, of judging people by appearances." La Fontaine

"Do not judge men by mere appearances; for the light laughter that bubbles on the lip often mantles over the depths of sadness, and the serious look may be the sober veil that covers a divine peace and joy." E. H. Chapin

"Appearances often are deceiving." Aesop (620 BC-560 BC), *The Wolf in Sheep's Clothing*

"Fashion is the science of appearances and inspires one with the desire to seem rather than to be." Michel de Montaigne (1533-1592)

"It is only shallow people who do not judge by appearances." Oscar Wilde (1854-1900)

Appearances, Image

Every organization must and should put its best face forward for the public. Perceptions are referred to as "credence goods." Every organization must educate outside publics about what they do and how they do it. This premise also holds true for each corporate operating unit and department. The whole of the business and each sub-set must always educate corporate opinion makers on how it functions and the skill with which the company operates.

Gaining confidence among stakeholders is crucial. Business relationships with customers, collaborators and other professionals are established to be long-term in duration. Each organization or should determine and craft its own corporate culture, character and personality, seeking to differentiate itself from others.

Beliefs, Convictions, Core Values

"The will to do, the soul to dare." Sir Walter Scott

"Stand. In the end, you'll still be you. One that's done all the things you set out to do. There's a cross for you to bear, things to go through, if you're going anywhere. There's a giant inside of you, about to grow. Stand. Don't you know you are free. Well, at least in your mind, if you want to be." Sly & the Family Stone (1970)

"Be always sure you're right, and then go ahead." Davy Crockett

"Men are alike in their promises. It is only in their deeds that they differ." Moliere

"One must learn by doing the thing. Though you think you know it, you have no certainty until you try." Sophocles

"I had rather be right than President." Henry Clay (1850)

"No act of kindness, no matter how small, is ever wasted. Kindness affects more than severity." Aesop

"If you will it, it is no dream." Theodor Herzl

"Our wills and fates do so contrary run that our devices still are overthrown. Our thoughts are ours, their ends none of our own." William Shakespeare

Beliefs, Convictions, Core Values

How organizations start out and what they become are different concepts. Mistakes, niche orientation and lack of planning lead businesses to failure. Processes, trends, fads, perceived stresses and "the system" force managers to make compromises in order to proceed. Often, a fresh look at previous knowledge gives renewed insight.

These are the key criteria for basing your professional vision:

1. Core Industry, The Business You're In.
2. Rendering the Service, Administering Your Work.
3. Accountability, Qualities with Which You Work.
4. Your Relationships and Contributions to Other People, Colleagues and Stakeholders.
5. Professional-Leadership Development, Your Path to the Future.
6. Your Contributions to the Organization's Overall Goals, Your Place in its Big Picture.
7. Body of Work, Your Accomplishments to Date and Anticipated Future Output.

Body of Knowledge, The Big Picture

"The cosmic process has no sort of relation to moral ends." T.H. Huxley

"Virtue, study and gaiety are three sisters who should not be separated." Voltaire (1737)

"My will was to live worthily as long as I lived, and after my life to leave them that should come after, my memory in good works." Boethius

"It is a far, far better thing that I do, than I have ever done. It is a far, far better rest that I go to, than I have ever known." Charles Dickens

"Wisdom comes only through suffering. Wonder is the beginning of wisdom." Greek proverbs

"The fox knows many things, but the hedgehog knows one great thing." Archilochus

"Knowledge comes, but wisdom lingers." Alfred, Lord Tennyson

"Nine-tenths of wisdom consists in being wise in time." President Theodore Roosevelt

"Be wiser than other people if you can, but no not tell them so." Earl of Chesterfield

"The highest wisdom has but one science…the science of the whole…the science explaining the whole creation and man's place in it." Leo Tolstoy

"The bitter and the sweet come from the outside, the hard from within, from one's own efforts." Albert Einstein

"Learning is a treasure which accompanies its owner everywhere." Chinese proverb

Body of Knowledge, The Big Picture

It seems so basic and so simple: Look at the whole of the organization, then at the parts as components of the whole and back to the bigger picture.

I advocate planning ahead and taking the widest possible view, utilizing a series of bite-sized chunks of business growth activity. This is the approach to clients that I have taken as a senior business advisor for 40 years. Even in times of crisis or when working on small projects, I use every opportunity to inspire clients look at their Big Pictures. The typical reaction is that my approach makes sense, and why haven't others taken it before.

The Big Picture can and does exist, though companies have not found it for their own applications very often. Organizations know that such a context is out there, but most search in vein for partial answers to a puzzling mosaic of business activity. The result, most often, is that organizations spin their wheels on inactivity, without crystallizing the right balance that might inspire success. Obsession with certain pieces, comfort levels with other pieces and lack of artistic flair (business savvy) keep the work in progress but not resulting in a finished masterpiece.

Businesses rarely start the day with every intention of focusing upon the Big Picture. They don't get that far. It is too easy to get bogged down with minutia. This book and my advising activities are predicated upon educating the pitfalls of narrow focus and enlightening organizations on the rewards of widening the view. Alas, the Big Picture of business is a continuing realignment of current conditions, diced with opportunities. The result will be creative new variations. Masterpieces are not stagnant paintings. They can be continually evolving works in progress.

Business

"No nation was ever ruined by trade. The first mistake in public business is the going into it." Benjamin Franklin

"Trade is a social act." John Stuart Mill

"The business of America is business." President Calvin Coolidge (1925)

"There is no such thing as a free lunch." Milton Friedman, economist

"If you pay peanuts, you get monkeys." James Goldsmith

"The big print giveth, and the fine print taketh away." Bishop J. Fulton Sheen

"If two men on the same job agree all the time, then one is useless. If they disagree all the time, them both are useless." Darryl F. Zanuck, film producer (1949)

"Business underlies everything in our national life, including our spiritual life. Witness the fact that in the Lord's Prayer, the first petition is for daily bread. No one can worship God or love his neighbor on an empty stomach." President Woodrow Wilson (1912)

"The harder the conflict, the more glorious the triumph. What we obtain too cheap, we esteem too lightly; it is dearness only that gives everything its value. I love the man that can smile in trouble, that can gather strength from distress and grow brave by reflection. It is the business of little minds to shrink; but he whose heart is firm, and whose conscience approves his conduct, will pursue his principles unto death." Thomas Paine

"No one can possibly achieve any real and lasting success or "get rich" in business by being a conformist." J. Paul Getty

"If I had to sum up in one word what makes a good manager, I'd say decisiveness. You can use the fanciest computers to gather the numbers, but in the end you have to set a timetable and act." Robert P. Vanderpoel

"The most successful businessman is the man who holds onto the old just as long as it is good, and grabs the new just as soon as it is better." Lee Iacocca

"Any business arrangement that is not profitable to the other person will in the end prove unprofitable for you. The bargain that yields mutual satisfaction is the only one that is apt to be repeated." B. C. Forbes

"The successful man is the one who finds out what is the matter with his business before his competitors do." Roy L. Smith

"A friendship founded on business is better than a business founded on friendship." John D. Rockefeller, Jr.

"The person who knows how will always have a job. The person who knows why will always be his boss." Diane Ravitch

"Politics is the art of preventing people from sticking their noses in things that are properly their business." Paul Valéry

Business

There is a difference between knowing a product-industry and growing a successful business. It is possible for a company and its managers to know much about certain arts and sciences without having the will to pursue them.

Much of the wisdom to succeed lies within. It must be recognized, fine-tuned and utilized. Much of the wisdom to succeed lies outside your company. It must be called upon, sooner rather than later.

People under-perform because they are not given sufficient direction, nurturing, standards of accountability, recognition and encouragement to out-distance themselves. Organizations start to crumble when their people quit on each other. Unhealthy organizations will always "shoot the messenger" when change and improvements are introduced. Healthy organizations absorb all the knowledge and insight they can, embracing change, continuous quality improvement and planned growth. Anybody can poke holes in an organization. The skill is to create programs and systems which do something constructive.

The level of achievement by a company is commensurate to the level and quality of its vision, goals and tactics. The higher its integrity and character, the higher its people must aspire.

Change, Progress

"Nature's mighty law is change." Robert Burns

"Nothing's the same when you see it again." Cat Stevens, from his song "Portobello Road"

"Change is inevitable in a progressive society. Change is constant." Benjamin Disraeli (1867)

"Change is not made without inconvenience, even from worse to better." Richard Hooker, 16th Century English theologian

"You can't step twice into the same river. Everything flows, and nothing stays still." Heraclitus

"The basic fact of today is the tremendous pace of change in human life." Jawaharlal Nehru

"He that will not apply new remedies must expect new evils. For time is the greatest innovator." Sir Francis Bacon

"All progress is precarious, and the solution of one problem brings us face to face with another problem." Martin Luther King, Jr.

"Human progress is furthered, not by conformity, but by aberration." H.L. Mencken

"Chaos often breeds life, when order breeds habit." Henry Brooks Adams

Change, Progress

Research shows that change is 90% positive and that individuals and organizations change at the rate of 71% per year. Change is necessitated by a natural flow of events, stemming from changes already made and realized. Some changes are mandated, and others are necessitated by circumstances outside your control.

The worst blockages of change come from people who possess the "been there, done that" attitude. 87% of the time, they really haven't. Other spoilers include middle managers who can't see the forest for the trees, don't want to see beyond the scope and are proud of it.

The mastery of change is to benefit from it, rather than become a victim of it. By arming ourselves with knowledge and strategies to succeed, then change occurs to our best benefit. Leaders who expose their teams to new territories enables them to see how they adapt within that framework. Championing change can mark the next tier in an executive's development.

A well-intentioned person may want and try so hard to do the right thing that he-she makes mistakes and ultimately does the wrong thing. It is the mark of a great person to admit mistakes, correct the course and move on. Another mark of a great leader is to let his people lead too…and give them the reins to do so effectively.

Change helps you do business in the present and helps plan for the future. Without mastering he challenges of a changing world, companies will not be optimally successful. The organization that manages change remains successful, ahead of the competition and is a business-industry leader. Meanwhile, other companies will have become victims of change because they stood by and did nothing.

Choices

"The United States will always make the right choice, but only after choosing other options first." Sir Winston Churchill

"If you limit your choices only to what seems possible or reasonable, you disconnect yourself from what you truly want, and all that is left is a compromise." Robert Fritz

"Because you are in control of your life, don't ever forget that you are what you are because of the conscious and subconscious choices you have made." Barbara Hall, "A Summons to New Orleans," 2000

"It is our choices that show what we truly are, far more than our abilities." J. K. Rowling, "Harry Potter and The Chamber of Secrets," 1999

"Honor isn't about making the right choices. It's about dealing with the consequences." Midori Koto

"In all things, there are three choices: Yes, No & no choice, except in this, I either choose the truth or I am deceit." Sovereign

"The future is not a result of choices among alternative paths offered by the present, but a place that is created first in the mind and will, created next in activity. The future is not some place we are going to, but one we are creating. The paths are not to be found, but made, and the activity of making them, changes both the maker and the destination." John Schaar, futurist

Choices

These are the seven levels of choices that we can make:

1. Past Choices Made and How You Have Evolved.
2. Good Choices and Why They Worked.
3. Bad Choices and the Lessons Learned.
4. Against Your Will.
5. For the Good of the Project, Career, Company.
6. For Your Own Good.
7. Taking Charge by Making Responsible Choices.

Courage

"Courage is resistance to fear, mastery of fear—not absence of fear." Mark Twain

"Courage is the price that life exacts for granting peace." Amelia Earhart, 20th Century aviator

"We could never learn to be brave and patient. If there were only joy in the world." Helen Keller (1890)

"In the dark days and darker nights when England stood alone, and most men save Englishmen despaired of England's life, he mobilized the English language and sent it into battle." President John F. Kennedy, upon proclaiming Sir Winston Churchill an honorary U.S. citizen, April 9, 1963

"I was not the lion. But it fell to me to give the lion his roar." Sir Winston Churchill

"Courage and perseverance have a magical talisman, before which difficulties disappear and obstacles vanish into air." President John Quincy Adams (1767-1848)

"Courage is the ladder on which all the other virtues mount." Clare Booth Luce (1903-1987)

"Life shrinks or expands in proportion to one's courage." Anais Nin (1903-1977)

"I wanted you to see what real courage is, instead of getting the idea that courage is a man with a gun in his hand. It's when you know you're licked before you begin but you begin anyway and you see it through no matter what." Harper Lee, *To Kill a Mockingbird*

"Every human being on this earth is born with a tragedy, and it isn't original sin. He's born with the tragedy that he has to grow up. That he has to leave the nest, the security, and go out to do battle. He has to lose everything that is lovely and fight for a new loveliness of his own making, and it's a tragedy. A lot of people don't have the courage to do it." Helen Hayes, actress

"If you explore beneath shyness or party chit-chat, you can sometimes turn a dull exchange into an intriguing one. I've found this to be particularly true in the case of professors or intellectuals, who are full of fascinating information, but need encouragement before they'll divulge it." Joyce Carol Oates

"Have courage for the great sorrows of life and patience for the small ones; and when you have laboriously accomplished your daily task, go to sleep in peace." Victor Hugo (1802-1885)

"Never discourage anyone who continually makes progress, no matter how slow." Plato

"You gain strength, courage and confidence by every experience in which you really stop to look fear in the face. You say to yourself, I have lived through this horror. I can take the next thing that comes along. You must do the thing you think you cannot do." Eleanor Roosevelt

"Keep your fears to yourself, but share your courage with others." Robert Louis Stevenson

"Discourage litigation. Persuade your neighbors to compromise whenever you can. As a peacemaker the lawyer has superior opportunity of being a good man. There will still be business enough." President Abraham Lincoln (1809-1865)

"Have patience with all things, but chiefly have patience with yourself. Do not lose courage in considering you own imperfections but instantly set about remedying them. Every day begin the task anew." Saint Francis de Sales

"Courage is doing what you're afraid to do. There can be no courage unless you're scared." Eddie Rickenbacker (1890-1973)

"It is curious that physical courage should be so common in the world and moral courage so rare." Mark Twain (1835-1910)

"Courage is being scared to death, but saddling up anyway." John Wayne

Courage

These are the stages in people's courage to learn and commit to new perspectives on life and business:

1. Cluelessness, Apathy. Henry Ford said, "90% of the American people are satisfied." Will Rogers said, "Mr. Ford is wrong. 90% of the people don't give a damn." Content with the status quo. Taking a vacation from thinking. Not interested in learning more about life or seeing beyond one's realm of familiarization.

2. Basic Awareness. Latent readiness. Not moved to think differently, take risks or make decisions until circumstances force it. 90% don't care about specific issues until events that affect their lives force them to care about something. 5% affect decisions. 5% provide momentum.

3. Might Consider. The more one gathers information, they apply the outcomes of selected issues to their own circumstances. Begin learning through message repetitions.

4. Taking in Information. Something becomes familiar after hearing it seven times. Gains importance to the individual through accelerated familiarity. The more one learns, the more one realizes what they don't know. At this plateau, they either slide back into the denial level of cluelessness or launch a quest to become mature via learning more about life.

5. Courage to Form Opinions. Triggering events or life changes cause one to consider new ideas, ways of thinking. Survival and the need-desire for self-fulfillment causes one to form strong desires to learn. Cluelessness and inertia are no longer options and are now seen as backward and self-defeating.

6. Thinking and Analyzing. Changing paradigms. Behavioral modification ensues. There are ways we used to think and behave. We do these things differently now because we have learned preferable ways that cause better outcomes. Thus, we don't revert to the old paradigms.

7. Behavioral Change and Commitment. Advocating positions. Creating own original ideas. Holding and further developing insights. Commitment to change and personal growth. Willing and able to teach and share intellect and wisdom with others.

Education, Professional Development and Training
"Soon learned, soon forgotten." Proverb

"Knowledge itself is power. Studies serve for delight, ornament, and ability." Sir Francis Bacon

"Education is the best provision for old age." Aristotle

"They know enough who know how to learn. A teacher affects eternity and can never tell where his influence stops." Henry Brooks Adams, 19th Century U.S. historian

"The direction in which education starts a man will determine his future life." Plato

"Education is simply the soul of a society as it passes from one generation to another." G.K. Chesterton (1924)

"I have learned since to be a better student, and to be ready to say to my fellow students, 'I do not know.'" William Osler

"He who can does. He who cannot teaches." George Bernard Shaw

"Training is everything. The peach was once a bitter almond. Cauliflower is nothing but a cabbage with a college education. Soap and education are not as sudden as a massacre, but they are more deadly in the long run." Mark Twain

"Human history becomes more and more a race between education and catastrophe." H.G. Wells

"Wisdom is oftentimes nearer when we stoop than when we soar." William Wordsworth

"What we have to learn to do, we learn by doing." Aristotle

"I am always ready to learn although I do not always like being taught." Sir Winston Churchill

Education, Professional Development and Training

Professional development is the most important ingredient in corporate progress. Today's workforce will need three times the amount of training that it now gets, if the organization intends to stay in business, remain competitive and tackle the future successfully.

Each year, one-third of the Gross National Product goes toward cleaning up problems, damages and the high costs of doing either nothing or the wrong things. Half of that amount goes toward some form of persuasion, instruction, spin-doctoring or educating.

More often that not, "training" is a vehicle to tout one's viewpoint, tinker with old problems or blame someone else for the course of events. If training is viewed as band-aid surgery to fix problems, then it will fail. Managers who have this "fix those people" mindset are, in fact, the ones who need substantive training the most. Professional development is rarely allowed to be extensive. It is usually technical or sales-marketing in nature. Employees and executives are rarely mentored on the people skills necessary to have a winning team. Thus, they fail to establish a company vision and miss their business mark.

There is a difference between how one is basically educated and the ingredients needed to succeed in the long-term. Many people never amass those ingredients because they stop learning or don't see the need to go any further. Many people think they are "going further" but otherwise spin their wheels. There is a large disconnect between indoctrinating people to tools of the trade and the myriad of elements they will need to assimilate for their own futures.

Ethics

"The end must justify the means." Matthew Prior

"If I am not what I say I am, then you are not what you think you are." novelist James Baldwin

"What is moral is what you feel good after. What is immoral is what you feel bad after." Ernest Hemingway

"Virtue is not always amiable. The happiness of man, as well as his dignity, consists in virtue." President John Adams (1779)

"Always do right. This will gratify some people and astonish the rest." Mark Twain

"The laugh is always on the loser." German proverb

"The function of wisdom is discriminating between good and evil." Cicero

"Ethical axioms are found and tested not very differently from the axioms of science. Truth is what stands the test of experience." Albert Einstein

"The humblest citizen in all of the land, when clad in the armor of a righteous cause, is stronger than all the hosts of error." William Jennings Bryan

"We can act as if there were a God; feel as if we were free; consider nature as if she were full of special designs; lay plans as if we were to be immortal; and we find then that these words do make a genuine difference in our moral life." William James

"We must learn to distinguish morality from moralizing." Henry Kissinger

"Any preoccupation with ideas of what is right or wrong in conduct shows an arrested intellectual development." Oscar Wilde

Ethics

Ethics is the science of morals, rightness and obligations in human affairs. Institutions must conduct many activities which impact their general welfare. Ethical issues go beyond nice rhetoric and must encompass duties, principles, values, processes, responsibilities and governing methodologies. Companies who fail to address ethical issues of the day are endangered species. Whatever the public expects of companies, then those companies should expect the same of themselves.

The company's Ethics Statement must be more than a terse branding slogan. Like the Mission Statement in the Strategic Plan, it is the amalgamation of careful thought, weighed insights and tests for fairness and durability. The Ethics Statement must be a part of the Strategic Plan, as are such other fundamental statements covering customer-focused management, diversity, valuing stakeholders, quality management and an empowered workforce.

Every organization differs in how it will implement Corporate Responsibility and Ethics programs. The differences are factored by the company's size, sector, culture and the commitment of its leadership. Some companies focus on a single area of operation. The Code of Ethics may include Fundamental Canons, Rules of Practice and Professional Obligations.

Business ethics encompass much more than accounting fraud and the publicly stated values of stocks. Ethics should be attached to many other important areas of business. Elements in the Ethics internal company review, which could subsequently be addressed in the full ethics plan, contained within the company's overall Strategic Plan.

The corporate ethics program may include a code of ethics, training for employees for ethical behaviors, a means for communicating with employees, reporting mechanism, audit system, investigation system, compliance strategy, prevention strategy and integrity strategy. The program seeks to create conditions that support the right actions. It communicates the values and vision of the organization. It aligns the standards of employees with those of the organization. The program relies upon the entire management team, not just the legal and compliance personnel.

A formal ethics program will prevent ethical misconduct, monetary losses and losses to reputation. If communicated well, it may breed customer trust. In fact, I highly recommend using executive summaries of the ethics program as a corporate communications tool. The sending of the Ethics Statement to customers, suppliers, regulators and other stakeholders demonstrates the extra length to which the company goes to become a model. It becomes a good marketing mailing, and it's the right thing to do.

Failure

"To do a great right, do a little wrong." William Shakespeare

"The only one who makes no mistakes is one who never does anything." President Theodore Roosevelt

"A life spent in making mistakes is not more honorable but more useful than a life spent doing nothing." George Bernard Shaw

"Tis better to have loved and lost than never to have lost at all." Samuel Butler

"A miss is as good as a mile." Proverb

"There's no success like failure. And that failure's no success at all." Bob Dylan

"Well, back to the old drawing board." Peter Arno, 20th Century cartoonist

"I'm grateful for all of my problems. As each of them was overcome, it made me stronger and able to meet those yet to come. I grew strong on my difficulties." J.C. Penney

"Failure, I never encountered it. All I ever met were temporary setbacks." J. Willard Marriott

"There's a little bit of success in every failure and a bit of failure in every success." O. Henry

"Life is sweetened by risks." Farrah Fawcett

Failure

Success and failure are a matter of perspectives. Out of every 10 transactions in our lives, five will be unqualified successes. One will be a failure. Two will depend upon the circumstances. If approached responsibly, they will become successful. If approached irresponsibly, they will turn into failures. Two will either be successful or will fail, based strictly upon the person's attitude.

A 90% success rate for a person with a good attitude and responsible behavior is an unbeatable percentage. There is no such thing as perfection. Continuous quality improvement means that we benchmark accomplishments and set the next reach a little further. Throughout our lives, we search for activities, people and meaning. We venture down roads where we find success. Other activities bring us failure, from which we learn even more what to do to achieve success the next time.

We learn three times more from failure than from success. The longer that success takes to attain has a direct relationship to how long we will hold onto it. Success is easily attainable. So, why do people psyche themselves into failing more often they have to, especially when they succeed much more often than they give themselves credit for. Learning the stumbling blocks of failure prepares one to attain true success. Fear is the biggest contributor to failure, and it can be a motivator for success. You cannot make problems go away, simply by ignoring that they exist.

Everybody fails at things for which they are not suited. Learn from the best and the worst. People who make the biggest bungling mistakes are showing you pitfalls to avoid.

These are the most common areas where most leaders and their businesses fail: Personal Abilities, Talents:

- Making the same mistakes more than twice, without studying the mitigating factors.
- Taking incidents out of context and incorrectly diagnosing situations.
- Rationalizing occurrences, after the fact.
- Appearing self-contained, therefore precluding others from wanting to help us.
- Inability to cultivate other people's support of me at the times that we needed it most.

Resources:

- Attempting projects without the proper resources to do the job well.
- Not knowing people with sufficient pull and power.
- Thinking that friends would help introduce us or help network to key influential people.
- Failure to learn effective networking techniques early enough in my career path.
- Inability to finely develop the powers of people participating in the networking process.

Other People:

- Accepting people at their words without questioning.
- Showing proper respect to other people and assuming that they would show or were capable of showing comparable respect to others.
- Doing favors for others without asking anything in return, if we expected quid pro quo at a later time. Not telling people what we wanted and then being disappointed that they did not read minds or deliver favors of their own volition.
- Befriending people who were too needy, always taking without offering to reciprocate.
- Picking the wrong causes to champion at the wrong times and with insufficient resources.
- Working with the false assumption that people want and need comparable things. Incorrectly assuming that all would pursue their agendas fairly. A better understanding of personality types, human motivations and behavioral factors would have provided insight to handle situations on a customized basis.
- Offering highly creative ideas and brainpower to those who could not grasp their brilliance, especially to those who were fishing for free ideas they could then market as their own.

Circumstances Beyond Our Control:

- Working with equipment, resources and people from a source without my standards of quality control, trying to make the best of bad situations.
- Changing trends, upon which we could not capitalize but which others could.

Wrong Calculations:

Incorrectly estimating the time and resources necessary to do something well.

Getting blindsided because we did not conduct enough research.

Failure to plan sufficiently ahead, at the right times.
Setting sights too low. Not thinking big enough.

Timing:

* Offering advice before it was solicited.
* Feeling pressured to offer solutions before diagnosing situations properly.
* Not thinking of enough angles and possibilities sooner.

Marketplace-External Factors:

* Not reading the opportunities soon enough.
* Not being able to spot, create or capitalize upon emerging trends at their beginnings.

Fear

"Fear has many eyes and can see things underground." Cervantes, *Don Quixote*

"It is a miserable state of mind to have few things to desire and many things to fear." Sir Francis Bacon

"You may take the most gallant sailor, the most intrepid airman, or the most audacious soldier. Put them at a table together. What do you get? The sum of their fears." Sir Winston Churchill

"To fight a bull when you are not scared is nothing. To not fight a bull when you are scared is nothing. But, to fight a bull when you are scared, that is something." Manolete, bullfighter

"Courage is resistance to fear, mastery of fear—not absence of fear." Mark Twain (1835-1910)

"The optimist proclaims we live in the best of all possible worlds; and the pessimist fears this is true." James B. Cabell

"It's the opinion of some that crops could be grown on the moon. Which raises the fear that it may not be long before we're paying somebody not to." Franklin P. Jones

"I do not fear computers. I fear the lack of them." Isaac Asimov

"You can discover what your enemy fears most by observing the means he uses to frighten you." Eric Hoffer

"Justice, like lightning, should ever appear to some as hope, to others as fear." Jefferson Pierce

"To suffering there is a limit; to fearing, none." Sir Francis Bacon, *Of Seditions and Troubles*

"A man's ethical behavior should be based effectually on sympathy, education, and social ties; no religious basis is necessary. Man would indeed be in a poor way if he had to be restrained by fear of punishment and hope of reward after death. If people are good only because they fear punishment, and hope for reward, then we are a sorry lot indeed." Albert Einstein

"Power does not corrupt. Fear corrupts, perhaps the fear of a loss of power." John Steinbeck

"We gain strength, and courage, and confidence by each experience in which we really stop to look fear in the face… we must do that which we think we cannot." Eleanor Roosevelt

"One ought to seek out virtue for its own sake, without being influenced by fear or hope, or by any external influence. Moreover, that in that does happiness consist." Diogenes Laertius

"The only thing we have to fear is fear itself—nameless, unreasoning, unjustified terror which paralyzes needed efforts to convert retreat into advance." President Franklin D. Roosevelt, first Inaugural address, Mar. 4, 1933

"Don't fear change, embrace it." Anthony J. D'Angelo, *The College Blue Book*

"Everyone believes very easily whatever they fear or desire." Jean de La Fontaine

"Government is not reason, it is not eloquence. It is force, a troublesome servant and a fearful master. Never for a moment should it be left to irresponsible action." George Washington

"Our doubts are traitors and make us lose the good we oft might win by fearing to attempt." William Shakespeare

"I expect nothing. I fear no one. I am free." Nikos Kazantzakis

"Let us never negotiate out of fear, but let us never fear to negotiate." President John F. Kennedy

"Don't fear failure so much that you refuse to try new things. The saddest summary of a life contains three descriptions: could have, might have, and should have." Louis E. Boone

"Our deepest fear is not that we are inadequate. Our deepest fear is that we are powerful beyond measure. It is our Light, not our Darkness, that most frightens us." Nelson Mandela

"Men fear thought as they fear nothing else on earth, more than ruin, more even than death. Thought is subversive, revolutionary, destructive and terrible. Thought is merciless to privilege, established institutions and comfortable habit. Thought looks into the pit of hell and is not afraid. Thought is great, free, the light of the world and the chief glory of man." Bertrand Russell

"Nothing in life is to be feared, it is only to be understood." Scientist Marie Curie

Fear

Fear is the biggest contributor to failure, and it can be a motivator for success. I use FEAR as an acronym for Find Excellence After Reflection. We are just as afraid of the things we don't know as the things in front of us. Most unknown fears turn out to not be as we had imagined.

Opportunists trade and capitalize upon fear. Several professions exist to help people get a grip on their fears. Those trying to sell will tell people what they want to hear or portray the product as being in their best interest. Some people and organizations turn others' fears into propaganda weapons for their own agendas (open or hidden). Some people and organizations take great delight in capitalizing upon the fears of others.

People are most afraid of what they don't understand. If a person scares easily, so will his neighbor. Both can know it, but they're more scared that each other will see it. After awhile, fearful people feel manipulated by others and don't know whom to trust. It is difficult to figure how people will behave when the chips are down. The definition of bravery is a person who is scared but still does what he-she has to.

Futurism, The Future

"The future ain't what it used to be." Yogi Berra

"The future is not a gift. It is an achievement." Robert F. Kennedy

"I never think of the future. It comes soon enough. The distinction between past, present, and future is only a stubbornly persistent illusion." Albert Einstein

"Tomorrow is another day." Margaret Mitchell, *Gone With the Wind*

"The future will one day be the present and will seem as unimportant as the present does now." W. Somerset Maugham

"You ain't heard nothing yet, folks." Al Jolson in *The Jazz Singer* (1927)

"You cannot fight the future. Time is on our side." William Gladstone (1866)

"I like the dreams of the future better that the history of the past." President Thomas Jefferson

"The fellow who can only see a week ahead is always the popular fellow, for he is looking with the crowd. But the one that can see years ahead, he has a telescope but he can't make anybody believe that he has it." Will Rogers

"The future, according to some scientists, will be exactly like the past, only far more expensive." John Sladek

"I have made good judgments in the past. I have made good judgments in the future. The future will be better tomorrow." Vice President Dan Quayle

"Everything flows and nothing abides; everything gives way and nothing stays fixed. The way up and the way down are one and the same. From out of all the many particulars comes oneness, and out of oneness come all the many particulars. A dry soul is wisest and best." Heraclitus

"So we beat on, boats against the current, borne back ceaselessly into the past." F. Scott Fitzgerald

"The only way to discover the limits of the possible is to go beyond them into the impossible. Any sufficiently advanced technology is indistinguishable from magic.

Arthur C. Clarke, "Technology and the Future":

"The best way to predict the future is to invent it." Alan Kay

"The trouble with our times is that the future is not what it used to be." Paul Valery

"The best thing about the future is that it comes one day at a time." President Abraham Lincoln

"There is always one moment in childhood when the door opens and lets the future in." Graham Greene

"Upper classes are a nation's past. The middle class is its future." Ayn Rand

"You can never plan the future by the past." Edmund Burke

"The empires of the future are the empires of the mind." Sir Winston Churchill

"The future belongs to those who prepare for it today." Malcolm X

"The illiterate of the future will not be the person who cannot read. It will be the person who does not know how to learn. Man has a limited biological capacity for change. When this capacity is overwhelmed, the capacity is in future shock." Alvin Toffler

"In a time of drastic change it is the learners who inherit the future. The learned usually find themselves equipped to live in a world that no longer exists." Eric Hoffer

"The only use of a knowledge of the past is to equip us for the present. The present contains all that there is. It is holy ground; for it is the past, and it is the future." Alfred North Whitehead

"The future is not something we enter. The future is something we create." Leonard I. Sweet

"I feel that you are justified in looking into the future with true assurance, because you have a mode of living in which we find the joy of life and the joy of work harmoniously combined. Added to this is the spirit of ambition which pervades your very being, and seems to make the

day's work like a happy child at play." Albert Einstein (referring to America)

"All human situations have their inconveniences. We feel those of the present but neither see nor feel those of the future; and hence we often make troublesome changes without amendment, and frequently for the worse." Benjamin Franklin

"It is because modern education is so seldom inspired by a great hope that it so seldom achieves great results. The wish to preserve the past rather that the hope of creating the future dominates the minds of those who control the teaching of the young." Bertrand Russell

"Many people think that if they were only in some other place, or had some other job, they would be happy. Well, that is doubtful. So get as much happiness out of what you are doing as you can and don't put off being happy until some future date." Dale Carnegie

"Look not mournfully into the Past. It comes not back again. Wisely improve the present. Go forth to meet the shadowy future, without fear." Henry Wadsworth Longfellow:

Futurism, The Future

Futurism is one of the most misunderstood concepts. It is not about gazing into crystal balls or reading tea leaves. It is not about vendor "solutions" that quickly apply band-aid surgery toward organizational symptoms. Futurism is not an academic exercise that borders on the esoteric or gets stuck in the realm of hypothesis.

Futurism is an all-encompassing concept that must look at all aspects of the organization, first at the Big Picture and then at the pieces as they relate to the whole. Futurism is a connected series of strategies, methodologies and actions which will poise any organization to weather the forces of change. It is an ongoing process of evaluation, planning, tactical actions and benchmarking accomplishments. Futurism is a continuum of thinking and reasoning skills, judicious activities, shared leadership and an accent upon ethics and quality.

I offer nine of my own definitions for the process of capturing and building a shared Vision for organizations to chart their next 10+ years. Each one gets progressively more sophisticated:

1. Futurism: what you will do and become, rather than what it is to be. What you can and are committed to accomplishing, rather than what mysteriously lies ahead.
2. Futurism: leaders and organizations taking personal responsibility and accountability for what happens. Abdicating to someone or something else does not constitute Futurism and, in fact, sets the organization backward.
3. Futurism: learns from and benefits from the past, a powerful teaching tool. Yesterdayism means giving new definitions to old ideas…giving new meanings to familiar premises. One must understand events, cycles, trends and subtle nuances because they will recur.
4. Futurism: seeing clearly your perspectives and those of others. Capitalizing upon change, rather than becoming a by-product of it. Recognizing what change is and what it can do for your organization.

5. Futurism: an ongoing quest toward wisdom. Commitments to learning, which creates knowledge, which inspire insights, which culminate in wisdom. It is more than just being taught or informed.

6. Futurism: ideas that inspire, manage and benchmark change. The ingredients may include such sophisticated business concepts as change management, crisis management and preparedness, streamlining operations, empowerment of people, marketplace development, organizational evolution and vision.

7. Futurism: developing thinking and reasoning skills, rather than dwelling just upon techniques and processes. The following concepts do not constitute Futurism by themselves: sales, technology, re-engineering, marketing, research, training, operations, administration. They are pieces of a much larger mosaic and should be seen as such. Futurism embodies thought processes that create and energize the mosaic.

8. Futurism: watching other people changing and capitalizing upon it. Understanding from where we came, in order to posture where we are headed. Creating organizational vision, which sets the stage for all activities, processes, accomplishments and goals. Efforts must be realistic, and all must be held accountable.

9. Futurism: the foresight to develop hindsight that creates insight into the future.

Genius

"Genius is 1% inspiration and 99% perspiration." Thomas A. Edison

"Genius is an infinite capacity for taking pains. The difference between genius and stupidity is that genius has its limits." Proverbs

"Mediocrity knows nothing higher than itself, but talent instantly recognizes genius." Sir Arthur Conan Doyle

"It takes people a long time to learn the difference between talent and genius, especially ambitious young men and women." Louisa May Alcott, novelist

"Genius does what it must, and talent does what it can." Owen Meredith, poet

"The true genius is a mind of large general powers, accidentally determined to some particular direction." Samuel Johnson, 18th Century British lexicographer

"When a true genius appears in the world, you may know him by this sign, that the duncesare all in confederacy against him." Jonathan Swift

"There's a fine line between genius and insanity. I have erased this line." Oscar Levant

"But the fact that some geniuses were laughed at does not imply that all who are laughed at are geniuses. They laughed at Columbus, they laughed at Fulton, they laughed at the Wright brothers. But they also laughed at Bozo the Clown." Carl Sagan

"Nobody in the game of football should be called a genius. A genius is somebody like Norman Einstein." Joe Theisman, football quarterback

"The public is wonderfully tolerant. It forgives everything except genius." Oscar Wilde

"Nothing in the world can take the place of persistence. Talent will not; nothing in the world is more common than unsuccessful men with talent. Genius will not; unrewarded genius is a proverb. Education will not; the world is full of educated derelicts. Persistence and determination alone are omnipotent." President Calvin Coolidge

"Since when was genius found respectable." Elizabeth Barrett Browning

"As it must not, so genius cannot be lawless; for it is even that constitutes its genius—the power of acting creatively under laws of its own origination." Samuel Taylor Coleridge

"Sometimes, indeed, there is such a discrepancy between the genius and his human qualities that one has to ask oneself whether a little less talent might not have been better." Carl Jung

"All the means of action—the shapeless masses—the materials—lie everywhere about us. What we need is the celestial fire to change the flint into the transparent crystal, bright and clear. That fire is genius." Henry Wadsworth Longfellow

"Genius without religion is only a lamp on the outer gate of a palace; it may serve to cast a gleam on those that are without while the inhabitant sits in darkness." Hannah More

"Common sense is instinct, and enough of it is genius." Henry Wheeler Shaw

"When a true genius appears in the world, you may know him by this sign, that the dunces are all in confederacy against him." Jonathan Swift

"Genius might well be defined as the ability to makes a platitude sound as though it were an original remark." L. B. Walton

"Let the minor genius go his light way and enjoy his life—the great nature cannot so live, he is never really in holiday mood, even though he often plucks flowers by the wayside and ties them into knots and garlands like little children and lays out on a sunny morning." W. B. Yeats

"Whereas in art nothing worth doing can be done without genius, in science even a very moderate capacity can contribute to a supreme achievement." Bertrand Russell

"Every gun that is made, every warship launched, every rocket fired signifies, in the final sense, a theft from those who hunger and are not fed, those who are cold and not clothed. This world is spending the sweat of its laborers, the genius of its scientists, the hopes of its children." President Dwight D. Eisenhower

"He who seldom speaks, and with one calm well-timed word can strike dumb the loquacious, is a genius or a hero." Johann Kaspar Lavater

"Talent, lying in the understanding, is often inherited; genius, being the action of reason or imagination, rarely or never." Samuel Taylor Coleridge

Genius
Ideas and concepts come to organizations in a variety of ways. Most have great thinkers inside and need to recognize the nuggets of gold that exist within. It is equally important to utilize consultants who really have insights and contribute original thinking, rather than those who are there to peddle off-the-shelf products and services.

Heroes, Mentors, Role Models
"We can't all be heroes because somebody has to sit on the curb and clap as they go by." Will Rogers (1879-1935)

"There are new words now that excuse everybody. Give me the good old days of heroes and villains. The people you can bravo or hiss. There was a truth to them that all the slick credulity of today cannot touch." Bette Davis, actress

"Nurture your mind with great thoughts. To believe in the heroic makes heroes." Benjamin Disraeli (1804-1881)

"Show me a hero, and I will write you a tragedy." F. Scott Fitzgerald

Heroes, Mentors, Role Models

Top executives were not taught to be leaders. They had few role models in equivalent positions. Thus, they get bad advice from the wrong consultants. In the quest to be a top business leader, one quickly reviews how poorly corporate executives were portrayed to the mass culture.

This progression of statements, validations and commitments is the premise of this book:

- Examine where you came from.
- Retread old knowledge.
- Apply teachings to today.
- Honestly evaluate your path to progress thus far.
- Affix responsibilities, goals and benchmarks to all intended progress.
- Find creative new ways to approach and conduct business.
- Proceed with zeal, commitment, creative instinct and boundless energy.
- Achieve and reflect upon successes.
- Learn three times more from failure than success.
- Plan to achieve and succeed in the future.
- Never stop researching, planning, executing and evaluating.
- Benchmarks of one phase, project or series of events drive the research and planning for the next phase.
- Futurism is not an esoteric concept. It is about planning to weather storms of the future and is directly applicable to daily success.

History

"History repeats itself." Proverb

"The Beat Goes On." Sonny Bono (1967)

"History will be kind to me, for I intend to write it." Sir Winston Churchill

"More than any other time in history, mankind faces a crossroads. One path leads to despair and utter hopelessness. The other, to total extinction. Let us pray we have the wisdom to choose correctly." Woody Allen

"It is not the neutrals or lukewarm people who make history." Adolph Hitler (1933)

"All things from eternity are of like forms and come round in a circle." Marcus Aurelius, Roman emperor (175 A.D.)

"History is philosophy teaching by examples." Dionsius of Halicarnassus, historian (8 B.C.)

"Man is a history-making creature who can neither repeat his past nor leave it behind." W.H. Auden

"Nothing has really happened until it has been recorded." Virginia Woolf

"History is nothing more than a tableau of crimes and misfortunes." Voltaire

"If Beethoven had been killed in a plane crash at the age of 22, it would have changed the history of music and of aviation." Tom Stoppard

"Whenever we read the obscene stories, the voluptuous debaucheries, the cruel and torturous executions, the unrelenting vindictiveness, with which more than half the bible is filled, it would seem more consistent that we called it the word of a demon than the Word of God. It is a history of wickedness that has served to corrupt and brutalize mankind." Thomas Paine

"Happy are the people whose annals are blank in history books." Thomas Carlyle

"Human history becomes more a race between education and catastrophe." H. G. Wells

"From their experience or from the recorded experience of others (history), men learn only what their passions and their metaphysical prejudices allow them to learn." Aldous Huxley

"A page of history is worth a pound of logic." Justice Oliver Wendell Holmes

"There is a history in all men's lives." William Shakespeare

"A true history of human events would show that a far larger proportion of our acts as the results of sudden impulses and accident, than of the reason of which we so much boast." Albert Cooper

"If, after all, men cannot always make history have meaning, they can always act so that their own lives have one." Albert Camus

"In studying the history of the human mind one is impressed again and again by the fact that the growth of the mind is the widening of the range of consciousness, and that each step forward has been a most painful and laborious achievement. One could almost say that nothing is more hateful to man than to give up even a particle of his unconsciousness. Ask those who have tried to introduce a new idea!" Carl Jung

"The history of human opinion is scarcely more than the history of human errors." Voltaire

"Books are the carriers of civilization. Without books, history is silent, literature dumb, science crippled, thought and speculation at a standstill. I think that there is nothing more opposed to poetry, to philosophy, to life itself than this incessant business." Henry David Thoreau

"History teaches us that men and nations behave wisely once they have exhausted all other alternatives." Abba Eban

"Hegel was right when he said that we learn from history that man can never learn anything from history." George Bernard Shaw (1856-1950)

"History is the version of past events that people have decided to agree upon." Napoleon Bonaparte (1769-1821)

History

From history, I've learned that there's nothing more permanent than change. For everything that changes, many things remain the same. The art of living well is to meld the changeable dynamics with the constants and the traditions. The periodic reshuffling of priorities, opportunities and potential outcomes represents business planning at its best.

One learns three times more from failure than from success. By studying and reflecting upon the events of the past and the shortcomings of others, then we create strategies for meeting the challenges of the future.

Human Nature

"Men and melons are hard to know." Benjamin Franklin

"The nature of men is always the same. It is their habits that separate them." Confucius

"Man is the only animal that blushes. If you pick up a starving dog and make him prosperous, he will not bite you. This is the principal difference between dog and man." Mark Twain

"We are usually the best men when in the worst health. It is almost impossible to smile on the outside without feeling better on the inside. It is a pleasure to give advice, humiliating to need it, normal to ignore it. Too many people confine their exercise to jumping to conclusions, running up bills, stretching the truth, bending over backward, lying down on the job, sidestepping responsibility and pushing their luck." Proverbs

"Most human beings have an almost infinite capacity for taking things for granted." Aldous Huxley

"Scenery is fine, but human nature is finer." John Keats (1818)

"A rarer spirit never did steer humanity. Give us faults to make us men." William Shakespeare

"Moral indignation is mostly 2% moral, 48% indignation and 50% envy." Vittorio De Sica

"Only the brave know how to forgive; it is the most refined and generous pitch of virtue human nature can arrive at." Sterne

"The sufferers parade their miseries, tear lint from their bruises, reveal their indictable crimes, that you may pity them. They like sickness, because physical pain will extort some show of interest from bystanders, as we have seen children, who, finding themselves of no account when grown people come in, will cough till they choke, to draw attention." Ralph Waldo Emerson

"Nature is trying very hard to make us succeed, but nature does not depend on us. We are not the only experiment." R. Buckminster Fuller

"Human nature is not of itself vicious." Thomas Paine

"It is often easier to fight for one's principles that to live up to them." Adlai E. Stevenson

Human Nature

It is customary to follow your gut and proceed along. Businesses cannot steer themselves just by coasting. Planning and strategy move that human nature into actionable results.

Human beings as we are, none of us do everything perfectly on the front end. There always must exist a learning curve. Research shows that we learn three times more from failures than from successes. The mark of a quality organization is how it corrects mistakes and prevents them from recurring.

Leadership

"A leader is a dealer in hope." Napoleon Bonaparte

"A president's hardest task is not to do what is right but to know what is right." President Lyndon B. Johnson (1965)

"When you're leading, don't talk." Thomas E. Dewey

"A leader who doesn't hesitate before he sends his nation into battle is not fit to be a leader." Golda Meir

"Leadership and learning are indispensable to each other." President John F. Kennedy, speech prepared for delivery in Dallas the day of his assassination, Nov. 22, 1963

"An empowered organization is one in which individuals have the knowledge, skill, desire, and opportunity to personally succeed in a way that leads to collective organizational success." Stephen R. Covey

"Men make history, and not the other way around. In periods where there is no leadership, society stands still. Progress occurs when courageous, skillful leaders seize the opportunity to change things for the better." President Harry S Truman

"Leadership should be born out of the understanding of the needs of those who would be affected by it." Marian Anderson

"Leadership has a harder job to do than just choose sides. It must bring sides together." Reverend Jesse Jackson

"I start with the premise that the function of leadership is to produce more leaders, not more followers." Ralph Nader

"Whether a man is burdened by power or enjoys power; whether he is trapped by responsibility or made free by it; whether he is moved by other people and outer forces or moves them—this is of the essence of leadership." Theodore H. White, The Making of the President, 1960

"You do not lead by hitting people over the head. That's assault, not leadership." President Dwight D. Eisenhower

"Good leadership consists in showing average people how to do the work of superior people." John D. Rockefeller

"There are no office hours for leaders." Cardinal James Gibbons

Leadership

The biggest problem with business stems from the fact that management and company leadership come from one small piece of the organizational pie. Filling all management slots with financial people, for example, serves to limit the organizational strategy and focus. They all hire like-minded people and frame every business decision from their micro perspective.

The ideal executive has strong leadership skills first. He or she develops organizational vision and sets strategies. Leaders should reflect a diversity of niche focus, guaranteeing that an overall balance is achieved. Those with strategies, process upholding and detail focus are all reflected. The best management team looks at the macro, rather than just the niche micro.

None of us was born with sophisticated, finely tuned senses and highly enlightened viewpoints for life. We muddle through, try our best and get hit in the gut several times. Thus, we learn, amass knowledge and turn most experiences into an enlightened life-like perspective that moves us "to the next tier." Such a perspective is what makes seasoned executives valuable in the business marketplace.

The most effective leaders accept that change is 90% positive and find reasons and rationale to embrace change. They see how change relates to organizations, realizing that the process of mastering change and turning transactions into a series of win-win propositions constitutes the real meaning of life.

Leadership is learned and synthesized daily. Knowledge is usually amassed through unexpected sources. Any person's commitment toward leadership development and continuing education must include honest examination of his-her life skills. Training, reading and pro-activity are prescribed.

Lies

"Little white lies are like little white rabbits. They multiply big." Charlie Chan

"He who multiplies riches multiplies cares." Benjamin Franklin

"White lies always introduce others of a darker complexion." William S. Paley, founder of CBS

"Oh what a tangled web we weave, when first we practice to deceive." Sir Walter Scott

"There is no one, says another, whom fortune does not visit once in his life; but when she does not find him ready to receive her, she walks in at the door, and flies out at the window." Montesquieu

"Man has three friends on whose company he relies. First, wealth which goes with him only while good fortune lasts. Second, his relatives; they go only as far as the grave, leave him there. The third friend, his good deeds, go with him beyond the grave." The Talmud

"When of a gossiping circle it was asked, 'What are they doing?' The answer was, 'Swapping lies'." Richard Brinsley Sheridan

"The man who is anybody and who does anything is surely going to be criticized, vilified, and misunderstood. That is part of the penalty for greatness, and every great man understands it; and understands, too, that it is no proof of greatness. The final proof of greatness lies in being able to endure continuously without resentment." Elbert Hubbard

"Lies are usually caused by undue fear of men." Hasidic saying

"Sin has many tools, but a lie is the handle which fits them all." Oliver Wendell Holmes, Jr.

"He who has not a good memory should never take upon himself the trade of lying." Michel De Montaigne

"Falsehood has an infinity of combinations. Truth has only one mode of being." Jean-Jacques Rousseau

"A liar begins with making falsehood appear like truth, and ends with making truth itself appear like falsehood." William Shenstone

"It is only necessary to make war with five things; with the maladies of the body, the ignorance of the mind, with the passions of the body, with the seditions of the city and the discords of families." Pythagoras

"I would make a proposition to my Republican friends that if they will stop telling lies about the Democrats, we will stop telling the truth about them." Adlai Stevenson

"There are three kinds of lies. They are lies, damned lies and statistics." Benjamin Disraeli

Lies

We live in a cliche oriented society. Without thinking, people say canned comments, often inventing contexts in which to frame them. Relationships of all kinds are generalized to death. Creativity often gives way to the familiar and the trite. It is amazing how often business discussions are derailed by cliches. Grasping for descriptive words, executives generalize with platitudes. Most commonly, without conscious intent, cliches are utilized as control mechanisms to shut down new, innovative discussion.

Once you rethink and reflect upon business lies heard, you will begin fashioning retorts to negative comments heard. It is when we recognize generalities as self-defeating and positively reframe, then pro-active change and continuous quality improvement will naturally occur.

Management

"Management is nothing more than motivating other people." Lee Iacocca

"In the modern world of business, it is useless to be a creative original thinker unless you can also sell what you create. Management cannot be expected to recognize a good idea unless it is presented to them by a good salesman." David M. Ogilvy

"A place for everything and everything in its place." Isabella Mary Beeton, 1861

"So much of what we call management consists in making it difficult for people to work. Management means, in the last analysis, the substitution of thought for brawn and muscle, of knowledge for folklore and superstition, and of cooperation for force. Management is doing things right; leadership is doing the right things. Management by objectives works if you first think through your objectives. Ninety percent of the time you haven't." Peter F. Drucker

"Good plans shape good decisions. That's why good planning helps to make elusive dreams come true." Lester R. Bittel, The Nine Master Keys of Management

"Good management is the art of making problems so interesting and their solutions so constructive that everyone wants to get to work and deal with them." Paul Hawken

"Nothing more completely baffles one who is full of trick and duplicity than straightforward and simple integrity in another. A knave would rather quarrel with a brother knave than with a fool, but he would rather avoid a quarrel with one honest man than with both." C. C. Colton

Management

Research tells us that 92% of all problems in organizations stem from poor management decisions. Having studied, worked with and mentored many managers over the years, I've concluded that few had sufficient management training up to that point. The system simply does not train executives, nor managers, nor leaders. Most corporate leaders are a management generation or two behind. Those who matured in the era of the Human Relations style of management were still clinging to value systems of Hard Nosed. They were not just "old school." They went to the school that was torn down to build the old school. That's Enron and their ilk in a nutshell. Similarly, baby boomer executives who were educated in the Management by Objectives era were still recalling value systems of their parents' generation before it. Baby boomers with a Depression-era frugality and value of tight resources are more likely to take a bean counter-focused approach to business. That's my concern that financial-only focus without regard to other corporate dynamics bespeaks of hostile takeovers, ill-advised rollups and corporate raider activities for business.

Mistakes

"Two wrongs do not make a right." Proverb

"Mistakes, we all make them. That's why we have erasers." James Garner, as Bret Maverick

"To err is human, to forgive, divine." Alexander Pope

"Experience is simply the name we give our mistakes. Nowadays most people die of a sort of creeping common sense, and discover when it is too late that the only things one never regrets are one's mistakes." Oscar Wilde

"A life spent making mistakes is not only more honorable, but more useful than a life spent doing nothing." George Bernard Shaw (1856-1950)

"If I had to live my life again, I'd make the same mistakes, only sooner." Tallulah Bankhead

"We're all capable of mistakes, but I do not care to enlighten you on the mistakes we may or may not have made." Vice President Dan Quayle

"When I woke up this morning my girlfriend asked me, 'Did you sleep good?' I said 'No, I made a few mistakes.'" Stephen Wright

"No man ever became great or good except through many and great mistakes." W. E. Gladstone

"Show us a man who never makes a mistake and we will show you a man who never makes anything. The only men who are past the danger of making mistakes are the men who sleep at Greenwood." H. L. Wayland

"The higher up you go, the more mistakes you're allowed. Right at the top, if you make enough of them, it's considered to be your style." Fred Astaire

"You will make all kinds of mistakes; but as long as you are generous and true, and also fierce, you cannot hurt the world or even seriously distress her." Sir Winston Churchill

"The only way to even approach doing something perfectly is through experience, and experience is the name everyone gives to their mistakes." Oscar Wilde

"The Athenians, alarmed at the internal decay of their Republic, asked Demosthenes what to do. His reply: "Do not do what you are doing now." Joseph Ray

"Do not look where you fell, but where you slipped." African Proverb

"When you make a mistake, admit it. If you don't, you only make matters worse." Ward Cleaver, on TV's "Leave It To Beaver"

"Mistakes are the portals of discovery." James Joyce

"Every great mistake has a halfway moment, a split second when it can be recalled and perhaps remedied." Pearl S. Buck, novelist

Negotiations, Compromise
"It takes two to tango." Proverb

"Never hold discussions with the monkey when the organ grinder is in the room." Winston Churchill

"Force without wisdom falls of its own weight." Horace

"Pure reason avoids extremes, and requires one to be wise in moderation." Moliere

"If you limit your choices only to what seems possible or reasonable, you disconnect yourself from what you truly want, and all that is left is a compromise." Robert Fritz

"Come, let us reason together." President Lyndon B. Johnson

"Discourage litigation. Persuade your neighbors to compromise whenever you can. As a peacemaker the lawyer has superior opportunity of being a good man. There will still be business enough." President Abraham Lincoln

Negotiations, Compromise

Research tells us that all of us agree on 95% of things. It's that 5% where we disagree that gets us into unnecessary confrontations. Too many organizations choose the wrong causes to fight, thus defeating the shared goals, opportunities and marketplace advantages they may have had. Business needs to pursue negotiations before resorting to litigation. Similarly, drawing one's line in the sand tends to negate future opportunities for negotiations and compromise.

Planning

"The beginning is the most important part of the work." Plato

"A good plan violently executed now is better than a perfect plan next week." General George S. Patton

"If I had known my son was going to be president of Bolivia, I would have taught him to read and write." Enrique Penaranda's mother

"You've got to be very careful if you don't know where you are going, because you might not get there." Baseball great Yogi Berra

"I always wanted to be somebody, but I should have been more specific." Lily Tomlin

"When we are planning for posterity, we ought to remember that virtue is not hereditary." Thomas Paine (1737-1809)

"Good plans shape good decisions. That's why good planning helps to make elusive dreams come true." Lester R. Bittel, "The Nine Master Keys of Management"

"If anything is certain, it is that change is certain. The world we are planning for today will not exist in this form tomorrow." Philip Crosby, "Reflections on Quality"

"What business strategy is all about; what distinguishes it from all other kinds of business planning is, in a word, competitive advantage. Without competitors there would be no need for strategy, for the sole purpose of strategic planning is to enable the company to gain, as effectively as possible, a sustainable edge over its competitors." Keniche Ohnae

"Men often oppose a thing merely because they have had no agency in planning it, or because it may have been planned by those whom they dislike." Alexander Hamilton

"In preparing for battle I have always found that plans are useless, but planning is indispensable." President Dwight D. Eisenhower

Planning

Getting the funds that you need from tight fisted management is an ongoing process. Cash outlays are justifiable either by dollars they bring in or dollars they stand to save for the organization. Cash outlays are always risks. Justify your risks in proportion to riskier ones they have previously funded. Validate your worth to the overall company operation. Under the rules of supply chain dynamics, one must study your supplier relationships, formalize a plan of outsourcing and develop collaborations.

Power

"Power corrupts, but lack of power corrupts absolutely." Adlai Stevenson

"Power corrupts the few, while weakness corrupts the many. Absolute faith corrupts as absolutely as absolute power." Eric Hoffer (1902-1983)

"Whenever there's a large group of powers, they always follow the one with the biggest bomb." John F. Kennedy

"Power does not corrupt. Fear corrupts, perhaps the fear of a loss of power." John Steinbeck

"Nearly all men can stand adversity, but if you want to test a man's character, give him power." President Abraham Lincoln

"Power does not corrupt men. But fools, if they get into a position of power, corrupt it. The power of accurate observation is commonly called cynicism by those who have not got it." George Bernard Shaw (1856-1950)

"Our scientific power has outrun our spiritual power. We have guided missiles and misguided men." Martin Luther King Jr. (1929-1968)

"If computers get too powerful, we can organize them into a committee. That will do them in." Bradley's Bromide

"If mankind minus one were of one opinion, then mankind is no more justified in silencing the one than the one, if he had the power, would be justified in silencing mankind." John Stuart Mill

"There is danger from all men. The only maxim of a free government ought to be to trust no man living with power to endanger the public liberty." John Adams (1735-1826)

Respect

"Respect a man, and he will do the more." James Howell

"If we paid more respect to the living than to the dead, then the world would be a better place." Sigmund Freud

"That you may retain your self-respect, it is better to displease the people by doing what you know is right, than to temporarily please them by doing what you know is wrong." William J. H. Boetcker

"If you want to be respected, you must respect yourself." Spanish proverb

"What you want, baby, I got. What you need, you know I got it. All I askin' is for a little respect. Find out what it means to me." Aretha Franklin

"We confide in our strength, without boasting of it; we respect that of others, without fearing it." President Thomas Jefferson (1743-1826)

"He that respects himself is safe from others. He wears a coat of mail that none can pierce." Henry Wadsworth Longfellow (1807-1882)

"In real life, unlike in Shakespeare, the sweetness of the rose depends upon the name it bears. Things are not only what they are. They are, in very important respects, what they seem to be." Vice President Hubert H. Humphrey (1911-1978)

"I respect faith, but doubt is what gets you an education." Wilson Mizner (1876-1933)

"The English have no respect for their language, and will not teach their children to speak it. The more things a man is ashamed of, the more respectable he is." George Bernard Shaw

"Some people have so much respect for their superiors they have none left for themselves." Peter McArthur

"To get back my youth I would do anything in the world, except take exercise, get up early, or be respectable." Oscar Wilde (1854-1900), *The Picture of Dorian Gray*

"I can win an argument on any topic, against any opponent. People know this, and steer clear of me at parties. Often, as a sign of their great respect, they don't even invite me." Dave Barry

"One should as a rule respect public opinion in so far as is necessary to avoid starvation and to keep out of prison. Anything that goes beyond this is voluntary submission to an unnecessary tyranny, and is likely to interfere with happiness in all kinds of ways." Bertrand Russell

"Self-respect is the fruit of discipline; the sense of dignity grows with the ability to say no to oneself." Rabbi Abraham Heschel

"Be peaceful, be courteous, obey the law, respect everyone; but if someone puts his hand on you, send him to the cemetery." Malcolm X (1925-1965)

"Never esteem anything as of advantage to you that will make you break your word or lose your self-respect." Marcus Aurelius Antoninus (121 AD-180 AD)

"I am a Conservative to preserve all that is good in our constitution, a Radical to remove all that is bad. I seek to preserve property and to respect order. I equally decry the appeal to the passions of the many of the prejudices of the few." Benjamin Disraeli (1804-1881)

"I owe my success to having listened respectfully to the very best advice, and then going away and doing the exact opposite." G. K. Chesterton (1874-1936)

"Self-respect is the cornerstone of all virtue." John Herschel (1792-1871)

Respect

The basics of good business are rooted in respect, a valuable commodity that caring professionals must nurture and show toward their colleagues, customers, industry, marketplace and stakeholders.

Responsibility and Accountability

"The buck stops here." President Harry S. Truman

"A bad workman always blames his tools." Proverb

"Each man the architect of his own fate." Appius Caecus, Roman statesman (4th Century, B.C.)

"You're either part of the solution or part of the problem." Eldridge Cleaver

"When your neighbor's wall is on fire, it becomes your business." Horace

"In dreams begins responsibility." W.B. Yeats, Irish poet

"There is no accountability in the public school system, except for coaches. You know what happens to a losing coach. You fire him. A losing teacher can go on losing for 30 years and then go to glory." H. Ross Perot

"We are at the very beginning of time for the human race. It is not unreasonable that we grapple with problems. But there are tens of thousands of years in the future. Our responsibility is to do what we can, learn what we can, improve the solutions, and pass them on." Richard Feynman

"The price of greatness is responsibility." Sir Winston Churchill

"You cannot escape the responsibility of tomorrow by evading it today." Abraham Lincoln

"Character—the willingness to accept responsibility for one's own life—is the source from which self respect springs." Joan Didion, "Slouching Towards Bethlehem"

"I think of a hero as someone who understands the degree of responsibility that comes with his freedom." Bob Dylan

"Liberty means responsibility. That is why most men dread it." George Bernard Shaw

"The fault, dear Brutus, is not in our stars but in ourselves. No one familiar with the history of this country can deny that Congressional committees are useful. It is necessary to investigate before legislating. But the line between investigating and persecuting is a fine one. And the junior senator from Wisconsin has stepped over it repeatedly. We must remember that accusation is not proof and that conviction depends on evidence and due process of law.

We will not walk in fear of one another. We will not be driven by fear into an age of unreason. If we dig deeply in our history and doctrines, we remember we are not descended from fearful men…not from men who feared to write, to speak, to associate with and to defend causes which were for the moment unpopular. This is no time for men who oppose Senator McCarthy's methods to keep silent.

We can deny our heritage and our history. But we cannot evade responsibility for the result of it. There is no way for a citizen of a republic to abdicate these responsibilities. We proclaim ourselves—as indeed we are—the defenders of freedom, what's left of it. But we cannot defend freedom abroad by deserting it at home. The actions of the junior senator from Wisconsin have caused alarm and dismay amongst our allies abroad…and given considerable comfort to our enemies.

And whose fault is that? Not really his. He didn't create this situation of fear. He merely exploited it and rather successfully. Cassius was right. The fault, dear Brutus, is not in our stars but in ourselves." Edward R. Murrow, 1953, analyzing the witch hunts of Senator Joseph McCarthy

Self Esteem, Confidence and Reliance

"If I am not for myself, who is for me?" Hillel

"To love oneself is the beginning of a life-long romance." Oscar Wilde

"To thine own self be true. And it must follow, thou canst not then be false to any man. Our remedies oft in ourselves do lie. We know what we are, but know not what we may be." William Shakespeare

"To know oneself is not necessarily to improve oneself. To enter one's own self, it is necessary to go armed to the teeth." Paul Valery

"Every man is his own worst enemy. God helps them that help themselves. He helps little that helps not himself. He travels fastest who travels alone." Proverbs

"When people do not respect us, we are sharply offended. Yet deep down in his heart, no man much respects himself." Mark Twain

"If you want a thing done well, do it yourself." Napoleon Bonaparte

"If the hill will not come to Mahomet, Mahomet will come to the hill." Sir Francis Bacon

"I am the master of my fate. I am the captain of my soul." W.F. Henley

Strength

"Speak softly and carry a big stick. You will go far." African proverb

"A nation does not have to be cruel to be tough. Physical strength can never permanently withstand the impact of spiritual force." President Franklin D. Roosevelt

"It is excellent to have a giant's strength, but it is tyrannous to use it like a giant." William Shakespeare

"If you can't stand the heat, get out of the kitchen." President Harry S. Truman

"Know how sublime a thing it is to suffer and be strong." Henry Wadsworth Longfellow

"My strength is the strength of ten, because my heart is pure." Alfred, Lord Tennyson

"This is the Law of the Yukon, that only the strong shall thrive, that surely the weak shall perish, and only the fit survive." Robert William Service, Canadian poet

"Our scientific power has outrun our spiritual power. We have guided missiles and misguided men." Martin Luther King Jr. (1929-1968)

"Rudeness is the weak man's imitation of strength." Eric Hoffer (1902-1983)

"We all have strength enough to endure the misfortunes of others." Francois de La Rochefoucauld (1613-1680)

"Let me tell you the secret that has led me to my goal. My strength lies solely in my tenacity." Louis Pasteur, scientist

"Life only demands from you the strength you possess. Only one feat is possible... not to have run away." United Nations Secretary General Dag Hammarskjold

"Difficulties strengthen the mind, as labor does the body." Seneca (5 BC-65 AD)

"You gain strength, courage and confidence by every experience in which you really stop to look fear in the face. You are able to say, 'I have lived through this horror. I can take the next thing that comes along.' You must do the thing you think you cannot do." Eleanor Roosevelt

"Look well into thyself. There is a source of strength which will always spring up if thou wilt always look there." Marcus Aurelius Antoninus (121 AD-180 AD)

"Dwell not upon thy weariness, thy strength shall be according to the measure of thy desire." Arab proverb

"Be a craftsman in speech that thou mayest be strong, for the strength of one is the tongue, and speech is mightier than all fighting." Maxims of Ptahhotep, 3400 B.C.

"Be entirely tolerant or not at all. Follow the good path or the evil one. To stand at the crossroads requires more strength than you possess." Heinrich Heine (1797-1856)

Strength

Companies say outlandish things in order to garner interest and support. They claim they are bigger and stronger, and prospective customers are to assume that backup systems are equally strong. When a company says they are the "Fastest Growing," beware! These circumstances are likely in place, each of which will defeat their claims:

1. Systems are not in place to handle rapid growth, perhaps never were.
2. Their only interest is in booking more new business, rather than taking care of what they've already got.
3. Management is relying upon financial people as the primary source of advice, while ignoring the rest of the picture (90%).
4. Team empowerment suffers. Morale is low or uneven. Commitment from workers drops because no corporate culture was created or sustained.
5. Customer service suffers during fast-growth periods. They have to back-pedal and recover customer confidence by doing surveys. Even with results of deteriorating customer service, growth-track companies pay lip service to really fixing their own problems.
6. People do not have the same Vision as the company founder, who has likely not taken enough time to fully develop a Vision and obtain buy-in from others.
7. The company founder remains arrogant and complacent, losing touch with marketplace realities and changing conditions.

Stress, Worry, Pain

"Time heals old pain, while it creates new ones." Hebrew proverb

"What deep wounds ever healed without a scar?" Lord Byron, poet

"If suffer we must, let's suffer on the heights." Victor Hugo

"Every little yielding to anxiety is a step away from the natural heart of man." Japanese proverb

"A man who fears suffering is already suffering from what he fears." Michel de Montaigne, 16th Century French essayist

"A trouble shared is a trouble halved. Don't meet troubles halfway. An hour of pain is as long as a day of pleasure. He that lives long suffers much. Take things as they come." Proverbs

"Nothing begins and nothing ends that is not paid with moan. For we are born in others' pain and perish in our own." Francis Thompson, poet and critic

"Over the years, your bodies become walking autobiographies, telling friends and strangers alike of the minor and major stresses of your lives." Marilyn Ferguson

"At the worst, a house un-kept cannot be so distressing as a life unlived." Dame Rose Macaulay

"If you are distressed by anything external, the pain is not due to the thing itself, but to your estimate of it; and this you have the power to revoke at any moment." Marcus Aurelius Antoninus (121 AD-180 AD)

"Indolence is a delightful but distressing state; we must be doing something to be happy." Mahatma Gandhi (1869-1948)

"The superior man is satisfied and composed. The mean man is always full of distress." Confucius (551 BC-479 BC)

"Like all weak men, he laid an exaggerated stress on not changing one's mind." W. Somerset Maugham (1874-1965), *Of Human Bondage*

"Small minds are much distressed by little things. Great minds see them all but are not upset by them." Francois de La Rochefoucauld (1613-1680)

"Music is a discipline, and a mistress of order and good manners, she makes the people milder and gentler, more moral and more reasonable." Martin Luther (1483-1546)

"What a distressing contrast there is between the radiant intelligence of the child and the feeble mentality of the average adult." Sigmund Freud (1856-1939)

"When anyone asks me how I can best describe my experience in nearly forty years at sea, I merely say, uneventful. Of course there have been winter gales, and storms and fog and the like. But in all my experience, I have never been in any accident... or any sort worth speaking about. I have seen but one vessel in distress in all my years at sea. I never saw a wreck and never have been wrecked nor was I ever in any predicament that threatened to end in disaster of any sort." E. J. Smith, 1907, Captain, RMS Titanic

Substance, Depth

"Those who go beneath the surface do so at their own peril." Oscar Wilde

"You can't do anything about the length of your life, but you can do something about its width and depth." Evan Esar (1899-1995)

"The most wonderful of all things in life, I believe, is the discovery of another human being with whom one's relationship has a glowing depth, beauty, and joy as the years increase. This inner progressiveness of love between two human beings is a most marvelous thing, it cannot be found by looking for it or by passionately wishing for it." Sir Hugh Walpoe

"The difference between a rut and a grave is the depth." Gerald Burrill

"Do not hover always on the surface of things, nor take up suddenly, with mere appearances; but penetrate into the depth of matters, as far as your time and circumstances allow, especially in those things which relate to your profession." Isaac Watts

"A little philosophy inclineth man's mind to atheism. But depth in philosophy bringeth men's minds about to religion." Sir Francis Bacon (1561-1626)

"Never offend people with style when you can offend them with substance." Sam Brown, Washington Post, 1977

"The meeting of two personalities is like the contact of two chemical substances: if there is any reaction, both are transformed." Carl Jung (1875-1961)

"Beware lest you lose the substance by grasping at the shadow." Aesop (620 BC-560 BC)

"The very essence of literature is the war between emotion and intellect, between life and death. When literature becomes too intellectual—when it begins to ignore the passions, the motions —it becomes sterile, silly, and actually without substance." Isaac Bashevis Singer (1904-1991), New York Times Magazine, Nov. 26, 1978

"I prepared excitedly for my departure, as if this journey had a mysterious significance. I had decided to change my mode of life. Until now, you have only seen the shadow and been well content with it. Now, I am going to lead you into the substance." Nikos Kazantzakis, Zorba the Greek

"Half the controversies in the world are verbal ones; and could they be brought to a plain issue they would be brought to a prompt termination. Parties engaged in them would then perceive either that in substance they agreed together, or that their difference was one of first principles. We need not dispute, we need not prove, we need but define. At all events, let us, if we can, do this first of all and then see who are left for us to dispute; what is left for us to prove." Cardinal John Newman

Success

"There are no gains without pains." Adlai Stevenson

"The desire for fame tempts even noble minds." St. Augustine

"Fame is like a river, that beareth up things light and swollen, and drowns things weighty and solid." Sir Francis Bacon

"Fame is a bee. It has a song. It has a sting. Ah, too, it has a wing." Emily Dickinson (1763)

"Oh how quickly the world's glory passes away." Thomas A. Kempis

"Be nice to people on your way up because you'll need them on your way down." Wilson Mizner

"Success has killed more men than bullets." Texas Guinan

"Nothing succeeds like success." Proverb

"The penalty of success is to be bored by people who used to snub you." Nancy Astor (1956)

"Success is counted sweetest by those who never succeed." Emily Dickinson

"Success is relative, what we can make of the mess we have made of things." T.S. Eliot, poet

"There are two reasons why I am successful in show business, and I am standing on both of them." Betty Grable, actress

"Victory has a thousand fathers, but defeat is an orphan." President John F. Kennedy

"There are two tragedies in life. One is to lose your heart's desire. The other is to gain it." George Bernard Shaw

"There is always room at the top." Daniel Webster

"Fame can never make us lie down contentedly on a deathbed." Alexander Pope (1713)

"Success is like a liberation or the first phase of a love affair." Jeanne Moreau, actress

"The secret of my success is that no woman has ever been jealous of me." Elsa Maxwell, actress

"What rage for fame attends both great and small. Better be damned than mentioned at all." John Wolcot

"The only place where success comes before work is a dictionary." Vidal Sassoon

"The only way to succeed is to make people hate you. That way, they remember you." Joseph von Sternberg, film director

"If you think you can win, you can win. Faith is necessary to victory." William Hazlitt

Success

Here are my suggested ingredients of success:

1. Finding knowledge in new and unique ways. Strive to learn something new everyday. Learn from examples (good and bad). Education leads to knowledge, which leads to wisdom. Develop continuing education, professional development and life philosophies.
2. Doing work that you're proud of. No matter what the job title, task or career orientation, work can be done professionally. If it doesn't mean something to you, it will not contribute to the marketplace or society at large. When you value it, they will begin to reciprocate.
3. Developing a philosophy, individually and organizationally. Analyze where you've been. Evaluate strengths and weaknesses. Analyze and strategize opportunities. Establish bigger goals this year than you had last ye, with means and reasons for reaching them.
4. Handling mistakes and crises. Everyone makes mistakes. The mark of Quality is how you handle them. Learn the art of diagnosing problems, taking input and effecting workable solutions. Planning for crises will divert them from occurring, 85% of the time. Waiting until the last moment to apply "band-aid surgery" is self-defeating and costly.
5. Dealing with fear. Everyone has fear. Those who deny it the most are detrimental to your success and that of your organization. Understand fears, and set plans to work with them. Remove barriers to success. Turn

internal fears into motivating forces. Fears will never go away but can facilitate the path toward success.

6. Learning to read others' screens. Put yourself in other people's shoes, and communicate in their sphere to achieve desired actions-results. Learn what motivates others and colors their take on life…in order to work well with diverse peoples and organizational cultures.

7. Self-fulfillment, purpose and commitment. Career-Life Vision, Body of Work. Develop a strategic plan, core values and action steps to accomplish your dreams. While others may roam aimlessly through life, you will achieve, sustain and share success. Commit to and thrive upon change.

Survival

"If you care to drive, drive with care. Leave blood at the Red Cross, not on the highway. On the road, it's not who's right that counts, it's who's left." Broderick Crawford (sign-offs to the 1950s "Highway Patrol" TV series)

"It isn't important to come out on top. What matters is to be the one who comes out alive." Bertolt Brecht, German dramatist

"People are not exterminable, like flies and bed-bugs. There will always be some that survive in cracks and crevices." Robert Frost, poet

"One can survive everything nowadays, except death." Oscar Wilde, dramatist

"When you get to the end of your rope, tie a knot and hang on." Franklin D. Roosevelt

Tact

"Leave well alone. Let sleeping dogs lie." Proverbs

"Tact consists in knowing how far we may go too far." Jean Cocteau, poet and artist

"One shouldn't talk of halters in the hanged man's house." Miguel de Cervantes, novelist

"Although there exist many thousand subjects for elegant conversation, there are persons who cannot meet a cripple without talking about feet." Chinese proverb

"Tact is a valuable attribute in gaining practice. It consists in telling a squint-eyed man that he has a fine, firm chin." J. Chalmers Da Costa

"Competence, like truth, beauty and contact lenses, is in the eye of the beholder." Laurence J. Peter, *The Peter Principle* (1969)

"Tact is the ability to describe others as they see themselves." President Abraham Lincoln

"Sometimes I think the surest sign that intelligent life exists elsewhere in the universe is that none of it has tried to contact us." Bill Watterson, cartoonist, *Calvin and Hobbes*

"A happy childhood is poor preparation for human contacts." Colette (1873-1954)

"Lying increases the creative faculties, expands the ego, and lessens the frictions of social contacts." Clare Booth Luce (1903-1987)

"Tact is the knack of making a point without making an enemy." Isaac Newton (1642-1727)

"It is an illusion that youth is happy, an illusion of those who have lost it. The young know they are wretched for they are full of the truthless ideal which have been instilled into them, and each time they come in contact with the real, they are bruised and wounded." W. Somerset Maugham

"Don't flatter yourself that friendship authorizes you to say disagreeable things to your intimates. The nearer you come with a person, the more necessary do tact and courtesy become. Except in cases of necessity, leave your friend to learn unpleasant things from his enemies; they are ready enough to tell them." Supreme Court Justice Oliver Wendell Holmes (1809-1894)

"The meeting of two personalities is like the contact of two chemical substances. If there is any reaction, both are transformed." Carl Jung (1875-1961)

"Step with care and great tact. And remember that Life's a Great Balancing Act. Just never forget to be dexterous and deft. And never mix up your right foot with your left." Dr. Suess, *Oh, the Places You'll Go*

"Tact is, after all, a kind of mind reading." Sarah Orne Jewett (1849-1909)

"A family is a place where minds come in contact with one another. If these minds love one another the home will be as beautiful as a flower garden. But if these minds get out of harmony with one another it is like a storm that plays havoc with the garden." Buddha (563 BC-483 BC)

Talent, Potential

"Talent develops in quiet places, character in the full current of human life." Goethe, 19th Century German poet and dramatist

"There is no substitute for talent. Industry and all the virtues are of no avail." Aldous Huxley

"Middle age snuffs out more talent than ever wars or sudden death do." Richard Hughes

"It's not enough to be Hungarian. You must have talent too." Alexander Korda, film director

"Let our children grow tall, and some taller than others if they have it in them to do so." Margaret Thatcher, British prime minister

"I am no more humble than my talents require." musician Oscar Levant (1906-1972)

"Getting ahead in a difficult profession requires avid faith in yourself. That is why some people with mediocre talent, but with great inner drive, go much further than people with vastly superior talent." Sophia Loren, actress

"The government consists of a gang of men exactly like you and me. They have, taking one with another, no special talent for the business of government; they have only a talent for getting and holding office." H. L. Mencken (1880-1956)

"It took me 15 years to discover that I had no talent for writing, but I couldn't give it up because by that time I was too famous." Robert Benchley (1889-1945)

"Mediocrity knows nothing higher than itself. Talent instantly recognizes genius." Sir Arthur Conan Doyle (1859-1930), *Sherlock Holmes, Valley of Fear*

"Man's main task in life is to give birth to himself, to become what he potentially is." Erich Fromm

"It seems to me that people have vast potential. Most people can do extraordinary things if they have the confidence or take the risks. Yet most people don't. They sit in front of the television and treat life as if it goes on forever." Philip Adams

"If I have ever made any valuable discoveries, it has been owing more to patient attention, than to any other talent." Sir Isaac Newton (1642-1727)

"Press on. Nothing in the world can take the place of perseverance. Talent will not; nothing is more common than unsuccessful men with talent. Genius will not. Unrewarded genius is almost a proverb. Education will not. The world is full of educated derelicts. Persistence and determination alone are omnipotent." President Calvin Coolidge (1872-1933)

"I don't measure America by its achievement but by its potential." Shirley Chisholm

"You must keep sending work out; you must never let a manuscript do nothing but eat its head off in a drawer. You send that work out again and again, while you're working on another one. If you have talent, you will receive some success, but only if you persist." Isaac Asimov

"The toughest thing about success is that you've got to keep on being a success. Talent is only a starting point in this business. You've got to keep on working that talent. Someday I'll reach for it and it won't be there." Irving Berlin (1888-1989)

"Toil to make yourself remarkable by some talent or other." Seneca (5 BC-65 AD)

"Whatever you are by nature, keep to it; never desert your line of talent. Be what nature intended you for and you will succeed." Sydney Smith (1771-1845)

"If you have a talent, use it in every which way possible. Don't hoard it. Don't dole it out like a miser. Spend it lavishly like a millionaire intent on going broke." Brendan Francis

"Hide not your talents, they for use were made. What's a sun-dial in the shade?" Benjamin Franklin (1706-1790)

"Everyone has talent. What is rare is the courage to follow the talent to the dark place where it leads." Erica Jong

Teamwork, Collaborations, Partnering

"All for one, one for all." Alexandre Dumas

"Never ask that which you are not prepared to give." Apache law

"Is there one word which may serve as a rule of practice for all one's life? Is not Reciprocity such a word? What you do not want done to yourself, do not do to others." Confucius (551 BC-479 BC)

"Whose bread I eat, his song I sing." German proverb

"A chain is no stronger than its weakest link. Union is strength. United we stand, divided we fall." Proverbs

"It takes more than one to make a ballet." Ninette de Valois, choreographer

"What I want is men who will support me when I am in the wrong." Lord Melbourne, 19th Century British statesman

"There are only two forces that unite men...fear and interest." Napoleon Bonaparte

"When bad men combine, the good must associate. Else they will fall, one by one, an un-pitied sacrifice in a contemptible struggle." Edmund Burke

"One man alone can be pretty dumb sometimes, but for real bona fide stupidity, there ain't nothin' can beat teamwork." Edward Abbey

"The finest plans have always been spoiled by the littleness of those that should carry them out. Even emperors can't do it all by themselves." Bertolt Brecht, German dramatist

"Everyone has observed how much more dogs are animated when they hunt in a pack, than when they pursue their game apart. We might, perhaps, be at a loss to explain this phenomenon, if we had not experience of a similar in ourselves." David Hume, 18th Century Scottish philosopher

Teamwork, Collaborations, Partnering

The biggest source of growth and increased opportunities in today's business climate lie in the way that individuals and companies work together. It is becoming increasingly rare to find an individual or organization that has not yet been required to team with others. Lone rangers and sole-source providers simply cannot succeed in competitive environments and global economies. Those who benefit from collaborations, rather than become the victim of them, will log the biggest successes in business years ahead.

Here are my definitions of three terms of teamwork, intended to help by differentiating their intended objectives:

Collaborations: Parties willingly cooperating together. Working jointly with others, especially in an intellectual pursuit. Cooperation with an instrumentality with which one is not immediately connected.

Partnering: A formal relationship between two or more associates. Involves close cooperation among parties, with each having specified and joint rights and responsibilities.

Joint-Venturing: Partners come together for specific purposes or projects that may be beyond the scope of individual members. Each retains individual identity.

The joint-venture itself has its own identity...reflecting favorably upon work to be done and upon the partners.

The benefits for participating principals and firms include:

- Ongoing association and professional exchange with the best in respective fields.
- Utilize professional synergy to create opportunities that individuals could not.
- Serve as a beacon for professionalism.
- Provide access to experts otherwise not known to potential clients.
- Refer and cross-sell each other's services.
- Develop programs and materials to meet new and emerging marketplaces.

Technology

"The machine threatens all achievement." Rainer Maria Rilke, poet

"Machines are worshipped because they are beautiful and valued because they confer power. They are hated because they are hideous and loathed because they impose slavery." Bertrand Russell

"Any sufficiently advanced technology is indistinguishable from magic." Arthur C. Clarke, science fiction writer

"Give me a firm place to stand, and I will move the earth." Archimedes

"Man is a tool-using animal." Thomas Carlyle, 19th Century Scottish historian-essayist

"The new electronic interdependence recreates the world in the image of a global village. For tribal man, space was the uncontrollable mystery. For technological man, it is time that occupies the same role." Marshall McLuhan, sociologist

"The machine does not isolate man from the great problems of nature but plunges him more deeply into them." Antoine de Saint-Exupery

"Our scientific power has outrun our spiritual power. We have guided missiles and misguided men." Martin Luther King, Jr.

"Technology: the knack of so arranging the world that we don't have to experience it." Max Frisch

"The real problem is not whether machines think, but whether men do." B.F. Skinner

"No man who has wrestled with a self-adjusting card table can ever quite be the man he once was." James Thurber, humorist

Temptation

"I generally avoid temptation unless I can't resist it." Mae West

"Tempt not a desperate man. The tempter or the tempted, who sins the most?" William Shakespeare

"Good habits result from resisting temptation. Forbidden fruit is sweet. If you can't be good, be careful." Proverbs

"I can resist everything except temptation. The only way to get rid of temptation is to yield to it. Resist it, and your soul grows sick longing for the things it has forbidden itself." Oscar Wilde

"Saintliness is also a temptation." Jean Anouilh, French dramatist

"I never resist temptation because I have found that things that are bad for me never tempt me. Virtue is insufficient temptation." George Bernard Shaw (1856-1950)

"Those who flee temptation generally leave a forwarding address." Lane Olinghouse

"There are several good protections against temptations, but the surest is cowardice." Mark Twain (1835-1910)

"There is not any memory with less satisfaction than the memory of some temptation we resisted." James Branch Cabell (1879-1958)

"We live in a time of transition, an uneasy era which is likely to endure for the rest of this century. During the period we may be tempted to abandon some of the time-honored principles and commitments which have been proven during the difficult times of past generations. We must never yield to this temptation. Our American values are not luxuries, but necessities—not the salt in our bread, but the bread itself." President Jimmy Carter, in his farewell address

"The last temptation is the greatest treason, to do the right deed for the wrong reason." T. S. Eliot (1888-1965)

"Why comes temptation, but for man to meet and master and crouch beneath his foot, and so be pedestaled in triumph?" Robert Browning (1812-1889)

"The devil made me do it." Flip Wilson, comedian

Thinking

"If two men agree on everything, you may be sure that one of them is doing the thinking." President Lyndon B. Johnson

"The man whose second thoughts are good is worth watching." J.M. Barrie

"Many people would sooner die than think. In fact, they do." Bertrand Russell

"I think. Therefore, I am." Rene Descartes, 17th Century French philosopher

"The most fluent talkers or most plausible reasoners are not always the justest thinkers." William Hazlitt, 19th Century British essayist

"Most of one's life is one prolonged effort to prevent oneself from thinking." Aldous Huxley

"There is nothing either good or bad, but thinking makes it so." William Shakespeare

"The significant problems we have cannot be solved at the same level of thinking with which we created them." Albert Einstein (1879-1955)

"A good listener is usually thinking about something else. Classical music is the kind we keep thinking will turn into a tune." Kin Hubbard (1868-1930)

"There is no expedient to which a man will not go to avoid the labor of thinking." Thomas A. Edison (1847-1931)

"Words ought to be a little wild for they are the assaults of thought on the unthinking." John Maynard Keynes (1883-1946)

"Few people think more than two or three times a year. I have made an international reputation for myself by thinking once or twice a week." George Bernard Shaw

"Too many people are thinking of security instead of opportunity. They seem more afraid of life than death." James F. Byrnes (1879-1972)

"The important thing in science is not so much to obtain new facts as to discover new ways of thinking about them." Sir William Bragg (1862-1942)

"There are two ways to slide easily through life; to believe everything or to doubt everything. Both ways save us from thinking." Alfred Korzybski (1879-1950)

"If you make people think they're thinking, they'll love you. But if you really make them think, they'll hate you." Don Marquis (1878-1937)

Time

"To choose time is to save time." Sir Francis Bacon

"Time keeps on slipping into the future." Steve Miller Band, 1976

"Men talk of killing time, while time quietly kills them." Dion Boucicault

"Dost thou love life? Then do not squander time, for that's the stuff life is made of. Time is money." Benjamin Franklin

"Time is a great teacher. Unfortunately, it kills all its pupils." Hector Berlioz, composer

"Time present and time past are both perhaps present in time future, and time future contained in time past." Poet T.S. Eliot

"I must govern the clock, not be governed by it." Golda Meir

"An hour in the morning is worth two in the evening. There are only 24 hours in a day. There is a time and place for everything. Time and tide wait for no man. Time cures the sick man, not the ointment. Time is a great healer. Time will tell." Proverbs

"Time ripens all things. No man is born wise." Cervantes, *Don Quixote*

"Time is the great physician." Benjamin Disraeli

"Come what come may. Time and the hour runs through the roughest day. I wasted time, and now doth time waste me." William Shakespeare

"Time eases all things." Sophocles

"The now, the here, through which all future plunges to the past." James Joyce

"Time wounds all heals." Groucho Marx

"We must use time as a tool, not a couch." President John F. Kennedy

"As if you could kill time without injuring eternity." Henry David Thoreau

"Take care of the minutes, for hours will take care of themselves." Earl of Chesterfield (1747)

Trust, Relationship Building

"If I have the public trust, then anything is possible. If I don't have it, then nothing is possible." President Abraham Lincoln

"A friendship founded on business is better than a business founded on friendship." John D. Rockefeller

"The body is shaped, disciplined, honored, and in time, trusted." Martha Graham (1893-1991)

"I know God will not give me anything I can't handle. I just wish that He didn't trust me so much." Mother Teresa (1910-1997)

"Trust men and they will be true to you; treat them greatly, and they will show themselves great." Ralph Waldo Emerson (1803-1882)

"Love all, trust a few. Do wrong to none." William Shakespeare

"Just trust yourself, then you will know how to live." Johann Wolfgang von Goethe (1749-1832)

"Put more trust in nobility of character than in an oath." Solon (638 BC-559 BC)

"Never trust the advice of a man in difficulties." Aesop (620 BC-560 BC)

"Love God and trust your feelings. Be loyal to them. Don't betray them." Robert C. Pollock

"If you wish in this world to advance, your merits are bound to enhance. Stir it and stump it, and blow your own trumpet, or trust me, you haven't a chance." W. S. Gilbert (1836-1911)

"Do not trust all men, but trust men of worth. The former course is silly, the latter a mark of prudence." Democritus (460 BC-370 BC)

"A human being is only interesting if he's in contact with himself. I learned you have to trust yourself, be what you are, and do what you ought to do the way you should do it. You have got to discover you, what you do, and trust it." Barbra Streisand, singer

Trust, Relationship Building
These are the seven stages of relationship building among collaborators and partners in business:

1. Want to Get Business. Seeking rub-off effect, success by association. Sounds good to the marketplace. Nothing ventured, nothing gained. Why not try!
2. Want to Garner Ideas. Learn more about the customer. Each team member must commit to professional development, taking the program to a higher level. Making sales calls (mandated or voluntarily) does not constitute relationship building.

3. First Attempts. Conduct programs that get results, praise, requests for more. To succeed, it needs to be more than an advertising and direct marketing campaign.

4. Mistakes, Successes and Lessons. Competition, marketplace changes or urgent need led the initiative to begin. Customer retention and enhancement program requires a cohesive team approach and multiple talents.

5. Continued Collaborations. Collaborators truly understand teamwork and had prior successful experiences at customer service. The sophisticated ones are skilled at building and utilizing colleagues and outside experts.

6. Want and advocate teamwork. Team members want to learn from each other. All share risks equally. Early successes inspire deeper activity. Business relationship building is considered an ongoing process, not a "once in awhile" action or marketing gimmick.

7. Commitment to the concept and each other. Each team member realizes something of value. Customers recommend and freely refer business to the institution. What benefits one partner benefits all.

Truth, Understanding

"Hell is truth seen too late." Tryon Edwards

"When you have eliminated the impossible, whatever remains, however improbable, must be the truth." Sir Arthur Conan Doyle

"And the lonely voice of youth cries, What Is Truth?" Johnny Cash

"The truth is always modern, and there never comes a time when it is safe to give it voice." Clarence Darrow

"Truth crushed to earth shall rise again." William Cullen Bryant

"Tis strange but true. For truth is always stranger than fiction." Lord Byron

"Truth is the only ground to stand upon." Elizabeth Cady Stanton

"Truth is the beginning of every good thing, both in heaven and on earth. And he who be blessed and happy should be from the first a partaker of truth, for then he can be trusted." Plato

"A great truth is a truth whose opposite is also a truth." Thomas Mann

"There is nothing so powerful as truth...and nothing so strange." Daniel Webster

"Better a lie that heals than a truth that wounds. Many a true word is spoken in jest. Tell the truth, and shame the devil. Truth fears no trial. Truth is stranger than fiction. Truth will out." Proverbs

"Let us begin by committing ourselves to the truth, to see it like it is and to tell it like it is, to find the truth, to speak the truth and live with the truth." President Richard M. Nixon (1968)

"Truth is no road to fortune." Jean Jacques Rousseau

"I never give them hell. I just tell the truth, and they think it's hell." Harry S. Truman

"Truth is mighty and will prevail. There is nothing the matter with this, except that it ain't so." Mark Twain

"Truth is on the march. Nothing can stop it now." Emile Zola

"The highest result of education is tolerance." Helen Keller

"The most comprehensible thing about the world is that any of it is incomprehensible." Albert Einstein

"No law or ordinance is mightier than understanding." Plato

Values, Ideals

"You get what you pay for." Proverb

"If you believe in an ideal, you don't own it. It owns you." Raymond Chandler

"A cynic is a man who knows the price of everything and the value of nothing." Oscar Wilde

"There ain't a wrong man in the world who can stand up against a right man who knows he is right and keeps on a-coming." Western movie cowboy star Lash Larue

"Good merchandise, even when hidden, soon finds buyers." Plautus

"Things are only worth what you make them worth." Moliere

"Imagine there's no heaven. It's easy if you try. No help below us. Above us only sky. Imagine all the people living for today." John Lennon (1971)

"A radical is a man with both feet firmly planted in the air." President Franklin D. Roosevelt

"People love high ideals, but they got to be about 33-percent plausible." Will Rogers

"Let us have faith that right makes might. And in that faith, let us do our duty to the end, as we understand it." President Abraham Lincoln

"You cannot hold a man down without staying down with him." Booker T. Washington

"The whole history of the American Revolutionary War is one of false hopes and temporary devices. We must champion more lasting solutions." President George Washington

Values, Ideals

Here are some examples of core values which could be embraced:

1. To be truthful, forceful and forthright in personal relationships.
2. To treat others as I would like to be treated.
3. To expect that I deserve and will receive the best out of life.
4. To be the kind of person that others can count upon, like, love and admire.
5. To be true to my word and consistent in my actions.
6. To show loyalty and commitment to those causes and projects which I undertake.
7. To show loyalty and commitment to family and those friends who are important to me.
8. To never stop growing emotionally and continuing my journey.

Here are some examples of Strategic Priorities that could be included:

1. To be the best that I can be.
2. To be the best in my chosen field.
3. To create new applications and set new standards for my chosen field.
4. To successfully mentor others.
5. To creatively approach projects in ways that others did not or could not do.
6. To achieve results that are realistically attained and honestly reached.
7. To continue building respect for myself and the self-assuredness to stay focused.

8. To know that I am doing the right things and taking the best possible courses of action.

9. To never stop growing professionally and continuing to evolve to the next tiers.

Vision

"I have a dream." Martin Luther King, Jr.

"Pure logic is the ruin of the spirit." Antoine de Saint-Exupery

"I've got vision, and the rest of the world is wearing bifocals." Paul Newman, in "Butch Cassidy and the Sundance Kid"

"The reasonable man adapts himself to the world. The unreasonable man persists in trying to adapt the world to himself. Progress depends on the unreasonable man." George Bernard Shaw

"People only see what they are prepared to see." Ralph Waldo Emerson (1863)

"A moment's insight is worth a life's experience." Supreme Court Justice Oliver Wendell Holmes

"A danger foreseen is half avoided." Thomas Fuller

"Vision is the art of seeing things invisible." Jonathan Swift

"Two men look out through the same bars. One sees the mud and one the stars." Frederick Langbridge

"If I can see so far, it's because I stand on the shoulders of giants." Sir Isaac Newton

"The four measures of a person's reason for being are courage, judgment, integrity and dedication." President-elect John F. Kennedy, Jan. 9, 1961

"You've got to have a dream. If you don't have a dream, how are you gonna have your dream come true?" Richard Rodgers and Oscar Hammerstein, from the musical "South Pacific"

"Every moment is a golden one for him who has the vision to recognize it as such." Henry Miller (1891-1980)

"You are not here merely to make a living. You are here to enable the world to live more amply, with greater vision, and with a finer spirit of hope and achievement. You are here to enrich the world. You impoverish yourself if you forget this errand." President Woodrow Wilson

Vision

Visioning is the process where good ideas become something more. Visioning is a catalyst toward long-term evaluation, planning and implementation. Visioning is a jump-off point by which forward-thinking organizations ask: What will we look like in the future? What do we want to become? How will we evolve? Vision is a realistic picture of what is possible.

The Vision describes what can and will happen, once everyone's energies are focused. Vision is not a financial forecast or a market analysis. Vision is less of a dream and more of a realistic picture of what is possible. When there is a genuine Vision (as compared to a terse "vision statement"), people are compelled to learn and excel, not because they are told to but because they want to.

The purposes and expected benefits of Visioning include:

- Taking hold of the future.
- Setting something in motion that will honor those who have built the organization.
- Involving the widest base of support in pro-active change and growth.
- Benchmarking the progress made and communicating it to outside constituencies.
- Nurturing the organization's image.
- Understanding the difference between good and bad handling of crises.
- Crisis follow-ups that help heal and rebuild after problems, versus those that fester and bring destruction to organizations.
- Study and ready the organization to make best advantage of bridge-building and problem remediation concepts.
- Methodologies to address problems sooner, rather than later.
- Establishing safeguards against future trouble.
- Putting more emphasis upon the positive ingredients and happenings.

Work

"There is no substitute for hard work." Thomas A. Edison

"I don't want to achieve immortality through my work. I want to achieve it through not dying." Woody Allen

"Blessed is he who has found his work. Let him ask no other blessedness. Work is the grand cure of all the maladies and miseries that ever beset mankind." Thomas Carlyle (1886)

"Work is not the curse, but drudgery is." Henry Ward Beecher

"More men are killed by overwork than the importance of the world justifies." Rudyard Kipling

"The best prize that life offers is the chance to work hard at work worth doing." President Theodore Roosevelt

"No bees, no honey. No work, no money." Proverb

"Work is much more fun than fun." Noel Coward

"When work is a pleasure, life is a joy. When work is a duty, life is slavery." Maxim Gorky

"It's been a hard day's night, and I've been working like a dog." Beatles song by John Lennon & Paul McCartney

"They say hard work never hurt anybody. But, I figure, why take the chance." President Ronald Reagan

"Work is the curse of the drinking classes." Oscar Wilde

"Work is necessary for man. Man invented the alarm clock." Pablo Piccasso

"Life is too short to do anything for oneself that one can pay others to do for one. It is not wealth one asks for, but just enough to preserve one's dignity, to work unhampered, to be generous, frank and independent." W. Somerset Maugham (1874-1965)

"If people only knew how hard I work to gain my mastery, it wouldn't seem so wonderful at all." Michelangelo Buonarroti (1475-1564)

"Temptation rarely comes in working hours. It is in their leisure time that men are made or marred." W. N. Taylor

"Working in the garden gives me a profound feeling of inner peace." Ruth Stout

"In reality, serendipity accounts for one percent of the blessings we receive in life, work and love. The other 99 percent is due to our efforts." Peter McWilliams

"Trouble is only an opportunity in work clothes." Henry J. Kaiser (1882-1967)

"I don't believe in intuition. When you get sudden flashes of perception, it is just the brain working faster than usual. But you've been getting ready to know it for a long time, and when it comes, you feel you've known it always." Katherine Anne Porter (1894-1980)

"The secret of joy in work is contained in one word—excellence. To know how to do something well is to enjoy it." Pearl Buck (1892-1973), "The Joy of Children," 1964

"I am doomed to an eternity of compulsive work. No set goal achieved satisfies. Success only breeds a new goal. The golden apple devoured has seeds. It is endless." Bette Davis, actress

Work
There is no substitute for good, hard work. These are the seven basic categories of the work force:

1. People who only do the things necessary to get by. Just a series of jobs, no more, no less.
2. People who are managed by others to meet quotas, schedules, procedures and statistics. People who do and make things.
3. Administrative, managerial support. They keep the boat afloat. They push paper, systems and technology. The process is the driving force.
4. System upholders. Don't rock the boat. Maintain the status quo. Resist change. Surround with like minds. They are motivated by survival.
5. People who sell something. Most companies have revenue-sales as their primary objective and measurement. To them, everything else is really secondary.
6. People in transition. Forced by circumstances to change (career obsolescence, down-sizing, marketplace factors). Some voluntarily effected changes, to achieve balance or new direction in life. Some do better in newer environments. Others cannot weather changes (too tied to staid corporate orientations).
7. Idealists, out to do meaningful things. They are deeply committed to accomplishing something special, beyond basic job requirements. They adapt to and benefit from change. They learn to take risks. They are motivated by factors other than money.

In each category of the work force, those employees subscribe to one of these seven plateaus of work ethic:

1. Just Enough to Get By. Getting paid is the objective. Don't know or have not learned anything further.
2. Taking Advantage of the System. Coffee break mentality. Abuse sick day policies, health benefits, etc. "Never gonna be" syndrome.
3. Inside the Box. Follow the rules but never consider formulating them. Subscribe to the philosophy: "There are no wise decisions, only activities carried out according to company procedures."
4. Don't Rock the Boat. Interested in remaining gainfully employed. Look forward in the short-term to the next paid vacation, in the long-term toward retirement.
5. Professional Is As Professional Does. Daily behaviors, achievements speak for themselves. Consistent in approaches. Never stop learning and growing.
6. Change Agent. Either forced by circumstances to change (career obsolescence, down-sizing, marketplace factors) or thrive upon change. As time progresses, become a mentor and champion for change.
7. Deep Commitments to Body of Work, Professionalism, Ethics. Don't know what a coffee break, sick day or vacation is. Give their lives, souls, expertise to careers and the lifetime results show positively. They make a profound influence.

Youth

"No wise man ever wished to be younger." Jonathan Swift

"Youth is something very new. Twenty years ago, no one mentioned it." Coco Chanel, French designer

"A majority of young people seem to develop arteriosclerosis forty years before they get the physical kind." Aldous Huxley

"No young man believes he shall ever die." William Hazlitt, 19th Century British essayist

"Youth is a malady of which one becomes cured a little every day." Benito Mussolini

"The young will always have the same problem…how to rebel and conform at the same time. They have now solved this by defying their parents and copying one another." Quentin Crisp, writer

"One starts to get young at the age of 60, and then it is too late." Pablo Piccasso

"Far too good to waste on children." George Bernard Shaw

"It is an illusion that youth is happy, an illusion of those who have lost it. The young know they are wretched for they are full of truth-less ideals which have been instilled into them, and each time they come in contact with the real, they are bruised and wounded." W. Somerset Maugham

"There's nothing that keeps its youth, so far as I know, but a tree and truth." Justice Oliver Wendell Holmes

"Young people are in a condition like permanent intoxication, because youth is sweet and they are growing." Aristotle (384 BC-322 BC)

"I do nothing but go about persuading you all, old and young alike, not to take thought for your persons or your properties, but and chiefly to care about the greatest improvement of the soul. I tell you that virtue is not given by money, but that from virtue comes money and every other good of man, public as well as private. This is my teaching, and if this is the doctrine which corrupts the youth, I am a mischievous person." Socrates (469 BC—399 BC)

"Praise youth and it will prosper." Irish proverb

"Don't laugh at a youth for his affectations. He is only trying on one face after another to find his own." Logan Pearsall Smith (1865-1946)

"Keep true to the dreams of thy youth." Friedrich von Schiller (1759-1805)

"Youth cannot know how age thinks and feels. But old men are guilty if they forget what it was to be young." J. K. Rowling, "Harry Potter and the Order of the Phoenix," 2003

"There are three things which the superior man guards against. In youth, lust. When he is strong, quarrelsomeness. When he is old, covetousness." Confucius (551 BC-479 BC)

Youth

Here are some characteristics of young people (rising stars) will make it as professionals and business leaders: